UNION PACIFIC COMMUNICATIONS HISTORY

Supporting Technological Leadership
in the Railroad Industry

GENE H. KUHN

GM Publishing Company LLC

Omaha, Nebraska

© 2020 GENE H. KUHN
ALL RIGHTS RESERVED. No part of this book may be used or reproduced by any means, graphic, electronic or mechanical, including photocopying, recording, taping or by any information storage retrieval system without the written permission of the publisher except in the case of brief quotations embodied in critical articles and reviews. All photographs contained herein, except those so noted, are the property of Gene H. Kuhn

Published by GM Publishing Co. LLC
FIRST EDITION

Kuhn, Gene H. 1930
ISBN 978-1-7337719-1-7
Union Pacific Communications History
Author - Gene H. Kuhn
Library of Congress Control Number 2020906783

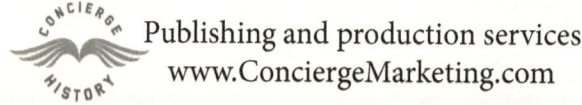
Publishing and production services
www.ConciergeMarketing.com

Printed in the United States of America
10 9 8 7 6 5 4 3 2 1

Foreword

Gene, my father, has been a dedicated engineer throughout his career spending 40+ years in communications spanning American Telephone & Telegraph (AT&T), Wabash Railroad, and then Union Pacific Railroad (UPRR) devoting his career to improving technology for these companies extremely reliant on effective communications. He always has and continues to be a loving husband to Mary Ann; supportive father for his sons, daughters, and their spouses - Steve, Kathy (Mike), Fred (Brenda), Anna (Wayne), and Ken; and a wise and intelligent grandfather for his eleven grandchildren.

Dad graduated with a Bachelor of Science Industrial Engineering degree from St. Louis University in 1952. Early in his career, he discovered his passion for communications. Communications became his career, especially microwave and fiber optics. Dad has other interests as well including geology and photography. Dad mentioned several times in years past he had considered becoming a geologist. After working for AT&T and Wabash Railroad in St. Louis, Dad was hired by the UPRR in 1966 and moved our young family west to Utah. His work assignments in Salt Lake City followed by Pocatello, ID provided numerous opportunities to mesh his work and hobbies. Microwave sites were located on the peaks of numerous mountains. There were numerous opportunities to photograph nature and enhance his understanding of rock formations all across the west. Dad loved to share these passions with his family (often to the point that my siblings and I wanted to change the subject). After having spent many years working in the field at numerous microwave sites, in 1974 the UPRR moved Dad and the family to Omaha where Dad would eventually manage and direct the Communications Department.

In 1984, I was home visiting the family for a week during Christmas. Eighteen months prior, I had been hired by a defense contractor in another city working with radar systems for fighter aircraft. Radar systems utilize microwave frequencies to detect and track enemy aircraft and ground based targets. One evening during my visit, several of us encouraged Dad to get out the slide projector and show some family photos. Dad obliged, set up the screen and projector, and proceeded to show a reel of photos from when we lived out west. There were pictures from a vacations, birthdays, and holidays. Everyone laughed and enjoyed seeing ourselves at much younger ages. There was a lot of enjoyment watching the slideshow until one photograph appeared on the screen…

While growing up, especially on car trips through the mountains, Dad would point out the rock formations we could see, varieties of trees, and the occasional eagle (that only he would see and the rest of us would be looking into the sky convinced none was to be found). Often, there would be microwave sites present at the top of a mountain and Dad would dutifully point it out. Then he would enlighten us on whose microwave it is - UPRR, AT&T, or another competing railroad. He still does this today, especially if we are on a trip to the western states.

Dad would tell us how the systems worked - transmitters, receivers, antennas, or whatever he felt we could understand. Many of the microwave sites he pointed out were places he worked at to make repairs—a transmitter down due to component failure, an antenna misaligned due to high winds, or some other problem. None of us really understood at that time what Dad was talking about. We just knew microwave sites allowed people or equipment to communicate across vast land masses. We often would plead Dad to change the subject to something else. Then there would be another eagle sighting.

When Dad would go to up to some of the microwave sites, he often had his camera with him. He would take a lot of pictures from the mountaintops; many of them were very serene landscapes of mountains and valleys. Some of his most interesting photographs would be winter scenes. He and his coworkers would have to take a Snowcat, a tracklaying vehicle for traveling through the snow, to reach the microwave site at the top of the mountain. I remember impressive pictures showing narrow trails up the mountain with snow towering over the Snowcat. Sometimes there would be a coworker standing in the picture to give one a perspective of the depth of the snow. One majestic photo Dad had taken was of a snow covered Mount St. Helens at sunrise many years before it erupted in May 1980. The photo was taken from Mount Skamania WA. This photo eventually appeared in the UPRR Employee's Magazine INFO.

Dad's photos weren't limited to scenery. His passion for communications and microwave sites led him to take numerous photographs of the equipment and buildings at the sites he worked. These included steel towers holding the antennas, racks of equipment, transmitters, receivers, power systems, and the small buildings holding all of the equipment.

During this festive occasion of watching the family slideshow, a rack of equipment from one of the many microwave sites appeared on the screen! This was a fairly common occurrence with the family slideshows. Dad started talking about this particular microwave site and the equipment in the rack. Everyone rolled their eyes upward... except for one.

I was now very intrigued because of my work as an engineer with radar systems. I asked numerous questions about the equipment.

How many channels?

What were the operating frequencies?

What bandwidths were typical?

Were spread spectrum techniques utilized?

Were there redundant systems to improve reliability?

Dad eagerly answered my questions. After all of these years, someone in the family finally showed an interest and appreciated his knowledge of the subject! In the middle of the questions and answers, Mom sighed with disbelief, "Oh my God, we have another one!"

For several years since retiring, Dad has wanted to document the history of communications of the UPRR. He had been writing notes of past experiences, talking with former co-workers, and conducting research for several years. This book captures in a documentary fashion many subjects including:

Key leaders in the UPRR associated with the development of telegraphs and communications;

Impactful judicial rulings and legislative actions;

The early years of telegraphs through radios and microwaves to the more modern use of fiber optics;

Relations with government agencies such as the Federal Communications Commission (FCC);

His experience as a consultant; and more.

Our family is extremely proud Dad had so much to offer the Communications Department at the UPRR. He's had a stellar career working on communications for the UPRR, Wabash, and AT&T, in addition to spending a few years as a consultant. Now he has achieved another milestone by documenting this history of telegraph and communications of the UPRR.

On behalf of our family, "Well done Dad!"

Fred Kuhn

Preface

> "The creativity of the communications engineer is vital to industrial progress. Advanced communications capability is generally high on the priority list of industry as industrial expansion occurs. It is clear to economists that a nation's communications capability is as much a part of its national resources as its coal and steel reserves, its port facilities, or the industriousness of its people."
> From C. O. Jett's 5 Year Plan

As C.O. Jett stated in his 1973 report for the Communications Department, *5 Year Plan,* advanced communication is vital to our culture and held aloft under the banner of "progress." The modern smart phone provides instant support of new ideas and communication methods for individuals in their quest for knowledge, information, and interaction. The telephone allowed people to talk across continents at real time. But even earlier, telegraph systems opened up the American West to business activity in the East, just as it bridged faraway parts of many countries with each other in ways that had taken days or weeks before. Almost overnight, business and personal lives were able to learn and react at speeds never before seen in human history. And railroads were some of the first adopters and innovators—telegraphs aided the movement of trains and improved safety, thereby protecting the people (and their cargo) who were coming to use the same technology at work and at home.

Improved communications, as you will see in this book, permitted improved decision-making, and this was nowhere more true than in the increase in speed of train movement, allocation of resources, and asset investments. At each step of railroad evolution, enhanced communications brought enhanced earnings. Telegraph systems became the telephone; carrier systems created the demand for microwave systems (Microwave systems are telephone radio equipment which combines many telephone lines into a very high frequency radio band technically called "microwaves". The number of telephone lines carried vary from six to six hundred allowed for railroads. The microwave signal is transmitted like a light beam between towers using an antenna like the reflector of a search light. Microwave radio equipment at each tower repeats the signal to the next tower). Expansion of microwave systems led to the need for greater communications capacity, and the railroad introduced fiber optics to their communications network.

Each department of the railroad expanded the general knowledge of their domain. The Mechanical Department improved locomotive performance through spectrum analysis of lubricants. The Signal Department introduced electronics to coded track permitting technology, which subsequently eliminated costly pole lines. The Computer Department (MIS) introduced computers to the railroad, subsequently becoming smaller, faster, with greater capacity, and more efficient, and with niche software dedicated to fine-tuning railroad operations.

You can go through each department and find similar examples of improvements. However, this book is primarily devoted to the Communications Department, which handled transfer of information both data and speech.

The authority to construct the transcontinental railroad was authorized by The Pacific Railroad and Telegraph Act of 1862, which as its name suggests, illustrates that Congress saw an opportunity for railroad and telegraph services to be expanded simultaneously. The goal was simple: "Construction of a Railroad and Telegraph from the Missouri River to the Pacific Ocean and to secure to the Government the use of same for Postal, Military and other Purpose". By granting this authority, the Communication Department of each railroad had equal status with the railroad's other Manifest Destiny-style operations by an act of Congress. In other words, Congress felt improved communications was as important to the economic and imperial health of the country as the movement of people and goods.

The author has reviewed many books on the history of the Union and Central Pacific Railroads. The story is a great story, well documented by numerous authors. Describing not only the railroads' history, but the development of the West and of the Nation.

Occasional references are made to the telegraph lines, and some document the developments in railroad communications. None of the books track the leadership of the department or development of the technology and services provided.

The author's goal is to record this leadership and their records found in the research to produce the book and the experiences he has which it is believed should also be recorded as outlined below.

The name of Union Pacific's Communications Department has changed over time from the "Telegraph Department" to the "Communications Department" to the "Telecommunications Department." Except where the distinction is necessary, it will be referred to in this book as the "Communications Department," or CD for short.

Realistically, the Communications Department has always been a supportive department to the movement of trains and business matters related to that function. But "Jay Gould, a railroad baron who took control of the Union Pacific Railroad in 1874, had plans to use the Congressional Act of 1862 to build on the company's telegraph and once set up, use that business to manipulate telegraph service along with the access the railroad had to shippers and people along the railroad, ultimately losing control of the UPRR, but maintaining great influence until his death in 1892.[1]" Ultimately, that "business" became Western Union.

In the end, WU became the principal common carrier telegraph service provider along the Union Pacific right-of-way, even for non-railroad communications. (Common carriers are government regulated companies which are to handle business presented to them without discriminations, communications common carriers are to handle voice, data or other communications presented to them. In the case of Western Union it was required to handle telegrams presented to them. The railroad is a common carrier for moving products presented to it.) The railroad Telegraph Department employees maintained the telegraph line to support the common carrier as well the railroad telegraph services. Roughly half of their salaries were paid by each company.

This book was written to preserve the historical period of the Communications Department of the C. Otis Jett era and subsequent period 1945-1992, and as much earlier history as can be identified, before it is completely lost. Much information in this book is taken from newspaper and journal magazine accounts and other publications, including some from Maury Klein, a history professor at the University of Rhode Island and an author of three books on the History of the Union Pacific Railroad that dealt with the years of operation between 1862 and 2011. (Union Pacific - The Birth of a Railroad 1862-1893 – Maury Klein, Union Pacific The Rebirth 1894-1969, Maury Klein, Union Pacific The Reconstruction from 1969 to the Present - Maury Klein). Many passages in his last book expanded the existing base of knowledge about the Union Pacific CD, and duplication of his information is avoided to the extent possible; however, some content will show up in both places to maintain the flow of this book. "However most of the content collected herein is from my personal experience as a communications engineer and as a manager, and director of the Union Pacific Communications Engineering Department between 1966 and 1992, and also from references of about 100 log books I maintained. The log books were personal notes from contacts with team members, (fiber optic team) and other communication employees and other railroad workers. Also with contacts with fiber optic contractors, communication equipment suppliers, other railroads officials and government workers, Association of American Railroad officials and their legal counsel. The notes were made from verbal reports, issues, discussions and observations."

Latter content collected herein is not attributed as it is from my personal knowledge, and references to the log books I maintained.

We are trying to preserve a list in sequence of department heads as best we can develop. A brief history of their service is included when available. Where to include this list in the book is a question we faced. The list is presented in an early chapter to avoid interruption to the flow of the Communications Department progress and improvements. Gaps in the sequence remain at this time.

This book is not authorized by the Union Pacific Railroad. The book is entirely the work of the author and is accurate as could be documented. Access to some early director's meeting minutes may have improved information on the leadership of the telegraph department in the early days.

DEDICATIONS

Dedicated to my wife Mary Ann Kuhn and my family, without whose love and patience it would not be possible.

As well, a special dedication to men I have known and worked with who have sacrificed their lives to provide support to the communications effort of the Department:

Joe Beach, Equipmentman, Yermo, CA, Died of Asphyxiation at Holiday Hill CA, date unknown, dealing with a power outage and maintaining the motor engine generator's operation during snow storm. Exhaust back fed into equipment building.

Paul Albert Rayko, radioman, Pocatello ID. Died May 11, 1983, of head-on vehicle crash on Highway 30, returning from communications equipment work near Kemmerer, WY.

Contents

Foreword..3

Preface...7

Dedications...13

Railroad Communications Industry Summary.......................17

Telegraph/Communications Department Leaders..................37

Union Pacific Telegraph and Related Telegraph Companies..57

Judicial and Legislative Government Actions..........................63

Technical Issues on Operation of Pole Lines...........................67

Carrier Telephone and Telegraphy..73

Union Pacific Railroad Officials' Involvement
   in Nebraska Telephone History..75

Early Union Pacific Railroad Telephone Service......................81

The Jett Era and Influence..107

Private Branch Exchanges PBX and the Jett Era
   Influence Telephone Switchboards (PBXs)....................... 135

Radio Systems in the Jett Era and Influence
   Early Radio Systems... 155

Communications Shop and the Jett Era and
   Influence Communications Shop..................................... 171

The Rise of Computers and Real Time Reporting in the
   Jett Era and Influence Data Transmission Systems......... 181

Expansion of Communications Systems and
  Jett Era and Influence 195

MoPac WP and UPRR Merger 209

Fiber Optic Cable Planning and Construction 219

Dispatcher Office Consolidations 245

Multipoint Distribution Radio System (MDS) and
  the Elimination of Pole Lines on the Union Pacific 253

Advanced Technologies ATCS Study....................................... 263

Solar Power Systems and Wind Generators........................... 271

UPRR Subsidiary Communications Expansion..................... 277

Government Relations... 281

Consulting – Union Pacific Communications 289

Education of a Communications Engineer............................ 293

Appendix A 297

Appendix B.. 303

Appendix C 319

Acknowledgments.. 327

Author Profile 331

Bibliography.. 335

Index 371

1

Railroad Communications Industry Summary

Telegraph lines were constructed simultaneously with the Union Pacific Railroad and Central Pacific Railroad between 1863 and 1869. The eastern railroads, with decades of experienced, provided standards for railroad construction and experienced men who subsequently planned, designed, and constructed the Pacific Railroads. This book is about the Union Pacific Communications Department and its leadership from the beginning of the railroad's construction until the end of 1992, with some additional references after that date.

1860s – 1900

During the 1860's expansion of telegraph systems, many telegraph companies associated themselves with already-built eastern railroads. The first experimental telegraph line, built by Samuel Morse, was built between Washington DC and Baltimore a distance of 38 miles along the Baltimore and Ohio Railroad right-of-way. The transcontinental telegraph construction, however, started in July 1861 and completed October 24, 1861, prior to construction of the Pacific Railroads. With construction of the Pacific Railroads, the Transcontinental Telegraph line was moved to the railroad right-of-way.

"Construction progress of the Pacific Railroads and their telegraph network was of great public interest at the time.

Industrial publications and newsletters such as the *Journal of Telegraph* and the *Telegrapher* had readerships primarily comprised of telegraphers, reported on organization of new telegraph companies, and expansion of their services to new towns, cities and countries. New telegraph equipment patents were frequently commented on in the publications like the *Telegraph Engineer*, through concern about the Western Union Telegraph monopoly and limited competition was often covered as well as documented in the following chapters 3 and 4," concern about the Western Union Telegraph monopoly and limited competition was often covered as well.

After the civil war, the public also closely followed construction of the Pacific Railroads and the expansion of the telegraph with daily reports. Construction of an Atlantic Cable to Europe, new telegraph technology such as with telegraph repeater, and expansion of the national telegraph across the West to Mexico were issues of great interest.[1]

Failure of the early Atlantic Cable installation led Western Union Telegraph, in 1865 to 1867, to plan to build a United States-European telegraph, from San Francisco, CA to Moscow, Russia. "The route was intended to travel from California via Oregon, Washington Territory, the Colony of British Columbia and Russian America (Alaska), under the Bering Sea and across Siberia to Moscow, where lines would communicate with the rest of Europe."[2] Negotiations with Russia for telegraph across Alaska led to the purchase of Alaska by the U.S. Government.

The July 2, 1866 issue of "The Telegrapher" featured the subject of government ownership of the telegraph industry promoted by "a gentleman who is well known to our readers"…"and we now learn one object of the National Telegraph Co., which is now asking Congress for certain rights and privileges, is to turn the vast line when constructed over to the Government, to be worked in conjunction with the Post Office."

A bill before the United States Senate, to establish telegraph lines by the government it be used in connection with the Post Office, was "killed" by the committee to which it was referred. The articles don't say, but presumably it was because of opposition by commercial telegraph interest. "The Telegrapher's" article goes on to criticize the Post Office's slow handling of the mail and potential higher rates, and government telegraph "would become a vast political machine of the most corrupt sort."[3]

The issue was left alone for several decades after, and throughout the 1880's the Union Pacific Railroad was highly involved with issues concerning telegraph service. But the issue of the Union Pacific and the Central Pacific Railroad requirement to construct "common carrier" telegraph lines as required by their charter was again raised in the House of Representatives by Representative Anderson of Kansas. The bill was submitted in opposition to the Western Union monopoly that "Jay Hawk Gould" had created.[4]

The national economy tanked in the summer of 1893, leading many railroads to bankruptcy; the Union Pacific Railroad went into receivership on October 13th, 1893, and remained in receivership until November 1, 1897, when Edward H. Harriman and a syndicate led by Kuhn Loeb an investment company purchased the railroad which began the Harriman Era of the Union Pacific Railroad.[5]

At that point, railroad telegraph service was under national scrutiny. Western Union Telegraph exercised a virtual monopoly, and many congressional leaders believed there should be a competitor in the field. Some congressmen wanted government control of the nation's telegraph service, placing it under control of the Post Office, similar to Great Britain. Others wanted full-fledge competition and looked to the western railroads to provide that competition, and they believed that the Pacific Railway Act demanded the railroads provide common carrier telegraph service.

The Federal District Court at St. Paul MN heard arguments brought by the government in 1890 to compel the Northern Pacific Railroad to operate its own telegraph system. "The action is brought under the land grant act of 1863, requiring the railroad company to maintain lines of telegraph for general business purposes along its route."[6]

1901-1910

"**Wants Uncle Sam to Buy the Telegraphs.** Representative Jackson of Kansas, has introduced a bill in Congress providing that the Government purchase the Western Union and the Postal

Telegraph-Cable companies and thereafter operate them in connection with the Post Office Department. Provision is made for appraisal of the property of the companies and for the payment of its appraised value when the amount is reported to Congress."[7]

Meanwhile, Postmaster General Thomas L. James wrote an article called "Why the Government Should Not Own and Operate the Telegraphs." In the article, he points out that "England so far has operated the lines at a loss," and, "The active competition between our two great telegraph companies has been not only been of economic advantage to our people, but it has assured them of the highest condition of efficiency. No commercial organization would contemplate or undertake to put distribution offices at points where they must be run at a loss, as hundreds of our smaller stations are."[8]

The issue of government ownership of the telegraph system arose again in the early 1900's with the introduction of bills in Congress with little success. Then in 1906 Congressman William R. Hearst from New York City introduced a bill to form a committee to evaluate takeover and determine a purchase price for the acquisition and authorize the Secretary of Treasury to borrow one hundred million dollars for that purpose which is about 2.79 billion in 2018 dollars[9]. Another debate in the House of Representatives in June 1906 was presented by Representative Samuel W. Smith of Michigan. "*The Telegraph Age*" a journal publication opposed both bills with strong objections to the takeover, primarily anticipating deficits accruing to the taxpayers."[10]

After the turn of the century and the end of bankruptcy of the Union Pacific Railroad, through Mr. E. H. Harriman's leadership, telegraph service for both the railroad and independent common carrier service was well established, and railroad telephone service was in early stages of development. Mr. Harriman used telephone service where available and encouraged is expansion on the Union Pacific Railroad.[11]

In remarks before the Convention of Railway Telegraph Superintendents held in Chicago June 18-20, 1902, Mr. J. J. Nate of Chicago described some early experiments conducted by a person described as an "inventive genius" using a self-constructed telephone instrument. The experimental telephone transmitted voice over telegraph wires. Nate went on to describe "train dispatching by telephone" on the Illinois Central-St. Charles Air Line in the Chicago area and concluded, "There is no valid reason why the telephone system may not be made as efficient in railroad service as the telegraph has become.[12]"

Nate's conclusion was only the beginning. In the decade following the turn of the century, considerable interest developed in the dispatching of trains by telephone and testing was done for the concept. For instance, the Illinois Central conducted a test with a telephone being carried in the cab of a locomotive. The train stopped at various locations and a telephone wire was strung to the existing telegraph line and was found capable of establishing voice communication with the train dispatcher's office over long distances. At the time, even with this success, there was no intention to replace the telegraph by telephone, but rather, the thought was to use the telephone for emergency purposes.[13]

But by 1900, the railroad industry was using and expanding telephone service on the eastern railroads. However, controversy over using the telephone to dispatch trains limited its use to ordinary business activities. For example, the Northern Pacific Railroad Company announced that it could substitute the telephone for telegraph along its line, and its officials identified a plan to connect each station with the general headquarters. This had been done by a number of large railroad companies and had been found to give general satisfaction,[14] but applying telephone service to the train dispatcher's office found considerable resistance. The Northern Pacific article continued, stating that the issue had been thoroughly discussed, however, it was determined to be simply "not practical."[15]

In fact, it was not intended to replace the telegraph by telephone, but the telephone could be used for emergency purposes.[16]

Dispatching of trains by telephone was resisted as much as earlier attempts to dispatch trains by telegraph. The first recorded dispatching of trains by telegraph was on the Erie Railway, on January 3, 1851. Engineers and trainmen talked about the movement of trains by wire, deciding that "they would not act upon such orders as there was nothing in the Rules and Regulations to warrant such action."[17]

During the 1901-1910 years telephone circuits were extended over many railroads. New telephone wires were added to telegraph pole lines, existing telegraph wires were transposed to telephone circuits and new technologies were added to use these wires for voice and telegraph through composite technology. Improvements in telephone communications permitted the business of railroads to be expedited by direct official-to-official communications.

For instance, L. B. Foley, Superintendent of Telegraph on the Delaware, Lackawanna, and Western Railroad Company, justified the use of telephone service on his railroad[18], and it quickly spread, until they'd equipped six hundred of their nine hundred and fifty miles of road with telephone circuits over three years.[19] Elsewhere, Mr. B. A. Worthington, First Vice President and General Manager of Wheeling and Lake Erie, described in a letter the advantages of telephone service in railroad operations. However, he had reservations about accuracy in dispatching trains by telephone even as he described the activity of several eastern lines using some telephone circuits in that fashion[20]. Mr. Worthington went on to explain himself about dispatching trains by telephone. "I believe the details of the train orders, with proper safeguards could be worked out, as under the present system train orders are repeated back by telegraph to the dispatcher issuing them; and while the present telephone system is not as accurate in the transmission as the Morse telegraph, yet, with the improvements that are constantly being made I am satisfied that the time will come when the Morse system will be entirely abolished in the handling of train orders and a telephone system substituted. [21]

With regard to securing business, the Burlington System reported on an extensive telephone network permitting traffic department officials to be in regular communications with local men of their departments. While the report didn't refer to dispatching of trains by telephone, it reported that the telephone circuit along the right-of-way permitted the "use of a portable telephone set carried by the conductor to get in communication with the dispatcher to run around an obstruction."[22] Here, we see the "emergency use" of the telephone in action.

Mr. L. H. Korty, superintendent of telegraph on the Union Pacific, discussed telephones with the following remarks in 1906: "Telephones are being introduced in connection with the automatic block system now being installed, as they will place the dispatcher in close touch with the non-telegraph stations. Portable telephones will be placed on trains. The movement of trains by telephonic orders in certain localities under proper safeguards is possible and is already being done on some roads. Long Distance telephone lines between division and district terminals," he goes on, "would afford invaluable service to operating and traffic departments...I look forward to the time, in the not distance future, when the telephone service of the Union Pacific will be co-extensive with that of the telegraph..."[23]

At a meeting of Railway Telegraph Superintendents in 1908, a general discussion was held by telegraph superintendents for a number of railroads, on the use of the telephone for train dispatching.[24] The companies reporting the installation of telephone lines for use in train dispatching included the Erie Railroad; Northern Pacific; Pennsylvania Lines; New York Central; Chicago and Northwestern; Delaware, Lackawanna, and Western Railroad; Union Pacific Railroad; and the Michigan Central.[25] In a paper read before the St. Louis Railway Club on February 12th, 1909, Mr. W. E. Harkness of NY presented a very detailed report on the subject of The Telephone for Train Dispatching". ." In the paper, he discusses the reason for the substitution of telephone in place of telegraph for directing of train movements and dispatching of trains, recent legislation limiting the work hours for railroad employees transmitting or receiving orders to nine hours a day. Another reason was the shortage of good telegraph operators and the expense of hiring additional operators. He described in great detail the procedures for safe operation and the experience of several railroads on the use of telephones in train dispatching toward that end. He also described equipment used for this service.[26]

There were many more references in *The Telegraph Age* on the use of telephone circuits for train dispatching through the balance of the decade including the Michigan Central (Nov. 1, 1909 Pg 774), Seaboard Air Line (Nov. 16, 1909 Pgs. 801-803), Illinois Central (Dec. 16, 1909 Pgs. 867-869), Chicago and Northwestern Railroad Company (Dec. 16, 1909 Pgs. 871-872), The Grand Trunk railroad, The Pennsylvania Railroad, and the Norfolk and Western (Jan. 1, 1910 pg 57), The Erie Railroad (Feb. 1, 1910 Pg. 122) and others.

1910 – 1920

Four issues were primary subjects within communications for the years between **1910** and **1920**: First, the expansion of power lines and their impact on the existing communications lines along the railroad rights-of-way. A meeting of the Western Division of the Association of Railway Telegraph Superintendents held in Chicago on January 19, 1910, a report was presented on high tension wire crossing. The Indiana Railroad Commission issued a circular calling attention to dangers arising from wire crossing the railroad tracks and common causes of defects in the construction of overhead wire crossings.[27] A Report of Committee on High Tension Wire Crossings laid out general requirements with specifications to apply for these crossings.[28]

Inductive interference was also of concern, as presented in a paper read at a meeting of Eastern Division Association of Railway Telegraph Superintendents in New York November 11th, 1914.[29]

The second issue consisted of reports by several railroads on use of telephone train dispatching. The Grand Trunk, Pennsylvania Railroad, and Norfolk and Western authorized use of telephone train dispatching,[30] with the Great Northern completing 2100 miles with the addition of the Spokane Division's 337 miles.[31] By the end of the decade, telephone train dispatching was common place.

The third issue was the development and implementation in the use of a printing telegraph machine. [32]

By 1915, the Morkrum telegraph printer was in common use as described in *Telegraph and Telephone Age*.

> THE PRINTING TELEGRAPH, during the five-year period 1912-1917, came into extended use by telegraph companies, press associations and the railroads. The printing telegraph consists essentially of a sending instrument, equipped with a keyboard similar to that of a typewriter, electrically connected with a receiving instrument in such a manner that the latter automatically reproduces what is typewritten on the sending instrument. Without the printing telegraph, if would have been difficult or impossible to handle the increased telegraph business during the Great War.[33]

The fourth issue that arose in this period was the interest in radio telegraphy and the radio telephone. Wireless experiments on the Union Pacific Railroad were frequently reported on and followed by the railroad industry. On December 23, 1912, the Union Pacific applied to the Department of Commerce and Labor for a license to operate and maintain a wireless telegraph system along its lines.[34] However, the Lackawanna Railroad had begun tests with wireless telegraphy in 1909; in 1913, they erected steel towers in Binghamton, NY and Scranton PA.[35] Mr. L. B. Foley, superintendent of telegraph on the Lackawanna Railroad at the time, read a paper on "Train Dispatching by Wireless" at the New York Railroad Club, February 19, 1915, describing work done on the Lackawanna in applying wireless to operations of trains. (It was a custom in the railroad and other industries to discuss improvements in their area of position or expertise to report on issues of common interest.) At the New York Railroad club men of responsibility and distinction were present such as David Sarnoff, Contract Manager, Marconi Wireless Telegraph Company of America (later President of RCA), J. L. Hogan Jr., National Electric Signaling Company and many other railroad telegraph superintendents.[36]

1921 – 1930

During the next decade, demand for more telephone service developed research and implementation of telephone and telegraph carrier systems. Many railroad officials complained that pole lines along the railroads were overburdened with a large number of wires. E. H. Colpitts and O. B. Blackwell, two Bell Telephone engineers, presented a paper on "Carrier Current Telephony and Telegraphy" at the Ninth Midwinter Convention of the American Institute of Electrical Engineers held in New York on February 17, 1921.[37] In the meantime, additions of copper wire to extend telephone service continued.[38] (Copper wire permitted longer telephone circuits compared with iron wire which was also used. More additional telephone service required more wires on telephone poles. Carrier systems discussed later in the book greatly expanded the number of telephone circuits a pair could handle. Iron wire severely limited the use of carrier systems).

The importance of pole lines to railroad service resulted in studies to extend the life of pole lines by treating the poles and improving line construction by using equipment to dig holes and set poles.[39] Pole line construction standards were developed, and classification of pole line grades of service. There were concerns over power line construction near the railroad pole line and associated induction, and hazards from wire line crossings resulted in establishing of standards for crossings and laws passed to enforce these standards. ("Every case of inductive interference along a railroad is due to the encroachment of the power lines and is not due to the telegraph and telephone lines which were there first."[40] "The problem confronting the railroad telegraph and telephone engineer is that situation involving inductive interference are becoming more numerous".[41]

Above, Mr. B. A. Worthington, of Wheeling and Lake Erie Railroad, discussed the procedure of using telegraph issued train orders being repeated back to the train dispatcher. When fully developed, the issuance of train orders by telephone incorporated the procedure of repeating the train order back. The details of which included the underling each individual word by the telegraph operator and the train dispatcher in his original train order, along with every telegraph operator on the dispatcher's telephone circuit.

"Prior to development of the vacuum tube and development of loud speakers, train dispatchers used a telephone style transmitter mounted in a harness on his chest, and a telephone style receiver mounted on a headband to permit hands free operation of his position allowing him to easily issues train orders and work permits.

"Prior to development of equipment to select a specific the telegraph operator (also referred as a train order operator) had to listen on the dispatcher telephone line for call by the train dispatcher. The telegraph operator could hear his station call sign within hearing distance of the telegraph sounder. Development of telephone selectors permitted the same freedom. This freedom permitted them to handle other business like selling passenger tickets."

Improvement in dispatcher telephone service resulted in its continued expansion, installation, and service improvements, with reliable selectors and loud speakers, which eliminated the headband receiver.[42] Meanwhile, transpositions schemes were standardized due to increased number of telephone circuits on the pole lines.[43]

(Telephone circuits added to pole lines with telegraph service experienced noise from electrical interference from adjacent telegraph lines in the form of "thumps". By periodically reversing the position of the wires on the pole line, called transpositions, these thumps were eliminated.

With the addition of multiple telephone lines on the same pole line telephone, voice from one line was induced into the other telephone line. The transpositions also eliminated this phenomenon. Each railroad initially developed their own pattern of transpositions. *Transpositions schemes were standardized due to increased number of telephone circuits on the pole lines.* A later chapter discusses transposition schemes more thoroughly.)

There was interest in radio communications between the head end of the train and the caboose at this time, but, besides some limited experiments, little progress had been made.[44] As well, new automatic telephone switching proved to be of interest to railroad communications officials, but only a few systems had been installed by 1930.[45]

1931 – 1940

Railway Signaling in 1935 reported, growth of train orders by telephone dispatch to exceed telegraph train orders on class I railroads, 151,103 miles (or 63.72%) were by telephone, compared to 93,907 miles by telegraph.[46]

A unique, four-station telephone system existed on Union Pacific Streamliners, which required no external power. The systems provided communications for trainmen; the four stations were between the engineman's seat, the second power car, the baggage car, and the buffet coach.[47]

Interest in telephone carrier systems continued with a number of papers: "Carrier Telephone for Railroads" by a representative of the American Telephone and Telegraph Company at the Telegraph and Telephone Section of the American Association of Railroads' October 1936 meeting.[48] At the following year's meeting, AT&T presented another paper, "Practical Application of Telephone Repeaters and Carrier Telephone."[49] Committee

IV, Research and Development, Subcommittee 4B reported a brief description of the AT&T "H" and "C" carrier systems and carrier transposition systems.

The "H" carrier was a single-channel, single-sideband carrier system operating 4,150-6,900 cycle and 7,400-10,150 cycle frequencies. The "C" carrier system was a three-channel carrier system operating in a frequency band of 5,000 cycles to 30,000 cycles.[50] At that time, 1937, no railroad systems were reportedly installed in railroad service, (the Union Pacific reported installing a "C" Carrier system in late 1937). The Rock Island Railroad reported installing several single-channel systems furnished by Communications Equipment and Engineering Company of Chicago, which operated in the 9 and 15 KHZ band.[51]

1941 – 1950

Continued interest in expansion of communications facilities occurred during this period in spite of or because of the war. All of the following saw improvements during the period: pole lines, wire lines, telegraph and telephone carrier systems, radio, printing telegraph, and yard speaker systems.

Proceeding the War, new and rebuilt pole lines continued, however, miles of new copper wire more than doubled between 1940 and 1941. During the recession the economic depression impacted railroad service; low profits or losses limited finance and incentives to expand train service and supporting communications services. Economic recovery and fear of war released funding for expansion of railroad service and supporting communications service. Installation of new railroad wire went from 4233 miles added in 1940 to 8504 miles in 1941 and another 8770 miles in 1942. It increased again with a further 1657.5 miles in 1943. Increase in gross mile of telephone dispatch quadrupled between 1940 and 1942, going from 519 miles to 2154 miles.[52]

During this period, development of wire-line carrier allowed for large expansion of telephone service, and concentration of carrier telegraphs on a single voice telephone circuit. Tracking of railroad carrier installations was first noticed in *Railway Signaling* in the January 1943 issue.[53] Development of signal CTC carrier systems were independent of communications carrier systems and designs were not always compatible. The first test of coded carrier control of CTC was conducted on February 11th, 1942, on "an Eastern Railroad" and the first actual service installation was on June 4, 1942, consisting of 60 mile of line circuit with 30 field stations.[54] As stated in *Railway Signaling*, "The Committee of Direction of the Telegraph and Telephone Section of the AAR appointed a Special Committee on Coded Carrier Control to investigate jointly with the Signal Section and report on possible interference between carrier systems for remote control of centralized traffic control and carrier communications systems of the Railroads." As the frequencies and power levels had been independently developed without regard to communication industry standards, at the time four installations were in service: one on the SP, two on the Seaboard, and the last on the Las Vegas-Yermo line of the Union Pacific, all on separate pole lines.[55]

While there had been earlier tests and some licenses had been granted, which were later withdrawn in 1930. Additional tests were conducted using higher frequencies. In the judgment of The Federal Radio Commission (now the FCC) other fields of activity, such as aviation and ship-to-shore, had greater need of the wave bands available than did the railroads. The use of radio for train communications was not revived until 1944, when the development of high-frequency equipment opened up vast new ranges of frequencies.[56] The Federal Communications Commission (FCC) granted the Rock Island Railroad four construction permits on May 30, 1944, and installation began June 5th of the same year at Burr Oak yard, south of Chicago. To understand the railroad radio needs, the FCC held an extensive hearing between September 13 and 18 in the US District Court House in Washington, DC, of railroad communications officials and manufacturers.[57]

A great number of opinions and facts were expressed and on January 16, 1945, the FCC issued a report proposing an allocation of frequencies for radio services including the railroads. A definite assignment of frequencies was made on May 17, 1945.[58] The FCC issued a final order governing the new Railroad Radio Service Effective December 31, 1945.[59] The first construction permit for the Railroad Radio Service was issued by the FCC on February 27, 1946, to the Denver and Rio Grande Western for thirty-two mobile units for end-to-end radio telephone service.[60] (Also see Appendix C of this book).

Several railroads opted for inductive radio for communications between head end (locomotive) and caboose and some communications to wayside stations. However, since the inductive radio usually required a pole line within two hundred feet for successful communications, this was not always practical for yard radio systems. Still, a number of railroads elected to install (space*) radio systems for yard service, including the Union Pacific.

*(Space radio is a term used to differentiate the radio system operating in the VHF and UHF frequencies from the inductive radio also used as described here. The term was used at this time, for the differentiation between the two systems. As "space" radio dominated the industry the term was dropped).

Yard Speaker system installations were expanding service to improve efficiency for the yardmaster to easily issue instructions to switchmen at trackside on car movements. Newly developed electronics were used to create yard speakers systems. Some of the railroads that reported talk-back and paging loud-speakers systems in 1947 included the C&O, the Illinois Terminal, Kentucky & Indiana Terminal, Louisville and Nashville, the Missouri Pacific, Southern, and the Union Pacific.[61]

American Telephone and Telegraph opened a microwave radio system between New York, NY and Boston on November 13th, 1947, and was introduced into the railroad industry following Western Union's Washington-and-Pittsburgh system.[62] Two papers were presented to the September 1949 Annual Meeting of the Communications Section AAR, one by Motorola and the other by Philco Corp., the latter of which was installing a microwave system for the Rock Island. The Rock Island system was between Goodland, Kansas and Norton KS a distance of 110 miles.[63] The Rock Island chose this installation due to severe ice damage to line wires and pole line as well as, sleet and snow storms.[64]

The railroad industry continued to automate the communications network with installation of Private Branch Exchanges (PBX*); the Illinois Central at several locations,[65] and the Union Pacific at North Platte.[66] "Many railroads have installed dial automatic exchanges which are connected by railroad-owned circuits. Such facilities not only permit the more rapid and efficient handling of calls, but enable the number of telephone operators to be substantially reduced."[67]

*(PBXs are further explained in Chapter 11 under the section on Telephone Switchboards).

1951 – 1960

At the October, 1950 annual meeting of the AAR Communications Section, Mr. E. M. Webster, Commissioner for the Federal Communications Commission (FCC) gave an address discussing the growing interest in Microwave Systems. "No attempt was made to establish technical standards, to limit the type of communication permitted-point-to-point, mobile, etc., or to sub-allocate the bands. The availability of the microwave region of the spectrum opens up an entirely new field."[68] At this point, several railroads had installed a number of limited systems; plans were under consideration to install more extensive ones. The Santa Fe had a 70-mile system between Galveston and Beaumont TX while the Southern Pacific made a survey for a 120 mile system between Crescent Lake and Eugene, OR.[69]

As described in *Railway Signaling and Communications*: "More railroad communications facilities, in the form of new equipment and miles of circuits, were installed in 1952 than in the previous year. The installation of road train radio communications continued at a high level, including 1,475 new units. New yard radio included 529 units, compared with 305 for the previous year. A total of 2,677 loudspeakers and control points were installed in yards, and 1,057 such units were included in new intercommunications systems in freight houses and locomotive shops. The railroads installed telephone train dispatching on 2,447 miles; built 7,101 miles of pole line and replaced 19,347 miles of copper wire. New mileage of long-distance telephone circuits totaled 50,909 miles telegraph circuits, 113,417 miles and printing telegraph circuits, 113,417 miles. A large percentage of these new circuit-miles were derived by installing carrier."[70]

The introduction of computer technology, and the information analysis it processed, drove the communications engineers to develop new and faster data transmission systems.[71] Various data transmissions systems were evaluated and used by different railroads. IBM card-to-tape, using teletype transmission, was one system, while The Union Pacific used the IBM transceiver system, which had direct connection to a voice channel and allowed up to four transceivers per telephone voice channel.[72]

Other new technologies were introduced during this period as well. Several railroads installed black-and-white TV for yard surveillance and others for car checking.

The balance of the decade showed continued expansion of communication facilities. Several railroads installed higher frequency wire line carrier systems between 30 KHZ and 150 KHZ. At the end of the decade, railroads found challenging decisions to be made between higher frequency wire-line carrier systems and microwave systems. A number of microwave systems were in service, usually for short-haul, including the Santa Fe, Rock Island, and the Southern Pacific (SP). The Denver and Rio Grande Western Railway had a 700 mile system under construction and the SP and UP were planning to install their own microwave systems.[73]

By 1960, automatic telephone exchanges (PBXs) had also increased substantially in the railroad industry. Thirty-three railroads had eighty-eight railroad-owned PBXs in service, which included about 6,900 lines. Many were connected by their own long-distance dial trunks, some interconnecting with other railroads, which permitted them to dial to cities on each other's line.[74]

1961 – 1970

During the '60s, railroad expansion of communications facilities increased greatly. Installation of road radios continued at a fast pace, with over 1,337 mobile radios installed and 263 fixed stations. Much of the radio equipment purchased in these years would subsequently meet the FCC deadline for split-channel radio operations, though many railroads with older equipment couldn't be converted.

In 1961, the railroad industry built or rebuilt 6,350 miles of telephone pole line and added 1383 terminals of carrier equipment and 690 talkback speakers[75] to meet demand for expanded communication services.

While railroad cost/benefit analysis studies between private microwave and AT&T Telpack services "trend heavily on each individual user's needs,"[76] plans for installation of microwave systems continued into the next decade. Nine railroads had planned 9,309 miles of microwave at the beginning of the decade and five railroads had 2,743 miles under construction[77] with forty-two microwave stations installed in 1962 alone. PBX installations continued with ten railroad PBXs owned and nine leased.[78]

The year 1962 also saw continued expansion of radio systems, with 3,806 mobile units and 430 base stations. Handietalkie radio expansion continued with 2,235 units. While some inductive radios continued to be installed, VHF radio greatly over shadowed inductive. Of the mobile units purchased, only 160 were inductive radios which were installed on subway cars where inductive radio continued to have an advantage.[79]

Through the balance of the '60s, communications installations remained strong, as reported by *Railway Signaling and Communications*: After 1963, locomotive radios averaged almost 4,000 per year. Fixed radio stations trended upward to 6667 in 1970, and handietalkie radios amounted to about 17,000 over the 8 years. (*Railway Signaling and Communications* for the years cited)

Pole line construction remained strong with new build and replacement of about 20,000 miles of pole line and 26,000 miles of new wire, some aluminum but mostly copper. New carrier terminals increased from 2,933 in 1963 to 6,229 in 1968, but dropping to about 2000 per year in the late '60s as more microwave system were installed. 156 microwave stations were installed in 1963, but dropped to 65 in 1964 and 1965. However, they expanded each year after to a total of 335 new stations in 1970. Almost 1000 were installed in the eight year period. (*Railway Signaling and Communications* for the years cited)

Other communications system also expanded through the period. About 14,000 talkback speakers and about 3,930 PBX systems were installed, of which 33% were leased and 66% were railroad owned.

1981 – 1990

This decade saw the railroad industry's interest in the expansion of Fiber Optic Cables became a significant new communications facility for railroad service or income. One of the first fiber-optic cable installation plans on a railroad right-of-way was an agreement between Amtrak and MCI in 1982.[80] The plan was to install a 225-mile cable in existing Amtrak ducts in the Amtrak trackage corridor between Washington and New York,NY, which allowed Amtrak to receive communication service in the MCI cable. Since the agreement was non-exclusive, Amtrak was able to lease service to other communications companies, such as Cable and Wireless, (an old British Company and an early entrant in using fiber optic technology).

Other agreements quickly followed: MCI with CSX, 4,000 miles of service in Florida and NY to Chicago; GTE/Sprint for 960 miles of Southern Pacific Transportation Co. in CA and Texas. Lightnet was formed as a joint venture between Southern New England Bell and CSX.

United Telecom Communication Inc. (later known as Sprint) signed lease agreements with the Milwaukee, the Illinois Central, Conrail and the Union Pacific and announced a 23,000 mile coast-to-coast, border-to-border network for the purpose of building a national fiber optic telecommunications network.[81]

Advanced Train Control Systems Project (ATCS) was pursued by the railroad industry during the 1980s, ARINC Research Corporation received a contract to develop the system. "In June 1984, the Association of American Railroads joined the Railway Association of Canada in inviting suppliers and consultants to a meeting in Toronto where broad goals of the program were stated."[82] The program envisioned the system to be capable of performing these main functions:

> *"They will specify the data links to the train control point, the operating plan in terms of arrival times dictated by the commercial needs of the traffic.*
>
> *"They will provide the means of detecting the location of the front and rear of a train and its direction and speed of movement and transmit this information to the control point.*
>
> *"The information will also include the position of all switches and reports from all detectors of snow and rock slides, or broken rails.*

> "They will include 'core control' to compute the most favorable sequences of decision concerning train movement over the next several hours.
>
> "They will include acceptable kinds of communications of instruction. This will include instruction to the enginemen in the form and electronic display...
>
> "And lastly, there will be some data link to the railway headquarters to let them know what is going on."[83]

Interest in consolidating dispatchers grew greatly into system-wide dispatch centers. Expansion and improved reliability of communications technology presented many railroads with the opportunity to improve scheduling and control of train movement. Mergers between railroads dictated a need to provide unified control of train operations, and computer-aided-dispatching permitted more efficient scheduling of trains and communications consolidation, as well as dynamic flexibility to change dispatch territories.

During this period, the Burlington Northern consolidated dispatch centers in Fort Worth, TX, while the Union Pacific consolidated dispatch centers at the Harriman Dispatch Center in Omaha.

1990 – 1992

The railroad industry, facing high costs to maintain and replace pole lines, began investigating in Supervisory Control and Data Acquisition (SCADA) systems to provide radio links to signal-control points. The Union Pacific installed a SCADA system to monitor, meter, and control to its CalNev pipeline subsidiary's pipeline between Colton, CA and Las Vegas in 1987. Between 1988 and 1990, the Union Pacific installed a SCADA system to CTC control points on the recently merged Missouri-Kansas-Texas Railroad. The exact date other railroads followed is not known, but reports presented at AAR Communications and Signals Regional Sections meeting demonstrated railroad interest in this technology. Presentations by the CSX and comments by their representatives indicated use of SCADA technology on the Santa Fe and Amtrak during this period.

Additionally, the railroad industry was faced with the interface of railroad communications with fiber optic company-provided services. Mr. William J. Scheerer, Assistant to Chief Engineer Chessie System, discussed the issue in a paper presented to the Association of American Railroads Communications and Signal meeting in Atlanta that took place between September 24-26, 1990. In it, he discussed the problem of furnishing drop- and insert-service along the right-of-way and "last mile interface." He identified three methods of interface for "last mile interface": 1) Lease of telephone services from local telephone company, 2) Direct interface with the fiber optic company POP near the railroad communications office, and 3) Microwave link. The Union Pacific chose to use direct interface with optical fibers for most all services, and microwave at a few locations where direct fibers were too expensive to provide.

Many railroads, experiencing a large increase in circuit availability, increased Exchange Of Services (EOS) with other railroads to serve off right-of-way offices. The Union Pacific established new or expanded EOS service with the Norfolk and Southern, the CSX, the Illinois Central, and the Southern Pacific.

Railroads continued expansion of microwave services across their network to reach and upgrade previously marginalized offices to expand data and voice facilities.

2

Telegraph/ Communications Department Leaders

Leadership of the Union Pacific Railroad Communications Department has always been in the hands of capable and knowledgeable individuals. Two Superintendents of Telegraph, for the Union Pacific Railroad, during construction of the railroad were identified as John D. Congdon and H. H. Cook; further information is listed below. John D. Congdon was identified as Superintendent in *"The Telegrapher,"* dated to July 2, 1866. Other than this listing extensive research could find no other information about him.

Little information about the H. H. Cook is available as Superintendent of Telegraph on the Union Pacific Railroad. In the *Journal of Telegraph* Vol. 1, from December 2, 1867. Several other references to Mr. Cook are listed below.

After completion of the railroad with the driving of the Golden Spike on May 10, 1869, Mr. Dickey and his assistant Mr. Korty were identified in August 1869, as being Superintendent and Assistant Superintendents of Telegraph both of whom had their headquarters at Omaha.[2] From then on we have identified these leaders and other leaders of Union Pacific Communications. These men, so identified, were early icons of industry, not only to the railroad but to the telephone industry in the West. Of course, through the years, not all Superintendents of Telegraph were enlightened managers. As with other railroad officials, some were dinosaurs, and were asked to step aside while their replacements proved to be enlightened managers who sought and hired excellent engineers.

Ed Creighton, while not employed by the Union Pacific, received contracts for pole line construction for Union Pacific telegraph lines simultaneous with railroad construction. "W. B. Hibbard," an associate of Creighton, "afterward became superintendent for Pacific Telegraph Company, first at Omaha and afterwards at Salt Lake."[1]

Ed Creighton

Ed Creighton was general manager of the original national telegraph line from Chicago to Salt Lake, and remained such from the time it was completed until 1867. He is credited with construction of the eastern half of the Transcontinental Telegraph Line in 1861; this subject is covered in more detail below. While he constructed telegraph lines for the transcontinental railroad initiative, there is no indication that he was employed by the railroad. When he turned over his responsibility to Mr. W. B. Hibbard, Hibbard was identified as Superintendent of the Pacific Telegraph Company, later to become part of Western Union Telegraph Company.[3]

W. B. Hibbard

Mr. Hibbard, while in the employ of Ed Creighton, constructed many lines for Creighton. He constructed the original telegraph line from Fort Kearney to Julesburg, while Creighton superintended the constructed the line from Julesburg to Salt Lake. Mr. Hibbard was never identified as an employee of the Union Pacific Railroad; however, he was at Promontory Point at the Last Spike Ceremony, and was identified as Superintendent of Telegraph Eastern Division for Western Union Telegraph.[4]

Others reported to be at the Last Spike Ceremony representing telegraph persons include E. Creighton, builder of telegraph from Omaha to Salt Lake, in 1861; F. T. Vandenburg, Superintendent Telegraph Central Pacific; Howard Sigler, operator Central Pacific; P. Kearney, operator for Western Union; and W. B. Fredericks, operator for Western Union.[5]

For the Golden Spike Ceremony, Mr. Hibbard had to construct a telegraph line from Salt Lake City to Promontory Point as the original Western Union transcontinental telegraph line routed through Salt Lake City. Mr. Hibbard arranged for the "wire to be attached to the golden spike so that when it was struck by Governor Stanford, that instant the electric spark communicated the cities east and west, announced the work was done"[6]

However, there was some controversy around the moment, as described in Chicago Tribune May 11, 1869:

> However, other reports indicated that the Western Union wire had just been extended as a branch of its transcontinental wire from Ogden to Corrine UT, east of Promontory. The Western Union transcontinental line was south of Salt Lake and the line north of the lake through Promontory was not completed until the summer of 1869. Who actually wired the hammer and spike is in dispute. Not in dispute is that the Central Pacific telegraph wire was wired to the hammer, and the Union Pacific telegraph wire routed through the telegraph table to a partly driven (if iron, or placed in the predrilled hole) spike, most likely the gold spike.
>
> Amos L Bowsher, Central Pacific foreman of telegraph construction, claimed to make the connections8, but as foreman, he probably oversaw the work. As was reported in the Chicago Tribune, the actual wiring was done by F. L. Vandenberg Superintendent of Central Pacific Telegraph.[9]
>
> Others reported as wiring the interconnection may have participated in stringing the wires and placement of the telegraph table.
>
> A laurel polished tie from CA had predrilled ¾ inch augur holes in it to receive the two Gold Spikes, Iron-Silver-Gold Spike and Silver Spike, which were the ceremonial last spikes completing the joining of the rails. The ceremony, with the

driving of the last spike and announcement "dot dot done" was completed.

After the ceremonial spikes were driven and the rails joined, the Union Pacific engine number 119 and the Central Pacific engine Jupiter were driven over the junction. The laurel tie and spikes were removed and a standard tie placed.

The iron spike (Lemon Spike, supposedly removed shortly after the event) was driven home after the ceremony was over and recovered later.[10]

John D. Congdon

The Union Pacific Railroad broke ground on December 3, 1863, but first started construction in Omaha on July 10, 1865. The first individual recorded as Telegraph Superintendent for the Union Pacific Railroad is John D. Congdon. An item in *"The Telegrapher,"* dated to July 2, 1866, lists Mr. John D. Congdon as "Superintendent of Union Pacific Railroad line at Omaha" and is the only reference which identified someone as the first Superintendent of Telegraph on the Union Pacific Railroad. Since this information was reported under the section "TELEGRAPHIC MISCELLANEA," it is presumed that Mr. Congdon was in charge of the Telegraph Department. Further search for hiring, work, or dismissal was elusive. Below is a reference to construction of a telegraph line for the Union Pacific between North Platte, NE, and Promontory Summit, UT by Ed Creighton.

H. H. Cook

Little information about the H. H. Cook is available as Superintendent of Telegraph on the Union Pacific Railroad. In the *Journal of Telegraph* Vol. 1, from December 2, 1867, wherein the Journal was tracking the construction of the railroad, it says on page 2: "The Union Pacific Railroad is being rapidly pushing forward to completion. Only last week, another section of 160 miles west of Laramie, of the road was opened with ten new offices requiring twenty operators. These have all been filled now at salaries varying from $65 to $85 per month.

"The great national iron thoroughfare that will soon span the continent, is now in operation 692 miles west of Omaha, the western terminus being a mushroom town called Benton. The road is divided up into divisions of equal distances, A, B, C, and D. The management of the telegraph line belonging to the railroad company is under the able superintendence of Mr. H. H. Cook, Esq. of Omaha, whose system of management precludes the possibility of the trains coming into collision on any part of the road. The boys all speak well of him."[11]

He was replaced by Mr. J. J. Dickey, of Chicago…appointment of General Superintendent of Union Pacific Railroad telegraph lines, vice H. H. Cook removed.[12]

John J. Dickey

John J. Dickey was born on April 11th, 1839, in Rushville, IL. John J. Dickey is the first Superintendent of Telegraph on the Union Pacific Railroad after completion of the railroad at Promontory Point on May 10, 1869, being promoted in August of 1869. In these early years as the Superintendent of Telegraph for the Union Pacific Railroad, he also simultaneously held the same title for Atlantic and Pacific Telegraph.

He held two jobs at once because of the private-public partnership of railroad telegraphs. At that time, many telegraph department employees were dual employees of the railroad and telegraph company, including Superintendents of Telegraph, linemen, Supervisors of Lines (exact title), and telegraphers. They received two paychecks. J. J. Dickey - Superintendent of Telegraph department (Union Pacific), and L. H Korty, Asst. Superintendent of Telegraph, has 14 offices in this city [Omaha], employing 45 operators and in the past year handled 12,000,000 messages, an average of 4000 words per day. John J. Dickey also held the title of Superintendent of Telegraph for the local Western Union Telegraph Company when it merged with the Atlantic and Pacific Telegraph in 1881. WUTC employed 46 operators, 41 clerks and office boys and 16 messengers in Omaha.[13]

During the summer of 1887, his position with Union Pacific was severed in order that he could devote attention to affairs of Western Union as General Western Superintendent which included Nebraska, Kansas, Colorado, Wyoming, Utah, Idaho and several more states. These changes in Colonel Dickey's (as he was known) position were due to changes of Union Pacific right of way contracts.

He passed away on December 29, 1903.[14]

Col. Dickey and L. H. Korty were instrumental in bringing telephone service to Omaha, NE and western states. This business and others is discussed in detail in chapter 8, however, these men were very prominent in Omaha business and social life as well.

Louis H Korty

Louis Korty was born Oct. 22, 1846, at Hanover, Germany. At the early age of 14, he became a telegraph operator working for the Illinois & Mississippi Telegraph Company.

At the age of 18, he was in the service of the United States Military Telegraph Corps working for General C. C. Washburn under General Sherman's Department of the Cumberland, Tennessee, Mississippi and the Gulf, as a cipher code operator who deciphered the secret papers taken from captured spies. He continued in military telegraph service as cipher clerk until 1865, to the age of 19; after the Civil War, he was appointed manager for the government of the joint office of the American and Southwestern Telegraph companies, a position which he retained until the lines were relinquished by the government and turned back to the companies.

In the fall of 1868, he came north and accepted a position with the Western Union Company, and for a year was one of the three operators who worked the overland circuit on which Omaha was one of the principle relay points. During the historic action at Promontory Point, Utah, when the Golden Spike was driven, he made the connection at Omaha whereby the hammer tap, signifying the joining of the rails at Promontory Point, was electrically transmitted to Washington. In the spring of 1870, at the age of 23, he entered the employ of the Union Pacific, serving as agent and telegraph manager at several stations in Wyoming and Utah. He was transferred to Omaha in October 1871 as chief operator; was appointed assistant superintendent of telegraph in 1881 at the age of 35; and on the resignation of Mr. J. J. Dickey in October 1887, as superintendent of the Union Pacific's lines. "He now enjoys the distinction of having charge of the largest railway telegraph system in the world," it was reported at the time by the Omaha Daily Bee.[15]

Mr. Korty, in conjunction with Mr. Dickey, introduced and developed the telephone in Nebraska, Wyoming, Utah, Idaho and Montana, and Western Iowa. He still retained a large interest in the two telephone companies opening that territory, and was secretary and treasurer of the Nebraska Telephone Company 1887.[16]

While Korty along with Dickey introduced the telephone industry to the Midwestern states, he was prominent in expediting telephone services to the Union Pacific Railroad as well. He saw the beneficial needs served by local and long distance service as important instruments to the Railroad. (Refer to comments by Korty in Chapter 9).

Due to health, Mr. Korty resigned his position as Superintendent of Telegraph of the Union Pacific Railroad Company in 1908. He died on May 16, 1921, at the age of 74.[17]

Mr. Sheldon

When Mr. Korty retired, the circular announcing his retirement read: "Mr. Sheldon is to succeed Mr. Korty, who voluntaries after a very successful administration of his department."[18]

Discussed below is Mr. Sheldon's approach to dispatching trains by telephone. He demonstrated organization ability in leadership in the Telegraph Department, and as member of the Association of Railway Telegraph Superintendents, he presented a paper on administration of the Telegraph Department. The paper, entitled "Efficiency of Office Organization" was very detailed about the organization of the management of the Superintendent of Telegraph's office,[19] which included such things which follows:

Several examples are taken from the paper which exemplify Mr. Sheldon's detail to management of his department:

> "The Superintendent of Telegraph, in order to exercise a proper supervision of his department, to have opportunity to look personally after many matters requiring attention along the line, to have time to meet and talk with callers who have ideas of interest and benefit to discuss, and to

> be able to keep posted on progress in our field of work, plan improvements, at5tend meeting of our associations regularly, etc., must not be tied down to close detains of office work, and office organization should be planned to afford him such opportunities. Otherwise, by tying him down closely to a desk, with barely time to wade through a mass of detail work, many larger things of importance and much value would be neglected through sheer lack of opportunity to them the attention required."

He goes on to discuss the responsibility of the Chief Clerk to handle the details of the operation and supervision of the staff.

The staff included positions of importance including a General Foreman to oversee construction and maintenance of the telegraph plant, positions responsible for the telegraph service and assorted stations, relay offices and department accounting.

One interesting position which is discussed in the paper is the Educational Inspector. This reflects Mr. Sheldon's attention to detail is included here:

> 2. "Closely connected with the employment bureau is the Educational Inspector, Who looks out specially for the student-helpers at stations, of whom we have about two hundred, and the students in various schools that we are encouraging, to see that satisfactory progress is made and that promotions are forthcoming as they are deserved. Until recently, but little attention has been paid to selection or education of those seeking to become operators and agents, most anybody strong enough to handle freight, baggage and express having been assigned to helpers positions, without regard to their qualifications for advancement or desire to advance. Then, when once employed, they were left to themselves to learn as much and how, as they saw fit, with no one specially interested to encourage and show them, to see that they had proper opportunities for study and practice and availed themselves fully of them. Now, helpers are selected from those who earnestly wish to become operators, being taken

generally from telegraph schools where some progress has been made, both in telegraphy and station work and accounts, and, before employment is given them, their fitness in general, in respect to education, physical condition, etc., is passed upon and decided..."

The discussion about the Educational Inspector continues to discuss the selection and motivational issues in employment of telegraph operators. Later in the paper many leaders in railroad industry and other industries come from telegraph operators. Thomas Edison, began employment as a telegraph as seen in the movie "Thomas Edison" starring Spencer Tracy as Thomas Edison.

A second paper, entitled "Organization for Wire Chiefs and Telephone Inspectors" outlined the responsibilities, selection of, and importance of the wire chiefs and telephone inspectors. The paper was presented at the St. Louis convention of the Association of Railway Telegraph Superintendents May 22, 1913.[20]

The exact date when train dispatching began on the Union Pacific using telephone circuits is not known, but Mr. Sheldon presented a paper before the Omaha Railway Club on March 9, 1910, describing the use of Telephone Train Dispatching. Further reference to the paper is covered in Chapter nine.[21]

Demonstrating a keen mind and organizational performance found Mr. Sheldon as a recognized leader in the railway telegraph industry. He served as vice president of the Association of Railway Telegraph Superintendents starting in June 20, 1910, and as president in June 4, 1912. At the Convention of Association of Railway Telegraph Superintendents held in Boston MA June 26-30, 1911, in the absence of the Association president, he served as chairman of the meeting.[22]

A telegraph office was established in the new Union Pacific headquarters building at 14th and Dodge Street, Omaha in November 1911 under Mr. Sheldon's supervision.[23] Further description is developed in Chapter 9 under "Early Union Pacific Railroad Telephone Service."

Mr. John B. Sheldon died at Wise Memorial Hospital July 30, 1914, and is buried at Forest Lawn Cemetery in Omaha. He was survived by niece Miss Lu. B. Sheldon, Chief of Telegraph at Union Station.[24]

Peter F. Frenzer

Peter Frenzer was appointed Supt. Telegraph for the Union Pacific on August 13th, 1914.[25] Mr. Frenzer was manager-in-charge of local operations during the installation of the new headquarters building in 1911. As Superintendent of Telegraph, he was one of the longest serving, his tenure running from August 13th, 1914 to December 31, 1938, a total of twenty-four years.

"Like all railroaders, he equated communications with telegraph, and he was close to Jeffers (president of Union Pacific), who took great pride in having started as a telegrapher and dispatcher.[26] Voice telephone service had been introduced to the railroad back in 1879, and in November of 1911, a new switchboard was installed in the new headquarters building as referenced above.[27] Direct long-distance telephone lines were in service for a number of years, but the poles could only handle a limited number of wires.

Little is known of the development of the Telegraph Department during his period as Superintendent. He made improvements to the Telegraph Department. During his administration, printing telegraph was installed; in 1917, the Union Pacific converted 492 miles of Morse telegraph circuits to printing telegraph circuits. The Union Pacific had 13,000 wire miles of copper at the start of 1921, and by the start of 1926, the Union Pacific had added another 4,363 mile of copper wire.[28]

Mr. Frenzer was elected to the Committee of Direction of the Telegraph and Telephone Section of the American Railway Association in 1919[29]. Progressing through Committee X - Education and Training as committee chairman, he became Chairman of the Telegraph and Telephone Section in 1929. During the 1920s, the railroad industry established and improved its pole line construction standards, treatment of poles for preservation, crossing standards for power lines, and induction mitigation during Mr. Frenzer's work on the committee.[30]

Improvements in communications which were not directly associated with Mr. Frenzer were also made. An intra-train telephone system between four stations was installed on the Streamliner, for instance.[31]

Telegraph managers apparently had freedom to act on their own initiative. Charley Sparr, a manager of telegraph at Los Angeles arranged to have some three channel-carrier systems installed between Los Angeles and Salt Lake City in 1937[32]. During a visit to Salt Lake, Jeffers, then Vice President of the Union Pacific Railroad, tried the telephone circuits out and hurried back to Omaha, where he called upon Frenzer and demanded to know about the newfangled system—and Frenzer didn't have a clue.

But he knew Sparr must be involved and said so. Subsequently, Sparr was summoned to Omaha at once, and naturally assumed he was being fired. "How soon," Jeffers barked at him, "can you have this all over the railroad?"

He asked Frenzer if he knew about the new phone system. Frenzer admitted he did, but reminded Jeffers how proud he was of his telegraph origins and insisted the road was doing fine with the telegraph alone.

It was then that Jeffers ordered his old friend to take retirement at once. With retirement, Union Pacific brought in Glen R. Van Eaton as Supt. of Telegraph.[33]

Frenzer's sudden retirement happened on December 31, 1938.[34] He died on March 16, 1941, at the age of 73.

A search of a replacement for Frenzer began by giving aptitude tests to the wire chiefs. Klein reports the winner to be G. R. Van Eaton, manager of the Las Vegas telegraph office, and he was handed Frenzer's position and told the job was to modernize communications on the Union Pacific Railroad.[35] However, according to newspaper accounts, there was a gap in the Superintendent of Telegraph position between December 31, 1938 and June 29, 1942 when Van Eaton was appointed.

Frank A. Coulter

During this gap in service between Frenzer and Van Eaton, Frank A. Coulter held the position. Coulter was appointed Superintendent of Telegraph January 1, 1939.[36]

During his period in office, there was significant expansion in development of wire carrier systems.

The installation of the first carrier system, Los Angeles to Salt Lake City, proceeded his term in office, but a number of carrier systems were subsequently installed, including the Salt Lake City to Omaha system in 1941, alongside development of plans to expand carrier systems throughout the railroad.

On November 25 & 26, 1941, a meeting was held in Omaha to develop coordination of carrier system design between Union Pacific Telegraph Department officials and high level officials of the Western Union Telegraph Company assembled from New York, NY, San Francisco, and Dallas. The details of the meeting are covered later in the book Chapter Nine with development of the wire line carrier system network.[37]

In May 1942, Mr. Coulter, Superintendent of Telegraph, retired and was replaced by Mr. Glen Van Eaton on May 29, 1942.

Glen R. Van Eaton

> "Mr. G. R. Van Eaton, Superintendent of Telegraph South Central District with headquarters Salt Lake City Utah, was promoted to Superintendent of Telegraph for the entire system with headquarters at Omaha, NE. Mr. Van Eaton entered the service of the Union Pacific in 1923 as station agent at Sloan, NV and in 1934 was promoted to wire chief at Las Vegas, NV. In 1937 he was advanced to manager of the telegraph office at Las Vegas and in June, 1941 he was promoted to assistant superintendent of telegraph, with headquarters at Salt Lake City. Two months later, his title was changed to superintendent of telegraph of the South-Central district."[38]

Van Eaton was appointed on May 29, 1942. The Announcement was made by E. J. Connors, VP of the railroad and A. C. Kronkhite, general manager for Western Union.[39] As was traditional, the Superintendent of Telegraph held the dual title for both the railroad and telegraph companies

The selection of Mr. Van Eaton is described above and his challenge "was to modernize communications on the Union Pacific Railroad."[40]

As stated in Klein's book "Union Pacific, The Rebirth 1894-1969", "Van Eaton knew nothing about the subject but he did know how to listen and learn. Above all, he recognized that the traditional system had failed completely in communications. As there was no one to bring up through the ranks, he had to go outside for people who knew electrical engineering. He recruited C. Otis Jett, an engineer with a diverse background. Of the six companies to which Jett applied for a job in 1945, only Van Eaton responded with a personal visit. "I won't take no for an answer," he reportedly said.[41]

During this Van Eaton/Jett period, communications on the railroad exploded. The title of superintendent was changed between February and June of 1957 to Superintendent of Communications. The exact date is unknown, but is determinable by the changes in title noted in Railway Signal and Communications articles of those months. It is not known when the dual office with Western Union ended, but references to the dual office also ended with Mr. Van Eaton.

Mr. Van Eaton served on several Association of American Railroads Communications Section committees. He was chairman of Committee Number 5, the Research and Development Committee.[42] In March of 1957 he became a member of the Committee of Direction[43] which reviews and directs policy and reports for communications and signal issues for the Association of American Railroads. In 1958, he became vice chairman of the Communications Section.[44]

Mr. Van Eaton Died January 21, 1978 at age 78.[45]

C. Otis Jett

Mr. C. Otis Jett had wide experience in communications and electronics. With degrees in law and electrical engineering (he studied at University of Kentucky, Eastern Kentucky State Teachers College and George Washington University[46]; the exact institution which awarded the degrees is not known), he exhibited knowledge beyond communications and provided Union Pacific management operational advice on many other business issues. His resume included such diverse employers as Bell System, the Forest Service, and the Tennessee Valley Authority Oak Ridge

Laboratory[47] (It is reported that he worked with Oppenheimer), before moving onto Union Pacific in 1945[48] as communications engineer. Though his exact title was unknown, an article in *World Herald* from 1949 identified him as system telephone and telegraph engineer.

Mr. Jett was appointed Assistant Superintendent of Communications in January of 1961, replacing John E. Fitzpatrick, who had retired. Mr. H. E. Froyd replaced Mr. Jett in his prior position.[49] During his work with the Union Pacific Railroad, he was responsible for the many improvements to the communications system, much of which is expanded upon later in the book Chapter Eleven According to Klein's book, "… The company's appetite (for communications) was voracious. More voice, data, and teleprinter channels were demanded faster than Jett could provide them. The pressure was intense; his operation was trying to do a decade's work in a year, every year."[50] These years of development of the Union Pacific Railroad Communications systems and his contribution to the introduction of computers to the railroad are widely covered in Klein's work, and not repeated here.

C. O. Jett Senior retired as Superintendent of Communications on June 30, 1973. With retirement, he submitted a detailed five-year plan (for improvements, planned for and recommended for the CD), which is widely referenced in this book.

Robert Brenneman

With Mr. Jett's retirement, Robert Brenneman was promoted to Superintendent of Communications, taking the helm on July 1, 1973. Mr. Brenneman started as a dishwasher in the Dining Car Department at a Union Pacific Railroad station restaurant. The secretary to the head of Dining Car and Commissary was drafted during World War II; Mr. Brenneman replaced the drafted secretary because of his knowledge of shorthand.

When former secretary for the Dining Car Department returned from service, he was reinstalled to his old job as secretary to the head of the Dinning Car Department. Mr. Brenneman transferred to the Communications Department in 1945 as secretary to Supt. of Communications, Van Eaton.[51]

Mr. Brenneman held an amateur radio license. Because of that, he became equipment supervisor in 1948,[52] and was picked to develop and implement radio systems for the Communications Department. In that year, the Union Pacific announced a $125,000 communications improvement program including the installation of two-way radio in yard offices and on diesel switch engines in the company's yard at Denver, Omaha, Salt Lake City, Seattle, Los Angeles, Portland, and Pocatello ID. The UP also equipped four road engines and four cabooses with two-way radio for operation between Maryville and Kansas City and fixed radio stations for communications with these trains at five points in Kansas. Mr. Brenneman was responsible for these radio improvements.[53]

By 1953, Mr. Brenneman was promoted to assistant system telephone and telegraph engineer. With introduction and expansion of radio systems on the Union Pacific, he was responsible for designing and supervising the installation of Union Pacific Railroad radio systems, including a novel car inspection system using a radio repeater and walkie-talkie radios.[54] In 1965, he was again promoted to communications engineer and later in the same year promoted to Assistant Superintendent-Communications under Mr. Jett.[55]

With Mr. Jett's retirement on June 30, 1973, Mr. Brenneman was promoted to Director Communications (Title change from Supt. to Director).[56] Under Mr. Brenneman's leadership, the microwave system continued expansion, including the building of a second microwave system between Omaha and Salt Lake City (called the "under-build"), replacement of early microwave equipment with upgraded equipment. Mechanical PBXs began to be replaced with electronic PBXs, and tube-type radios replaced with transistor radios.

Mr. Brenneman retired from Union Pacific Railroad in 1978 with 41 Years with the Railroad.

Hugh Robertson

Born December 14, 1920, Mr. Robertson was a U.S. Coast Guard electronic technician during World War II. Following military service in 1945, he joined the Union Pacific Communications Department as an equipmentman. He was promoted to

Communications Engineer in Salt Lake City and later to Assistant Superintendent Communications in January 1967.[57]

In 1972, he left the Union Pacific to serve as Director of Communications and Signals, Association of American Railroads from 1972 to 1975.[58]

He returned to the Union Pacific in January 1, 1976 and was appointed Director of Communications UPRR. While Director of Communications, he also served as President of the Land Mobile Communications Council and a member of the Department of State, World Administrative Radio Conference (1979).[59]

Mr. Robertson retired from the Union Pacific Railroad in 1981. He died on July 4, 1998.

John J. Jorgenson, Vice President Management Information Services

In December of 1978, the Communications Department was moved from direct report of Vice President of Operations to Mr. Jorgenson, Vice President of Management Information Services Department (MIS). This was the Computer Department. Data transmission heavily supporting the MIS Department was the *raison d'etât* for the move. Both departments were closely technology dependent.

With the Missouri Pacific and Western Pacific Railroad merger which occurred on December 22, 1982, the name was changed to Information Technologies Department.

Mike Ahern

Mr. Ahern was hired by the Union Pacific about January 5, 1959 as an equipmentman after serving in the United States Navy between 1953 and 1955[60]. He was promoted to Communications Engineer about 1965. In this capacity he installed much microwave equipment as the railroad expanded its communications services.

Mr. Ahern was appointed Assistant Director Communications Facilities in December of 1979, one of three promotions to Assistant Director Communications. The other two Assistant Director Communications were Jim May, Assistant Director Communications Services, and the Author, Assistant Director Communications Engineering and Planning all directly reporting to Vice President John Jorgenson.

Mr. Ahern was later promoted to Director Communications Department in December 1982 and to General Director Telecommunications after the merger with the MP & WP.

He retired from the Union Pacific Railroad November 30, 1988, and died September 17, 2009

Gene H Kuhn

Advanced through several communications engineering positions in the Union Pacific Railroad between 1966 and 1992, and detailed at the end of the book under "Author's Profile."

Jim May

Hired as a telegrapher at Laramie in July of 1961, he worked the extra board (railroad employees who do not have a specific employment location and are moved from place to place to fill a need), for a year or so and then moved onto being wire chief in Cheyenne, Kansas City, and Denver. He resigned in 1964 but returned as wire chief in September 1969 in Omaha. He was promoted to Office Manager in Omaha in 1971, and with installation of AAS and TIS computers, he was promoted to Assistant Manager Telecommunications to oversee the Communications Department's installation responsibilities, and prepare an AAS/TIS training program for the Wire Chiefs.

He was appointed to Asst. Director of Communications Services in December 1979, and later Director Communications Services. He was sent by John Jorgenson, V. P. Management Information Services, to Harvard Business School between September and December of 1980 to prepare Mr. May for future assignments.

He retired in 2004.

Jim Merrick

With the merger of Union Pacific with the Missouri Pacific Railroad and Western Pacific Railroad the communications and computer operations were merged and a new organizational structure created with Mr. Merrick appointed Asst. V.P. of Communication in December 1982. Mr. Merrick came from the MIS Department and had prior experience with the AT&T Western Electric subsidiary. Mr. Merrick led the Communications Department for ten years until his retirement in December 1992. During that period, he oversaw the merger of the three communications departments. Mr. Merrick provided leadership to leverage the asset value of the Communications Department by seeking commercial opportunities. The Department used its facilities to serve the communications needs of the Union Pacific Company's subsidiaries and its technical knowledge to furnish advice to outside companies, including the Ferrocarilles De Mexico.

3

Construction of the Transcontinental Telegraph

Railroad communications in the era of modern computer technology may have improved the scheduling, research, expansion, planning, analysis, and processing of inventory control of dispatcher operations, but railroad communications to trains began with the telegraph in the form of train orders issued by the dispatcher and passed to train crews by the telegrapher.

The transcontinental telegraph proceeded railroad telegraph on the Union Pacific Railroad but became an integral part of the history of the railroad.

The Pacific Telegraph Act of 1860 called for the construction of communications that could bridge the east and west coasts of the United States, most pressingly to integrate CA (which had previously become a state in 1850) into the Union. The original Transcontinental Telegraph was constructed by Western Union Telegraph Company between St. Joseph, Missouri and Sacramento, CA. The initial pole line was constructed of native poles (trees cut down in nearby forests for use as telegraph Poles) and plain #9 gauge iron wire.[1]

Omaha had been connected to the East Coast via a telegraphic wire from St. Joseph. During 1860, this wire had been extended to Ft. Kearny, NE. Edward Creighton, a Western Union general agent acting for the Pacific Telegraph Company, oversaw building of the line from Salt Lake City to Omaha. In the winter of 1860-61, Creighton surveyed the balance of the route of the proposed Transcontinental Telegraph Line between Omaha and Sacramento, to be built with the financial support for which he arranged. He continued to San Francisco to meet with investors, who agreed to extend the line from Sacramento to Salt Lake City.

The Nebraska Territorial Legislature authorized the incorporation of the Pacific Telegraph Company in January 11th, 1861. Most of the incorporators, including Edward Creighton, were Western Union executives. Creighton contracted construction of the line from Fort Kearny to Julesburg, while he would supervise the operation from Julesburg to Salt Lake City.[2]

Creighton dug the first post hole for the telegraph line on July 2, 1861; the line was completed on October 24, 1861. A week later, the Overland Telegraph Company of California completed the circuit to Salt Lake City from Carson City. On October 23, 1861, Stephen J Field, the chief justice of California wired Abraham Lincoln to assure him of Californians' "loyalty to the Union."[3] Due to disruptions in Missouri, because of the Civil War, the line was constructed into Omaha and extended to Chicago. Meanwhile, the western part of the line was built by the Overland Telegraph Company between Salt Lake City Utah and Carson City NV.

When Creighton became general superintendent of the Pacific Telegraph Company telegraph system, repair became a priority, and he built branches to many western cities.

Upon completing the transcontinental telegraph line, Mr. Creighton developed many business activities. He invested in the cattle business, banking and other telegraph expansion. He continued in construction business especially building telegraph lines (Sorenson, Alfred, History of Omaha 1889)

In 1869, he also built a line for Pacific Telegraph Company from Laramie, WY to Promontory Summit and he also constructed a railroad line for the Union Pacific from North Platte, NE to Promontory Summit.[4]

4

Union Pacific Telegraph and Related Telegraph Companies

In 1862, Abraham Lincoln signed The Pacific Railroad and Telegraph Act, which subsequently became the charter for the Union Pacific Railroad and Telegraph Company. This act of Congress placed telegraph services on equal footing with the railroad in terms of the importance of the creation, implementation, and maintenance of a nationwide system. At last, the President's desire for the transcontinental railroad and the unifying of the United States was fulfilled.

The original overland telegraph was operated until 1869, when it was replaced by a multi-line telegraph that had been constructed alongside the route of the Union Pacific and Central Pacific railroads.[1] As the line was moved onto the right-of-way of the Union Pacific, railroad wires were added and became the first wire line communication facilities of the Railroad. Over the years, more and more wire was added to the line for train dispatching, operating, and administrative purposes.

A copy of a "Western Union Inventory of Pole Lines" dated 1912 in the UPRR Headquarters files recorded history of the lines. In it was described the original transcontinental telegraph line construction across the west, with pole replacements and line-wire additions included up to that date in 1912. It also recorded that the pole line and wires were moved to the railroad right-of-way with construction of the railroad.

The inventory showed the Western Union wire (for commercial service) and the dedicated railroad wires used for train operations. Poles were replaced and wires added and all was recorded therein. After discovery of telephone service, certain wires were transposed for train dispatcher service. Thus, a continuation of railroad dedicated service and commercial telegraph service existed on the same pole line. (Western Union Inventory of Pole Lines on Union Pacific Property, dated 1912 (at the time of this writing the inventory has been lost. Notes referring to it were prepared a number of years earlier)[2].

Railroad clerks operated agencies which sold train tickets, aided in the dispatch of trains, and provided common carrier message services, including Western Union Telegrams. These agents received a percentage of the business they handled (essentially a commission), thus, Linemen and Supervisors of Lines served as dual employees of the Union Pacific Railroad and Western Union Telegraph. They served the day-to-day effort to maintain the wire line service, repair broken wires, and replacement of individual poles. Western Union maintained line gangs for major pole line replacements. These arrangements continued into the 1960s on the Union Pacific.

Union Pacific telegraph business was not to be developed commercially as envisioned by Congress. However, it played a significant role in the development of the railroad operationally and progressively. Management of the railroad operations through communications facilities was also impacted by the inclusion of "telegraph" in the act. Gould used this authorization to take control of the railroad telegraph and spun it off the railroad telegraph into a common carrier. *(Gould's control of the Union Pacific and subsequent control of the Atlantic and Pacific Telegraph are documented in Maury Klein's The Life and Legend of Jay Gould, Pg 141, and Maury Klein, The Birth of a Railroad 1862-1893 pgs. 337)*[3].

One of Gould's most distinctive talents was an ability to make a single action to simultaneously serve several purposes. At the time he was trying to cement an alliance with the Baltimore & Ohio, which had decided to operate its own express service. At Chicago and St. Louis the Union Pacific could exchange both traffic and express business with the B & O. Nowhere did Gould display this talent more brilliantly than in his handling of the company's telegraph business.[4]

The charter required the Pacific roads to build a telegraph as well as a railroad. Like most roads, the Union Pacific went out of the commercial telegraph business early; unlike most, it did not sign on with Western Union, already the industry giant. General Dodge, Chief Engineer of the railroad, raised so many objections to Western Union's proposal to build a telegraph line on the Union Pacific that it was rejected. In 1869, the UP got much better terms from a small firm called Atlantic & Pacific Telegraph and received 24,000 shares of A & P stock in the bargain. Three years later, the Union Pacific made peace with Western Union through an agreement giving Union Pacific and A&PT a telegraph wire from Omaha to Chicago in return for allowing Western Union one from Omaha to Ogden.[5]

A writer in the "Telegrapher, Volume VIII – No. 63" (dated to November 2, 1872) described a trip on the Union Pacific Railroad:

> "An hour's ride brought us to the famed Platte Valley, up whose broad fertile bosom we travelled nearly four hundred miles. On the right hand are the Union Pacific wires – number one and two under control of the Atlantic and Pacific Telegraph Company. They are well put up on cross-arms, with flint glass insulators of the best quality, and supported by good pine and cedar poles about twenty feet in length. Twenty-five to thirty are used to the mile. Number one wire is used by the railroad company and is divided into four sections, to correspond to the divisions of the road between Omaha and Ogden. Number two wire is used as a through wire between Chicago and Ogden by the A. & P. T. Co., but is hardly adequate for their largely increasing business. A third wire to Julesburg, thence new wires into Colorado, are contemplated next year. On the left side to the track are the Western Union wires, three in number. They are built in a very substantial manner, but in many places the poles have been reset so often as to leave nothing but short stubs, ten or twelve feet in height. This is no serious objection

on the plains. One of the company's wire is used as a through wire between Chicago and San Francisco, but unless the weather is excellent the entire distance, hard work and poor time is the result. The other two wires are worked in short sections, as it has been found impracticable to work more than one long circuit on the poles in this climate. Western Union offices are from forty to eighty miles apart, and operators are in most cases repairmen."[6]

This description of the lines is the only report to verify that there were two pole lines along the Union Pacific Railroad at that time. (This also verifies the report of Creighton building a line for Western Union between Laramie WY and Promontory Summit for the Pacific Telegraph Company (as a contractor for Western Union) and a railroad line for the Union Pacific from North Platte, NE and Promontory Summit, Utah (as a contractor for the Union Pacific).

Until 1874, A&PT limped along in obscurity. Several Union Pacific Directors held the Union Pacific's shares as collateral for an exchange loan made during the hard times of 1873. The company thought so little of the stock it gave the Directors an option to purchase half of the shares, but before the options were exercised, Gould took charge of Union Pacific in March 1874.[7]

Gould's keen eye seized at once on the telegraph stock as too valuable an asset to let go. After a stiff fight he compelled a reluctant a Director to surrender his option on the A&PT shares. With his two adversaries routed from the field, Gould launched his own campaign to transform A&PT into a serious competitor of Western Union. His Boston associates lent their support on the promise that he would perform no less a miracle with the little telegraph company then he had with Union Pacific.

In May 1875, the executive committee authorized Gould to sell the company's shares at $25, the current market price (about $570 in 2018 money). Gould personally took sixteen thousands of the shares while the Bostonians divided the remaining eight thousand. "I don't think an amalgamation of the Western Union Telegraph Company and Atlantic and Pacific Telegraph Co.'s far off," Gould noted hopefully in July 1875.[8]

In fact, it took Gould another two years of grinding struggle to force a merger with Western Union in August 1877. Western Union bought a majority interest in A&PT at $25, the same price Gould had paid Union Pacific for its shares and considerably more than the stock had ever been worth before his arrival on the scene. In this campaign, Gould realized handsome profits for himself, the railroad, and those who followed his lead, along with some important fringe benefits.[9]

5

Judicial and Legislative Government Actions

The telegraph requirement in the Pacific Railroad and Telegraph Act of 1863 resulted in many Legislative bills and court rulings in the early years of the Union Pacific. These had a distinct effect on railroad property rights with regards to the right-of-way. While these issues were mostly settled by the early 1900s, they became important to later issues, such as when the Railroad's officials considered installing a coaxial cable on the right-of-way for common carrier or private carrier communications services. While these plans were not implemented, fiber optic cable installations did result as technology developed in 1984 and the resolution of these legislative and judicial rulings were referenced in the justification to proceed with its installation along the railroad right-of-way.

Almost from the beginning of the national expansion of the telegraph systems to the west coast, issues of exercise of monopoly power, government operation of a national telegraph system, and the Pacific Railroad and Telegraph Act of 1862 dominated the national discussion. In 1870 the Postmaster General, though favorable to a Postal Telegraph system, did "not consider it judicious…at this time."[1] In 1873, Western Union threatened to cut off Pacific Coast newspapers' discussion and promotion of a postal telegraph service.[2]

In 1880, as reported in the *New York Times*' "The War of the Telegraphs" article, the case before the US Circuit Court in St.

Louis of *Atlantic and Pacific Telegraph versus the Union Pacific Railroad* concerned the perpetual lease of telegraph: The American Union Telegraph Company had built lines from the east into Omaha, and insisted that under the terms of the Act of Congress that charted the railroads and telegraph, they should have their telegraph business forwarded by the railroad wires. Acting under this opinion the Union Pacific was preparing to take full control of their wires, but Atlantic and Pacific Telegraph obtained a temporary injunction.[3] In 1883 a House Bill was entered to prevent discrimination in handling of telegraph messages or price.[4] In December of the same year, an experimental Postal Telegraph was proposed to operate in competition to existing telegraph systems. Senator Edmunds proposed taking the entire telegraph system away from private corporations and made a part of the Postal Service.[5]

In 1884 Louis H. Korty, Assistant Superintendent of Telegraph for the Union Pacific Railroad and Secretary of the Nebraska Telephone Company, spoke in opposition to the proposed telegraph bill.[6]

Another issue of access to the telegraph lines west of Omaha was raised by the B&O Telegraph in 1885 similar to the American Union Telegraph issue in 1880. Western Union Telegraph had an exclusive contract with Union Pacific. As a result, the Union Pacific denied service to B&O Telegraph.[7] B&O continued to try to gain access to Union Pacific Railway for a telegraph connection, but Western Union still had an exclusive contract with the Union Pacific. Further discussion in the second session of the 49th session of Congress contended that "if forced to operate its road in accordance with its obligations as a common carrier…laws of the United States, the Union Pacific would…in short be bankrupt."[8]

In a series of Congressional bills starting in 1887 and court actions starting in 1892, which rose all the way to the Supreme Court, raised the issue of the railroad being required to provide telegraph service. A Congressional bill on August 7, 1888 was introduced on the calendar of the House of Representatives; it required the Union and Central Pacific Railroads to construct telegraph lines by their charters instead of contracting with Western Union Telegraph and thereby giving that company a monopoly west of the Missouri River. A discussion of government telegraph also arose. Representative White of NY said it was unwise for the Government, which was the largest creditor of the Pacific Railroads, to reduce profits of the railroads.

In January of 1889, The Union Pacific filed an answer in United States Court which defended its agreement with Western Union Telegraph. The railroad avers it constructed railroad and telegraph line which was so required by the act, further, the "Defendant admits that in September 1869 it entered into a contract with Atlantic and Pacific Telegraph...undertook to lease and devise to the said telegraph all..."[9]

"When the federal court at the instance of the father of the Union Pacific, the general government, sought to sunder the bonds between the road and telegraph in 1892, an appeal was taken to the circuit court, which two years later reversed the district and upheld the contract. Then an appeal was taken to the Supreme Court, which had nullified the contract between the railroad and telegraph. (The Supreme Court in a ruling in 1895, struck down the Union Pacific Railroad and Western Union Telegraph Agreement.[10]) Finally, Judge W. D. Cornish, was handed the case as master in chancery. In 1898 he reported that the original Union Pacific company having passed through bankruptcy, was out of existence and a new company organized. This finding was approved. Petitions, cross-petitions, bills of exceptions and a mass of legal documents were filed following this decision and thus the case has stood until the present. [...] A special examiner from the Department of Justice at Washington has recently been in Omaha going over this court dockets and has devoted considerable time to the Union Pacific, Western Union case-the oldest one on the docket-and it is said that his aim was to clear up this maze of litigation."[11]

In the end, Atlantic and Pacific telegraph lost its case and a new agreement with Western Union Telegraph giving exclusive use of telegraph lines "in so far as the law allows" on the Union Pacific land was signed in 1901; the issue of the Union Pacific Railroad now being a Utah Corporation * was a considering point.[12]

*The Union Pacific was sold out of receivership on November 1, 1897 and chartered as a Utah corporation on January 31, 1898 as a new corporation. (Klein, Maury, The Union Pacific Rebirth 1894-1969, p.28.)

These issues and rulings played an important role in how the Union Pacific has used its right-of-way for communications other than the operation of the railroad itself. Considerable contracts, legislative bills, petitions and more were reviewed and litigated in courts all the way to Supreme Court, as well as by Congress and the Union Pacific Law Department itself. The net result is the Union Pacific determined it had the right to exercise its own decision as to the use of its right-of-way.

In 1966 the Union Pacific Railroad, along with several other railroads including the Southern Pacific and Penn Central, considered the issue of expansion of assets by use of the right-of-way for a transcontinental communication company using coaxial cable technology for long distance communications services. This plan is discussed later in detail.

The act's provisions were reviewed again with the advent of fiber optic communications technology. This time the railroad took advantage of the opportunity to latch onto a new technology which aided the merged railroads communications systems (Union Pacific, Missouri Pacific, Western Pacific) that, without which, the advantages of merger would have developed more slowly.

In the beginning, constructing telegraph alongside initial railroad infrastructure gave the company managers reports of construction progress on track and building while expediting orders needed for construction materials. The telegraph also aided in train movement and car accounting. Communication systems and services thus began with the very start of the railroad and improved control of the process and operation ever since. Through the years, as technology progressed, the railroad has introduced new communications technology and services simultaneously with expansion of railroad service.

6

Technical Issues on Operation of Pole Lines

Many persons looking at pole lines fail to appreciate the thoughtful engineering which goes into their design. The initial telegraphic line construction was expedited for business and financial reasons, and so the original transcontinental telegraph was constructed from locally available trees. Too, these poles were cut and placed without preservatives, such as creosote, to extend their useable life.

The initial telegraphic line construction was expedited for business and financial reasons, as well to unite California with the East. The movement of information was valuable and the quickest installation was most rewarding. Reliability of performance shortly became just as important, however, when loss of service meant loss of income. Structural engineering integrity improved as original pole line builders learned from experience; telegraph system operators sought to improve reliability by hiring engineers to introduce standards of construction based on sound engineering principles.

Insulators were used from the early days of telegraph. In addition to the insulating properties of glass, they were designed to provide a "dry spot" during rain to limit leakage of the electric current. Later insulators were designed with a "double petticoat insulator," which provided a longer leakage path and improved transmission performance of the electric current.

Wire line technology also improved with operational experience in these early years of pole line operation. Glass insulators first produced in the 1850s underwent many improvements and patents over 100 years. Other insulators were developed by the Bell system for improved performance of carrier systems.

In these early days, weather played an important factor in circuit reliability. Hoar frost reduced voice (and telegraph) performance, in some cases reducing or eliminating service until the frost vanished. Icing of the lines brought the wires down completely, in some cases causing poles to break off for miles. In April 1917, storms raged into spring, climaxing in a sleet barrage that knocked out 1,500 telegraph poles.[2]

To avoid these conditions and limit destruction, storm breaks were provided as lines were upgraded. Double pole "H" fixtures with so-called "head guys" and "side guys" were installed in the pole lines at half-mile intervals to limit line failures from storms such as wind or icing. Side guys were installed periodically to strengthen the line. Additional poles were selected for head and side guys at quarter-mile intervals and others were only side guyed for line protection in a defined structural pattern.

With the introduction of voice circuits on the pole line, a need developed to avoid the induction of the telegraph transmission into the voice circuit, and as more voice circuits were added to the pole line, cross-induction (crosstalk) occurred between the voice circuits. (Crosstalk occurs when a voice conversation from one pair of telephone wires is heard on another pair of wires. Thumps from a nearby telegraph wire could also be heard.)

Voice transposition plans were developed to avoid this problem. A transposition is a transfer of one wire of a voice circuit to the pin position occupied by its pair on a crossarm, and the transfer of its pair to the original wire's location. The induction which is induced between wires in one transposition section is reversed in the next section, thereby eliminating crosstalk from one voice circuit to another and the clicks heard in the voice circuit from the telegraph circuits. (Below is a description of some interesting tidbits concerning a couple of pole lines and unique issues on transpositions from the author's experience.

Square Poles

Some pole lines were constructed around 1915 with sawed redwood trees.

On the Union Pacific Railroad the pole line north of Pocatello to Butte Montana was constructed with "square" redwood trees. Also the pole line from Shoshone to Ketchum ID was redwood. These lines lasted into the 1990's when they were replaced with microwave and radio systems as was the Butte line or were abandoned as was the Ketchum line.

The Western Pacific Railroad, acquired in 1982, had a pole line west of Winnemucca constructed in the same period with sawed redwood trees. This line was replaced with microwave and radio systems in 1992.

Transpositions

Early voice circuits operated to provide voice communications between the designed terminals. However success with converting telegraph wires to voice resulted in more telegraph wires being converted to voice circuits while allowing the "simplex" [the mid- point repeating coils (transformers)] of the voice circuit still carrying a telegraph circuit resulted in cross talk between the voice circuits. The amount of crosstalk depended upon the separation on the pole line between the circuits and the level of balance each circuit had.

To avoid the crosstalk a transposition scheme was developed. Most pole line crossarm pin positions were numbered looking east from left to right as 1 to 10.

Wires were generally paired on pins 1 & 2, 3 & 4, 7 & 8, 9 & 10 were spaced at 12." Some circuits were installed on what are called the pole pins 5 & 6 were separated by a pole and were more prone to crosstalk due to the wider spacing. They were initially integrated into the transposition pattern. In later years with transposition patterns designed for higher carrier patterns whey were eliminated.

Transpositions were made by crossing the wire on one pin of the pair to the other pin, i.e. wire on pin 1 was moved to pin 2, and the wire on pin 2 moved to pin 1. Likewise transpositions occurred on the other pairs. The frequency of transpositions on pin pairs varied in a pattern developed by the communication engineers of the designing companies.

Early transposition schemes eliminated crosstalk between the voice circuits. As higher frequency carrier systems were installed on wirelines, more complex systems were developed. A Western Union 30 Khz transposition scheme was installed on the Union Pacific Railroad. In answer to a question in Railway Signaling and Communications, Mr. Van Eaton responded "When installing a new wire or rebuilding a pole line, we do not transpose any additional pairs for 30 kc operation or higher operation unless there is a requirement. Transposing is ordinarily completed prior to the time new carrier installations are made. We do not have a regular program in which a certain amount of transposing is done each year."[3]

While this system was developed to avoid crosstalk between carrier systems up to 30 KHz, certain patterns radiate certain carrier frequencies which caused absorption into the atmosphere, causing holes in carrier frequencies at certain frequencies. The pattern, while designed to avoid this phenomenon, caused problems in certain carrier systems installed on circuits beyond their design. However even these transposition patterns had pairs which could handle the carrier. The Union Pacific usually conducted tests to find circuits to handle the higher carrier systems (up to 150 KHz) on the Western Union 30 KHz pattern avoiding the cost of installing more frequent transposition required by higher frequency designs.

The Bell system designed transposition systems for "J" carriers for non compandered carrier systems up to 150 KHz, and "O" carriers for compandered carrier systems. The J carrier system required 8 inch pin spacing and extremely tightly controlled transposition spacing. The O transposition pattern continued to use 12 inch pin spacing (although sometimes using 8" spacing).

The J scheme was designed for transcontinental circuits, while the O scheme was for shorter haul circuits.

Compandered channels was mostly used on wire line carrier systems. The word compandered is a composite word of "compressed, and expanded." The spoken word was compressed into the higher frequencies at the input and expanded at the output restoring lower frequencies to normal. This technique was to suppress crosstalk and other noise inputted between terminals. As frequency shifting of data tones were constant in level the compandered techniques had no impact on them.

7

Carrier Telephone and Telegraphy

Carrier multiplexing is the transmitting of several voice or telegraph circuits over one circuit (or pair of wires) and can be likened to an AM broadcast radio in that each radio channel is tuned to a discrete frequency.

Carrier current multiplexing dates back to the early days of the invention of the telephone. Bell's original experiments in vibration-reed-type telegraph led to the invention of the telephone.[1] As these systems were invented, a transmission plan was developed where a voice circuit (or telegraph circuit) was transmitted in one direction (a channel) and another voice circuit was transmitted on the same physical circuit in the opposite direction (channel) at a different carrier frequency. A number of carrier multiplexing systems were developed where the channels were directionally interlaced, or the channels were grouped in one frequency band for transmission in one direction, and their paired channels were grouped in a higher frequency band and transmitted in the opposite direction. Filters in the carrier equipment prevented these channels from interfering with each other.

With advent of carrier multiplexing, induction from one carrier system on a physical circuit induced its system easily into another adjacent or nearby physical circuit, causing corresponding crosstalk. To counter this effect, carrier transpositions schemes—as opposed to earlier voice transposition schemes—were developed, and transposition brackets were improved. Early transposition schemes were developed by Western Union and later systems were developed by Bell Laboratories.

Western Union transposition schemes to 30 KHz were installed on the Union Pacific Railroad, while the Bell System developed transposition schemes to 150 KHz for use on their toll lines. Some railroads used the higher Bell System transposition schemes only.

The frequency of transpositions varied between circuits in a pattern to avoid crosstalk between adjacent pairs and to a lesser extent between more remote pairs. The greater distance between the more remote pair lessened the inherent crosstalk. Generally, the carrier transposition schemes were designed for a full complement of carrier systems; however, not all circuits were fully transposed to the carrier scheme, only those necessary for the carrier systems planned.

Also, certain pin-position schemes allowed for higher frequency system than the scheme was originally designed. This became important when electrical effects know as absorption was considered—due to the transposition pattern, some circuits tended to radiate electrical energy into the atmosphere at certain frequencies; this phenomena resulted in a loss of energy (holes) in a frequency attenuation pattern (the tendency for higher frequencies to have greater attenuation (loss)). These holes could prevent some channels in a carrier systems pattern to be usable.

8

Union Pacific Railroad Officials' Involvement in Nebraska Telephone History

In 1876, Louis H. Korty, then Chief Operator of Telegraph for the Union Pacific Railway, was one of the founders of the telephone industry in Nebraska. He had become acquainted with Mr. Theodore N. Vail while the latter was a resident in Omaha.

Mr. Vail was a one-time Iowa farmer and NE railway mail clerk. He was chief clerk in a mail car running from Omaha to Cheyenne. His genius for organization, great executive ability, and ceaseless energy soon brought him promotion to division superintendent, then shortly thereafter to superintendent of the railway mail service of the United States.

The Boston men—Bell, Watson and others—who were trying hard to make the telephone popular and successful financially, concluded that they must secure the best general manager possible, so Thomas A. Watson, who had heard the first words ever spoken in a telephone, was sent to Washington to interview and report on the noted railway superintendent, Mr. Vail. He would soon be asked to come to Boston, organize the telephone business, plan its future, and further its development.[1]

Mr. Korty, while visiting the Centennial Exhibition at Philadelphia in the summer of 1876, saw Dr. Alexander Graham Bell and his invention of the telephone. He saw the potential of the telephone and kept an eye on its development. He convinced his superior, Mr. J. J. Dickey, of the possibilities of the instrument that was causing telegraphers to question whether it would supplant the telegraph.

In 1877, he secured two telephones from Bell. On November 18, 1877, the two telephones were connected between his office in the Union Pacific Office in Omaha, and Mr. Dickey's office at the Union Pacific Transfer in Council Bluffs.[2]

Mr. Korty and Mr. Dickey formed a partnership and acquired the license rights for a portion of Iowa, all of Nebraska, Wyoming, Utah, Montana and Idaho. During the following year they established various private lines throughout western Iowa and eastern Nebraska. *The partnership between these two men was disrupted for a short time as a result of the strong competition and fight for patent rights between the Western Union and the Bell people. Mr. Korty was employed in the telegraph department of the Union Pacific Railroad, while Mr. Dickey was superintendent of the Atlantic and Pacific Telegraph Company.[3] The later firm was sold to the Western Union Telegraph Company. They required Mr. Dickey to make an end his relationship with the Bell Company, and to support the inventions of Thomas A. Edison and Elisha Gray.[4]*

After cessation of hostilities in the East between the two competitors, Mr. Dickey and Mr. Korty resumed their alliance.[5]

On April 15, 1879, Mr. Vail wrote Mr. Korty appointing him agent of the National Bell Telephone Company; "I enclose your appointment as agent as made with Mr. Madden. It is affording me more than usual pleasure in doing this for I had some fears that Omaha would not avail herself of the advantages of our systems for some time to come and, remembering all the associations I had more than the usual desire to see Omaha provided. Trusting you will succeed."[6]

Mr. Korty and John J. Dickey, who was the district superintendent of the Western Union Telegraph Company and Superintendent of Telegraph of Union Pacific Railroad, as founders of the telephone industry in the west, organized the Omaha Electric Co. and opened Omaha's and Nebraska's first telephone exchange early in 1879. Thereafter, the demands of other Nebraska cities for telephone service became insistent and Messrs. Dickey and Korty, with their associates Silas H. H. Clark (president of the Union Pacific Railroad), Thomas L. Kimball (passenger agent), and J. W. Gannett, incorporated the Nebraska Telephone Co on July 1, 1882.[7]

In 1879, with cooperation of Mr. S. H. H. Clark, then president of the Union Pacific Railroad, the organized and opened the first telephone exchange, known as the Omaha Electric Company. Omaha Electric Company received the appointment as agent for the surrounding territory from the National Bell Telephone Company.[8]

Mr. Theodore Vail advised the gentlemen to consult Mr. Watson about the installation of a switchboard and let him supervise the construction of the central office system. A letter dated April 15, 1879 from Vail to Korty reads, "...I think it would be well to let our Mr. Watson supervise the construction of the apparatus for your central office system, as he can bring upon it an experience of over two years."[9]

Not long after bringing the telephone to Omaha, the following occurrence was reported in the Omaha Daily Bee:

> "The value of the telephone exchange system was admirably demonstrated Wednesday morning. Upon the receipt at 3 o'clock of the dispatches concerning Ute Indians, the central telephone office called Fort Omaha. The regular operator was in the city, but the constant ringing of the signal bell awakened the night watchman, aroused General Williams who was telephonically informed of the dispatches, which were repeated to him word for word by C. E. Mayne at the central office. Mr. J. J. Dickey superintendent of Union Pacific telegraph service was then awakened by telephone, and informed that communications was desired with Major Furay, depot quartermaster. Mr. Dickey then awoke Major Furay, next door, and in a few moments Major Furay came into Mr. Dickey's residence and was put in communications with Gen. Williams who issued orders to him to arrange transportation of the troops. To do this, communications had to be obtained with Mr. Nash, secretary of assistant general superintendent J. T. Clark of the Union Pacific. Mr. Nash has no telephone in his house, but Mr. Korty, living

> next door, has one, and therefore, Mr. Korty was awakened by telephone and upon learning what was wanted, he called Mr. Nash into his house, and then Major Furay arranged the transportation with him. All this was done in the course of half an hour."[10]

While Mr. Dickey, Mr. Korty, and Fort Omaha had telephones, many officials on the Railroad and in the military did not.

Other exchanges were established in the same year. Korty, Dickey, General G. M. Dodge and others built the Council Bluffs Telephone Exchange Company. The Lincoln Telephone Exchange Company was created in Lincoln as the second Nebraska telephone exchange. Exchanges were established in other Nebraska towns: Fremont and Grand Island in 1880; Stuart 1883; North Platte 1885; Norfolk and West Point 1888; Lexington and McCook 1897; Sidney 1898; Alliance and Broken Bow 1899. "The beginning of telephones in most Nebraska towns…was a pay phone for community use in the town's drug store. The popularity of the town's one phone caused rapid expansion."[11]

The first telephone directory for Omaha was published on July 10, 1879 with only 124 names. Soon others towns and communities in eastern Nebraska were demanding telephone service and a telephone exchange. Mr. Dickey and Mr. Korty were kept busy during the next few years supplying this call for service.[12]

The demands of several Nebraska towns became so insistent that the Nebraska Telephone Company was incorporated July 1, 1882. Those who signed their names to the Articles of Incorporation were L. H. Korty, J. J. Dickey, S. H. H. Clark, Thos. L. Kimball, and J. W. Gannett. The general nature of the business was to build and operate telephone and telegraph lines within the state and between other states, to establish and maintain systems of messenger service, and to deal in telephone and electrical supplies. The amount of capital stock prescribed by the Articles was seven hundred-thousand dollars, divided into shares of one hundred dollars each, subject to be increased to a total of one million dollars' worth of shares. The highest amount of indebtedness or liability to which the Nebraska Telephone Company could at any time subject itself was fifteen thousand dollars.

This corporation quickly absorbed all the other telephone companies then existing in Nebraska. On August 7, 1882, the company purchased the property of the Beatrice Telephone Company; December 27, 1882, it purchased properties belonging to L. H. Korty at Blair and Arlington: on February 14, 1883 it purchased certain toll lines and on April 14, 1883, the Nebraska Company purchased the property of the Omaha Electric Company. Other properties were soon purchased across the state.[14]

Thoughts on Corporate Leadership by Telegraphers

Andrew Carnegie's first employment was in telegraph service. Reportedly, he served as a telegraph messenger boy.[15]

Edgar Eugene Calvin, President of Union Pacific Railroad, served as President of the Union Pacific from July 1916 to November 1918. "**It is Second Nature**... Why do telegraph operators become railroad presidents?"

Besides listing UP President Calvin, the article lists 10 other telegraphers who became railroad presidents.[16] Other notables who began careers as telegraphers was Edwin M. Herr President of Westinghouse Electric Company, and Honorable Emanuel S. Philipps, governor of Wisconsin, who began his business career as a telegraph operator. Both Mr. Herr and Governor Philipps worked for the Union Pacific Railroad at one time, Mr. Herr as a telegraph operator, and governor Philipps as a general agent.[17]

William Martin Jeffers, President of Union Pacific Railroad, started at age twenty as a telegraph operator in Sidney, NE. He became president of the Union Pacific in October 1937 and remained in that position until February 1946.[18]

As stated above, the railroad industry had a tradition of recognizing talent within its organization and promoting individuals to leadership positions. However, some individuals started on the railroad and rose to positions of great leadership elsewhere. For example, Theodore Vail rose from being a railroad mail clerk on the Union Pacific to president of AT&T and Western Union Telegraph (holding the positions at one time simultaneously).[19]

Similarly, the Communications Department promoted men like John B. Sheldon, who rose from being a clerk in the Telegraph Department to Superintendent of Telegraph, as well as Glen Van Eaton to the same position from his humble start as station agent in Sloan, NV. In 1934, Van Eaton was promoted to wire chief in Las Vegas. In 1937, he was promoted to manager of telegraph; in June 1941, he was promoted to Assistant Superintendent of Telegraph with headquarters in Salt lake City; and two months later, his title was changed to Superintendent of Telegraph of the South-Central District until his promotion to Superintendent of Telegraph with headquarters at Omaha, NE. (This was later changed to Superintendent of Communications).[20]

Robert H. Brenneman rose from dishwasher to Superintendent of Communications.

Hugh Robertson, after serving time in the US Coast Guard, was hired as an equipmentman, communications Engineer, Assistant Superintendent Communications, and eventually rose to Superintendent of Communications.

Mike Ahern, after serving in the US Navy, was hired as a groundman, rose through equipmentman, Equipment Supervisor, Communications Engineer, Assistant Director of Communications, and then to General Director Communications.

Recognition of talent, and regular promotion up the ranks, provided incentive for all employees to do a sure and diligent job and use their own initiative to perfect their role.

As the Bible says, "To one who is given talent, much is expected."

9

Early Union Pacific Railroad Telephone Service

As mentioned earlier, in 1877 Mr. Korty secured two telephones from Bell. On November 18, 1877 these telephones were connected between his office in the Union Pacific Headquarters in Omaha and Mr. Dickey's office at the Union Pacific Transfer in Council Bluffs, thereby becoming the first telephones installed on the Union Pacific Railroad. The Union Pacific's headquarters at that time was located in the former Herndon Hotel building at Ninth and Farnam Streets, to which the Union Pacific moved to in 1869 from the old territorial building on Ninth and Douglas. [1]

From the "History of Telegraph Lines" Western Union Telegraph Company April 1, 1912:

1. The first copper wire installation, #9 gauge, was completed in 1890;

2. The first telephone line was constructed in 1890 (on the telegraph line) and was .17 miles long;

3. and extensive construction of dispatcher and other phone circuits was completed during 1909 and 1910 (also see Harriman years).

In July 1904, telephone service along the Union Pacific was initially installed in offices and shops between Cheyenne and Laramie, with a drop at the gravel pit siding in Buford, WY. The experiment was so successful that plans were developed to extend the system between Omaha and Green River, WY. Delays in handling telegrams between various officials proved that repairs in locomotive shops could be expedited by use of the telephone between district superintendents and locomotive shop bosses.[2]

In 1904, the Union Pacific Railroad installed its own telephone exchange in Omaha. With 40 individual Nebraska Telephone Company exchange numbers, these were converted to the newly installed Union Pacific 200-line exchange equipped initially with 72 lines and 15 trunks to the Nebraska Telephone Company.[3] There is no confirmation that the Omaha Green River circuit was terminated in the switchboard. However, with information below confirming Mr. Harriman's addiction to the telephone, it seems logical that this circuit was terminated in the switchboard. *Telegraph Age* reported the Union Pacific Railroad had a telephone circuit in operation between Omaha and Cheyenne since June 1908 and was used for official conversations between division headquarters.[4]

Indeed, the new 1911 switchboard had long distance circuits terminated in the switchboard (below).

Telegraph Age reported a meeting of Union Pacific officials and employees at Omaha for the consideration of practical subjects; Korty, then Superintendent of Telegraph, introduced the discussion with the following remarks: "The telephone is becoming a most valuable aid in the operation of trains in large yards and terminals. Quick expansion is necessary because of the constantly increasing volume of business.

"Telephones are being introduced in connection with the automatic block system now being installed, as they will place the dispatcher in close touch with the non-telegraph stations. Portable telephones will be placed on trains for use on the wires of the system in emergency cases."

Continuing, he explained, "Experiments with telephones on trains are in progress on this road which it is hoped may result in devising apparati what will make it possible for the engineer and conductor to successfully carry on conversations and compare their understanding of orders." (Possibly a reference to Dr. Milliner's radio experiments which started in 1906.)

"The movement of trains by telephonic orders in certain localities under proper safeguards is possible and is already being done on some roads. On the Union Pacific between Council Bluffs and

Gilmore (a station in the Omaha area) in conjunction with the block signal system the movement of trains is very greatly facilitated by use of telephones by the dispatcher in one of the towers...

"Long Distance telephone lines between division and district terminals would afford invaluable service to operating and traffic departments in giving orders and exchanging information which now overburdens the telegraph wires. I look forward to the time when the telephone service of the Union Pacific will be co-extensive with that of the telegraph; with long-distance telephone circuits along the main lines capable of satisfactory us between the extreme limits of the road, not as a rival of the telegraph, but rather as an auxiliary thereto, and as a direct and quick means for personal conversations between officials, agents and others. Each system has its particular advantage over the other, the telegraph being the best where a record is required."[5]

As mention in above discussion on Mr. Sheldon's term as Superintendent of Telegraph, the exact date when train dispatching began using telephone circuits is not known.

The Union Pacific Railroad was not a leader in the introduction of dispatching trains by telephone. In the period between1908 to 1915, reports of telephone dispatching were frequently reported on. *Telegraph Age* reported on use of telephone dispatching on the Erie Railroad, Northern Pacific, Pennsylvania, and New York; Great Northern Railway;[7] and Canadian Pacific, Louisville & Nashville, Baltimore and Ohio and many other railroads.[8] The statistical report offered in the article on dispatching trains by telephone and telegraph reported the Union Pacific with 3,310 miles of track, dispatched trains by telephone only 123 miles, while the remaining 3,187 miles was done by telegraph. Many other railroads greatly exceeded that mark—the Chicago Burlington and Quincy Railroad had 1,926 miles and the Great Northern had 1,294 miles of railroad dispatched by telephone. However, most railroads, including the Union Pacific, planned expansion of the use of telephone system dispatching.[9]

Reported in the *Telegraph Age*, "The Union Pacific is erecting a telephone line to be used in train dispatching from North Platte, NE, westward to Sidney, 123 miles. This line is all single-track and is equipped with automatic block signals."[10] Subsequent reports showed a moderate increase in telephone dispatch circuits of: 492 miles, June 1910; 709 miles, May 1913; 721 miles, June 1915.[11]

Mr. Sheldon presented a paper "Telephone Train Dispatching" before the Omaha Railway Club on March 9, 1910.[12] Further reference to the paper is covered below. The paper was very detailed in its description of the service, its operational requirements, the equipment and the success of this service.

He introduced the paper with comments that "For the past two years, the subject of telephone train dispatching (the paper uses "despatching" throughout) has been prominently before the railroad world... Trial circuits that were established by some of the more venturesome roads, but not without some misgiving as to the ultimate and complete success of the innovation, proved so thoroughly reliable, expeditious and economical in operation that telephone train dispatching was soon accepted as standard by the very conservative American Railway Association, and since then upwards of forty of the leading railroads in the United States and Canada have gone into it and are constantly putting this system into more extensive use...

"The telephone was found so beneficial in these ways, especially by trainmen, who could not operate the telegraph, that its development and enlarged use in the movement of trains was naturally only a matter of time...

"The Union Pacific management early became convinced, after careful investigation, of the desirability of this new system and authorized the construction and equipment of a circuit between North Platte and Sidney, a distance of 123 miles that has been in successful operation for more than a year..."

In this paper he goes on to describe the plans for expansion of this service across the railroad to Ogden. He further discussed the cost of construction and equipment for the North Platte to Sidney system. His discussion referenced the formation of an auxiliary telephone message circuit to be transposed with the dispatcher circuit for use in an emergency—which in the end became common practice.

He also described in detail the equipment provided for the dispatcher, the stations, and a new concept--the "booth phone," to be used by trainmen and the advantage of them being able to talk directly to the dispatcher.

Further in the paper he describes the design in detail of the station equipment and problems and solutions in the design of multiple stations on the line. He also describes the protection of the equipment from high voltage using carbon block arrestors. (High voltages from induction, or contact from nearby electrical power lines, or lighting).

He introduced the practice of using selector equipment for the dispatcher to select the desired station he wanted to speak to. He also described in detail the use of the equipment, and the protocol for transmitting and repeating train orders, which continues today.

Mr. Sheldon said, "The dispatching of trains by telephone is, all told, at least one-third more rapid that the use of the telegraph for that purpose." He also describes the impact on the dispatcher: "The telephone also contributes greatly to ease the work of the dispatcher. The quickening of the work gives him more time for figuring out the problems of train movements, which greatly reduces the stress, and the ease of talking, compared with telegraphing, affords much relief." He goes on to say, "Experience has shown that, expensive as it is to install, the operation of a telephone train-dispatching circuit can usually be carried on with such economy, altogether, as to make up the cost of it within practically the first year of its use."

In conclusion, Mr. Sheldon comments: "We have a number of such circuits, by some the use of two existing parallel iron wires, that are transposed for the telephone circuit, but the most valuable are had from our four through copper duplex telegraph circuits [circuits designed with special equipment to simultaneously transmit message in both direction on a single wire] between Omaha and Ogden that, by transposing, give us two splendid telephone circuits all the way that are capable of satisfactory use for long distances. Conversations on these circuits are frequent between Omaha and Cheyenne—516 miles—and talks have been had as far as Rawlins, 690 miles.

> *"The principle use for these telephone circuits, however, is for conversation by officials and the handling of regular messages by telephone operators between district or division terminals.*

"For the message business, roomy, ventilated and nearly noise-proof booths are provided for the operators. These operators handle messages by telephone that otherwise would be put upon the telegraph. They take them directly off typewriter as transmitted and the speed of the service is approximately three times that of the telegraph. Both day and night service is maintained at most of the ten division and district terminal points between Omaha and Ogden.

"Although the duplex telegraph circuits on these four wires, making eight telegraph circuits in all, are worked for long distances, one as far as from Omaha to San Francisco and another between Omaha and Salt Lake City, with repeaters every 500 miles, we divide up the telephone service generally into five separate circuits on each pair of wires, thus giving us in all on these four through-wires a total of eight telegraph and ten telephone circuits. These circuits are connected with our Private Branch telephone Exchange (PBX) switchboard at Omaha, through which connections can be made with any of the telephones in our exchange, or through the city, for conversational; purposes."[13]

"The wire line plant reached a peak in miles of pole line and wire mileage in the early 1920s. Many single-wire Morse telegraph circuits were paired for telephone operation, voice transposed, and additional telephone instruments installed."[14]

Progress on expansion of telephone circuits was at hot topic in industry journals. *Railway Signaling* followed industry progress and reported on this topic. Under a column titled "General Outlook Shows Increasing Demand for Communications," the journal reported, "The majority of the railroads are recognizing the need for the betterment and extension of modern communication facilities. The conscientious work of the members of the American Railway Association, Telegraph and Telephone Section during the past few years has produced in ready form circuits, data and general information regarding telegraph and telephone developments…"

Furthermore, on request of the journal, letters were received from 50 superintendents of telegraph of the leading railroads, giving detailed accounts of the recent developments of special interest in the field and outlining the general prospects for 1924. In brief, this single statement reveals the fact that the growth of traffic and the increasing demand for quick, reliable, satisfactory communications is outstripping the expansion of telegraph and telephone construction, and that a radical increase in the construction program is necessary.[15] This same article presented tables showing the industry work completed in 1923 and contemplated for 1924. The prominence in expansion of telephone train dispatching compared with telegraph is reflected in construction plans for 1924 of 1657.7 miles of telephone, versus 30 miles of telegraph.[16]

Ed Harriman

In December of 1897, Ed Harriman was appointed to the Union Pacific Railroad executive committee and on May 23, 1898, was elected its chairman. His first act was to summon Union Pacific's secretary, Alexander Miller, and announce that he had taken charge of the company's affairs.[17] Harriman had a vision for improvement in the railroad "which flowed one gigantic plan after another.[18]

At a July 14, 1898, meeting the only expenditure approved was the purchase of 30,000 tons of steel rail. Before Harriman was done, he would spend $98 million for improvements and equipment.[19] He instructed chief engineer J. B. Berry to lay out a plan to reduce grades, straighten curves, and shorten the distance of the line. By 1909, the Union Pacific had shortened the main line by 54 miles, had 4,470 feet of less grade and eliminated 9,255 degrees of curvature or nearly twenty-six complete circles.[20] Even the telegraph line was spruced up. The original line amounted to two wires strung on small poles of different sizes. Under Harriman, the line was redone with larger poles and heavier copper wire, 30,000 miles of it. The telegraph system was run by dynamos instead of batteries, with circuits every 500 to 1,000 miles. Even a modern telegraph system was not enough to suit Harriman, who was personally addicted to the telephone. At the time of his death in 1909, the Union Pacific was stringing 2,000 miles of telephone train-dispatching lines alone the system.[21]

In the late 1800s, many experiments in telegraph carrier technology were made, some very crudely by today's standards. The phonopore and the phonoplex were both systems introduced in 1885 for providing additional telegraph channels in the frequency range above that of the ordinary D.C. or Morse channels. The phonopore, was developed by Charles Langdon-Davis in England and Edison developed the phonoplex. Phonopore and phonoplex Frequency Division Multiplex, (F.D.M.) telegraph systems were used on railways in the late 19th century.[22]

The Union Pacific Railroad installed the Edison phonoplex system between Laramie and Cheyenne to relieve the burden of telegraph business, which at times was too great for the regular channels. The system was also in use between Rock Springs, Green River, Granger, and Evanston, WY and Ogden, Utah.[23]

Alexander Graham Bell was experimenting with this technology when he discovered the telephone. Initial telephone circuits were limited by the characteristics of the wire line. Early experiments in carrier technology lead to scientists devoting attention to wireless telegraphy in 1905 before applying this technology to wire lines. Originally invented by Edison, the thermionic tube was improved by DeForest by adding the grid which laid the foundation of the electronic amplifier. The amplifier became the foundation of the voice repeater.[24] Voice repeaters extended the length of telephone circuits by increasing the volume of the weak voice signal. In the late 1920s, voice repeaters were installed on the Union Pacific Railroad on a number of circuits to permit direct telephone communications from headquarters at Omaha to points as far west as Salt Lake City.[25] In November of 1911, the Union Pacific moved to a new headquarters building a 14th and Dodge. A new telegraph test board and telephone switchboard was installed in the new building under the supervision of Mr. Jack Sheldon, then Superintendent of Telegraph.

The following is an excerpt from the *Omaha Daily Bee*, Nov. 5, 1911:

> *"Where every modern feature of the latest design been provided…some details of the telegraph department*

will be worth reading. It is installed on the fourth floor, with twenty-three operators now at work. Approximately 9,000 separate messages are handled every day by the telegraphers in the headquarters office. Necessarily, then a very large proportion of the wires making up the total of nearly 35,000 miles of telegraph circuits and approximately 8,000 miles of telephone circuits on the Union Pacific center in this office. Wires enter this building in twisted pair cables in underground conduits and the exposed wiring in the office all laced openwork, in accordance with the latest modern method. Approximately 40,000 feet of wire were used in making connections throughout the office, of which about 35,000 feet are in conduits under the floor.

"The (telegraph) switchboard, a Union Pacific special design, something on the order of a telephone switchboard, is different in many ways and more modern than anything of the kind heretofore placed in service. It has a present capacity of forty telegraph wires and is fully equipped with volt meter, milli-ammeter, Wheatstone bridge, galvanometer, telephone set, etc. for the testing and measuring of wires and circuits. The cords and plugs are on the telephone order, instead of peg plugs or, wedges, as ordinarily used in telegraph switchboards. There are four sets of telegraph instruments with a telephone set conveniently arranged in connection with the board for testing. The circuit designs in the board, and in connection with multiplex and other telegraph tables, are special and in advance of previous practice. A coil rack of special design has been provided for equipment used in connection with simultaneous telegraph and telephone service on the same wires, which cares for this equipment in a most up-to-date manner.

"A wire distributing frame is also of special design, to take care, in a comprehensive manner, of all the incoming wires in cables and the distribution in the *switchboard, lamp panel and tables. This frame has an ultimate capacity for 700 pairs of wires.*

"A lamp panel of slate, a Union Pacific design, has a capacity for seventy multiplex circuits. The main dynamo currents for operation of the multiplex circuits feed through the lamps connected with this panel for the purpose of protection in case of overload.

"Provision has also been made, through special relay equipment installed on the lamp panel, for distribution of time signals with a capacity for equipment of 114 wires for this service. Through this equipment, the naval observatory time signals from Washington, D. C. are distributed upon every circuit and to every office on the road at 11 a. m. central time each day. By these signals the standard clocks, from which trainmen and others in the service regulate their watches, are regulated at all the different division, and district terminals on the road.

"The designing an installation of this splendid telegraph plant is an achievement reflecting much credit on J. B. Sheldon, superintendent; A. O. Nichols, chief clerk, and John Hilbert, who was actively in charge of the work.

"In a corner of the main operation room of the telegraph department is the pneumatic tube terminal. This system, comprising of two and three quarters miles of three-inch brass pipe, was furnished by a Chicago firm. Donald C. McLaughlin, superintended the work, but a genius in pneumatic engineering, Frank Novak, executed the plans. The distribution of mail and telegrams throughout the building will be accomplished by means of this pneumatic tube system. Vacuum power will propel articles through the tubes at the rate of ninety feet per second, vacuum force of each tube being about five horse power.

"Thirty-five departments will be reached by the pneumatic tube system, and it is hoped by this means to get an almost instantaneous distribution of telegrams and important mail inter-office messenger service and important mail. Inter-office messenger service will be practically eliminated by this means.

"Many a good sized town that feels a trifle proud of its telephone system has a less pretentious plant than that required to keep things on the move in the Union Pacific headquarters, it is the most complete in use in any office building in Omaha; in fact, will stand close comparison with the plant of any skyscraper in the land. Its installation was supervised by the engineers of the Nebraska Telephone Company, and they are authority for the above statement.

"The telephone exchange is on the fourth floor of the building, in close proximity to the telegraph offices, and is a complete exchange in every particular. It has a capacity of 600 individual lines and 170 have already been placed in service. In addition to the city telephone service, connections with the long distance circuits are reserved for the exclusive use of the railroad company. Two of these run direct Cheyenne and other Wyoming points, one to Grand Island and western Nebraska towns and the fourth to Lincoln and stations in southern Nebraska. During the day six girls will serve at the switchboards and during the night, while the service will be light, connections be had to every department."[26]

Peter Frenzer succeeded Mr. Sheldon upon his death on July 30, 1914 and was appointed Superintendent of Telegraph Union Pacific Railroad on August 13, 1914.[27] Mr. Frenzer served on the AAR Telegraph and Telephone Section Committee 10, Education and Training.[28] At the September 20, 1929 meeting of the Telegraph and Telephone Section of the A. R. A. in St. Paul MN, Mr. Frenzer was elected chairman of the Committee of Direction for 1929 to 1930.[29]

During Mr. Frenzer's administration, pole line improvements were continually made and additional wires added to the poles. At the end of December 1920, there were 5,674, miles of pole line jointly owned with Western Union, 581.4 miles owned exclusively by the railroad and 1,430.3 miles owned exclusively by Western Union. There were 19,815 miles of iron wire of mixed gauges, and 13,314.3 miles of copper wire.[30]

There were 3,279.9 miles of telephone circuits, and 3,323.4 miles of train dispatcher voice circuits. Most telephone circuits were identified as conversation circuits, which like the train dispatcher circuit served the same offices as the train dispatcher and served as a backup to the train dispatchers' voice circuit in case of failure.[31]

In subsequent years over 4,000 miles of copper wire was added to the pole line and almost 900 miles of dispatcher voice circuits were added, including 333.6 miles of telephone circuits.[32]

During 1925, "Two units of the Union Pacific system, the Oregon Short line and the Oregon-Washington Railroad and Navigation Co. completed 495.1 miles and 398.9 miles respectively of multiplex printing telegraph."[33]

Mr. Frenzer, one of the longest-serving Superintendents of Telegraph, served from August 13, 1914 to December 31, 1938. Like all railroaders, he equated communications with telegraph, and was close to Jeffers (president of the railroad), who took great pride in having started as a dispatcher.

Voice telephone service had been introduced to the railroad back in 1879. Direct long-distance telephone lines were in service for a number of years with addition of wires and crossarms, but the poles could only handle a limited number of wires.

Charley Sparr, a manager of telegraph at Los Angeles, arranged to have a three-channel carrier system. (In his "Five Year Plan," Mr. Jett reported the Western Electric CN-4 was installed by Western Electric between Los Angeles and Salt Lake City, the Carrier System having been installed in the fall of 1937.) During a visit to Salt Lake, Jeffers tried the telephone circuits out and hurried back to Omaha. He called up Frenzer and demanded to know about the newfangled system. Frenzer didn't have a clue. But he knew Sparr must be involved and said so. Sparr was summoned to Omaha at once, and naturally assumed he was being fired. "How soon," Jeffers barked at him, "can you have this all over the railroad?"

Jeffers asked Frenzer if he knew about the new phone system. Frenzer admitted he did, but reminded Jeffers how proud he was of his telegraph origins and insisted the 'road was doing fine with the telegraph alone. Jeffers ordered his old friend to take retirement at once.[34] He did so on December 31, 1938.[35]

The search for a replacement for Frenzer was begun by giving aptitude tests to the wire chiefs. Klein reports the winner to be G. R. Van Eaton, manager of the Las Vegas telegraph office; he was handed Frenzer's position and told the job was to modernize communications on the Union Pacific Railroad.[36] However, according to newspaper accounts there was a gap in the Superintendent of Telegraph's office between December 31, 1938 when Peter Frenzer retired and June 29, 1942 when Glen R. Van Eaton was appointed Superintendent of Telegraph.

During this gap in the office of Superintendent of Telegraph identified in Klein's book, Frank A. Coulter, held the position of Superintendent of Telegraph and was appointed so on Jan. 1, 1939, the day after Frenzer officially retired.[37] "Frank A. Coulter Assistant Superintendent of Telegraph with headquarters in Omaha was promoted to Superintendent of Telegraph with same headquarters, succeeding P. F. Frenzer, who retired on December 31."[38]

During Coulter's period in office there was substantial movement in development of wire carrier systems. High-level officials from Western Union's New York, San Francisco, and Dallas offices met with Union Pacific officials in Omaha on November 25 and 26, 1941, to develop fundamentals issues of coordination of carrier system design.

Considering that the Union Pacific was an important segment of Western Unions network and these carrier systems were in early stages of development, it is not too surprising that the meeting drew such a diverse group of Western Union officials. A memorandum was issued following the meeting which outlined technical matters which were agreed to concerning operation of carrier systems on the jointly owned wire lines.[39]

The Western Union officials were:

Messrs. Donaldson	New York
Hanks	New York
Norton	San Francisco
Sikora	San Francisco
St. Cyr	Chicago
Blain	Dallas

The Union Pacific Railroad Company:

Messrs., Coulter,

    Fitzpatrick,

    Hilbert,

    Frederick,

    Petrie.

The names listed here, on the memorandum, do not identify their official responsibilities. However, Frank Coulter, the Superintendent of Telegraph, is one of the UPRR's officials. Other UPRR individuals identified were Joseph N. Petrie, System Telegraph and Telephone engineer appointed to the position in 1942,[40] who left the Union Pacific Railroad in November 1945 to take a position with Automatic Electric;[41] Mr. John E. Fitzpatrick, Assistant Superintendent Telegraph,[42] who retired December 1960 and was replaced by C. O. Jett;[43] and Mr. John Hilbert, an engineer on Mr. Sheldon's staff during construction of the new headquarters building in 1911.[44]

Because of the significance of this meeting and its impact on carrier operations, the entire memorandum is herein quoted:

> "The purpose of this conference is to consider problems of multiple carrier system operation on the jointly owned lines of the Union Pacific Railroad Company and the Western Union Telegraph Company, and to provide solutions for such problems in accordance with the principles of the various contracts applicable.

"Both Companies contemplate large investment in carrier systems on the jointly owned lines and in order that each Company may realize the full benefit from such investments, it is necessary that the systems of both Companies be designed, installed and operated in coordination with other carrier systems on the same line. The effective and economical operation of these systems requires the fullest cooperation between the two Companies in the planning and installation of their respective systems in order that these large investments may not be jeopardized and in order to avoid alterations at a later date.

"In order to effect such coordination, it is recommended that the following practices be adopted by the two Companies:

Prompt exchange of information regarding present and future plans for carrier operation.

Joint planning in the matter of location of repeater stations and carrier test points, frequency directions, and signal levels.

Where both Companies plan to operate carrier systems on the same line, the cost of chaining and laying out the line for carrier transpositions shall be divided equally between the two Companies. Where such expense has been assumed by one Company and the other Company later decides to install a carrier system on the line, the second Company shall reimburse the first Company at the rate of $5.00 per mile as its share of the chaining and laying out costs of the transposition system.

Each Company, shall at its expense, transpose its wires used for carrier operation the pattern specified in the transposition design, for the carrier frequency utilized. Each Company shall also bear the entire cost of placing its wires in standard pair positions.

> *Whenever one Company decides that its circuits require loading in jointly owned cables, the other Company shall be consulted, and if practicable, a mutually acceptable plan for loading all carrier circuits in such cables shall be developed. In such cases, each Company shall pay for its own loading coils and the costs of labor and other materials shall be shared by the two Companies in proportion to the number of load points required by each Company.*

> *If at any time the best engineering solution of specific problems encountered in the design of plant for carrier operation requires alterations of jointly owned structures such as: enlargement of man holes, construction of additional man holes, additional poles or "H" fixtures, crossarms, etc., the expense of such changes shall be divided between the two companies in accordance with the contract applying thereto."*[45]

Shortly after the Western Union-Union Pacific meeting, Mr. Van Eaton (Manager of Telegraph Salt Lake City) sent a telegram on March 3, 1942 from Salt Lake City to Mr. Coulter in Omaha outlining budget planning to greatly expand the number of carrier systems for the Union Pacific.

In the message Mr. Van Eaton mentioned the existing three-channel carrier from Salt Lake to Los Angeles (CN-4 installed by Western Electric), and the single-carrier channel from Salt Lake to Lund UT—which he planned to extend to Las Vegas—and a single-channel carrier to be added between Las Vegas and Los Angeles. He planned a three-channel carrier from Salt Lake to Ogden and on to Omaha, and single-channel carrier from Salt Lake to Pocatello. He included a three-channel carrier from Salt Lake to Huntington, OR and a single-channel carrier from Pocatello to Nampa, both in ID. Several of these carrier systems were already budgeted for and several were new additions he recommended. His telegram identified cable pairs to be loaded at each location for the carrier systems. He also requested a copy of the Memorandum Agreement of November 26, 1941 with Western Union Telegraph Company on coordination of the carrier systems and expense sharing.

Mr. Van Eaton was apparently aware of a proposal to add an additional three-channel carrier between Omaha and Salt Lake, reserving one channel for telegraph circuits. Mr. Van Eaton assumed that Mr. Colter would include costs for loading cable pairs at Ogden and Salt Lake in his estimate.

Mr. Jett identified a three-channel Western Electric C-5 carrier system installed in 1941 just prior to World War II between Omaha and Salt Lake with terminals installed back to back at Cheyenne to provide much-needed additional facilities. He goes on to say "In rapid succession, a 3 channel carrier system (Western Electric C-5) was installed between Salt Lake City and Portland OR, and a second 3 channel system (Western Electric C-5) was installed between Omaha and Salt Lake City to provide direct circuits from Omaha to Los Angeles, Salt Lake City and Portland."[46] The Van Eaton message to Colter apparently It was apparently part of an effort to connect Omaha to Portland via the Salt Lake-to-Huntington three-channel carrier, and to Los Angeles via the new Salt Lake-to-Los Angeles three-channel carrier system.[47]

Like many other things in the country, the '40s and '50s were a time of rapid expansion of carrier systems. Between 1942 and 1956 the Union Pacific Railroad installed 41,252 circuit miles of telephone carrier channels and 111,072 miles of telegraph carrier channels. During World War II, limited availability of copper wire prevented additions of copper wire, however pairing of telegraph wires and transposing thereof, permitted expansion of communications carrier systems in support of the railroads war effort. Despite the addition of only 25.8 miles of new copper wire, 3,170 telephone carrier circuit miles were installed.[48]

After the war ended, between 1946 and 1960 8,450 miles of new copper wire were added. During this same period, 4,391.4 miles of new and rebuilt railroad-owned pole lines were constructed as well as 397.5 miles of pole line jointly owned with Western Union Telegraph Company.[49]

Mr. Coulter served as Superintendent of Telegraph until Mr. Glen Van Eaton replaced him on May 29, 1942. Coulter retired in May 1942.

Glen R. Van Eaton was appointed Supt. of Telegraph Union Pacific Railroad May 29, 1942. The announcement was made by E. J. Connors, VP of Railroad and A. C. Kronkhite, general manager for Western Union.[50] As was traditional, the Superintendent of Telegraph held the dual title for both the railroad and telegraph companies.

Some of these early carrier systems were installed on the dispatchers' talk circuit, as they were the first wires to be transposed. On branch lines, the dispatcher circuit may have been the only voice circuit, as it had many drop wires into telegraph offices, telephone booths, and other buildings.

The large number of drops greatly attenuated any carrier system superimposed on them. Mr. Jett designed a pole top filter to isolate these "drops" from the carrier systems thereby avoiding attenuating the carrier signal. He described the need to clean up the pole lines for the application of carrier systems. He added that, with 1800 pole-top filters, they had more filters between Los Angeles and San Bernardino than between San Bernardino and Omaha.[51] In a July 1956 feature article, he described "The Union Pacific's Methods for Line Treatment of HF Carrier.[52]

10

Early Radio Experiments and Developments

The Union Pacific Railroad Company has long been at the forefront of railroad radio communications. In 1906, the railroad funded experiments by Dr. Frederick H. Millener for radio communications to trains, but the experiments were controversial within the company's management. Some felt him a genius, some felt him a crank. Needless to say, the experiment continued for ten years and by all accounts were at the leading edge of radio technology for the time.

At the Railway Signal Association meeting at Louisville, KY, October 12-14, 1909, *Telegraph Age* reported that "The Union Pacific Railroad is the first railroad in the west to take active steps to show the applicability of wireless to railroad service. Soon they will begin the erection of a large and powerful wireless station at their Omaha shops and conduct extensive experiments in the way of communications with moving trains both by telegraph and by telephone."[1]

> "Dr. Frederick H. Milliner, of Omaha, experimental engineer of the Union Pacific Railroad, has received orders to proceed at once with the installation of a wireless telegraph system at Omaha. The first new stations to be equipped will be at Sydney, NE and Cheyenne, WY."[2]

"WIRELESS EXPERIMENTS ON UNION PACIFIC. - The Union Pacific Railroad Company on December 23, (1912) applied to the Department of Commerce and Labor at Washington for a license to operate and maintain a wireless telegraph system along its lines. The company wishes to install an experiment station, and the Government is requested to give permission for such a station. Several wireless stations, it is stated, will be constructed when the license is issued."[3]

"It has been known for some time that the Union Pacific is experimenting to determine the possibilities of using the wireless telegraph in the operation and control of trains, and Dr. Millener, experimental electrician for that company at Omaha, has made some exceedingly interesting experiments along this line. Some of these have attracted world-side attention, as, for instance, his feat of controlling the movements of a truck equipped with wireless apparatus by means of other wireless apparatus situated at a distant point. The Union Pacific has applied the wireless to sending train dispatches, and wireless stations for use in case the regular telegraph wire are interrupted for any reason are now being constructed. Dr. Millener read an instructive address before the New York Railroad Club recently on this subject, in which he dwelt upon the possibilities of the wireless telephone and telegraph in train handling and the experiments his road is now conducting."[4]

The Union Pacific had been a pioneer in the development of "wireless telegraph" or telephone communications, thanks to Dr. Frederick H. Millener, who was in charge of the general office building in Omaha. Since 1906 Millener had been experimenting with a device he claimed would allow moving trains to communicate with stations thirty or forty miles away. In 1914 he announced that his system was functional and commercially feasible.[5]

Dr. Millener's initial instructions from Union Pacific management were to develop a radio-controlled cab signal system (See Wabash Railroad Side Bar). In his report he discussed the problems associated with this effort. It was recognized early that the cab signals need to be extremely reliable—a reported "100,000 operations without failure," but the technology available in that era had not yet progressed to that level of reliability. The "coherer or valve detector, which we were able to secure actually, or to learn of would not last for anything like 100,000 operations without a failure, work was discontinued on the mechanical radio cab signal. Lighting of an arc light, atmospheric disturbance or casual spark would sometimes cause the signal to operate." Millener, Dr. Frederick H., Paper "RADIO COMMUNICATION WITH MOVING TRAINS, Presented before the Institute of Radio Engineers, NY, December 5, 1917).

In addition to the technological problems with radio technology at this early period, legal issues arose concerning patents and ownership of them. This was a concern of Dr. Millener and rather than purchase equipment developed by others, he preferred to develop systems in-house.

During the cab system experiments, Dr. Millener developed a radio-controlled rail truck with four speeds ahead and four speeds back and ring a bell. He believed from these experiments a commercial cab signal could be developed. He further believed this technology was the first application of radio technology to control heavy machinery.

Radio Controlled Cab Signals

In April 1965 L. B. Yarbough, Engineer of Signals and Communications, for the Norfolk and Western Railroad (Formerly Wabash Railroad) working with WABCO developed a system of radio controlled cab signals. The system was based upon the Ford Motor Company's radio controlled locomotives at their production plant at River Rouge Michigan. While this system was a step down from a fully radio controlled locomotive such as is used at the Union Pacific yard at North Platte in the 2000s. Mr. Yarbough was of the opinion that introduction of cab signals was more palpable to the Brotherhoods than a complete replacement of locomotive engineers. The radio controlled cab signals allowed a switchman with a remote unit to signal switching movements to the locomotive engineer on a long string of cars without needing additional switchmen to pass the hand signals to the engineer.

The radio system signalled forward and reverse movements and speeds, along with a signal to stop. Indeed loss of the radio signal resulted in an immediate stop cab-signal.

Unlike the current system which use coded pulses, the WABCO system used a continuous carrier modulated with unique tones. Loss of the carrier caused the stop signal to be indicated.

Dr. Millener's report discussed the need for a ground counterpoise on his radio systems. An interesting occurrence with the WABCO system developed when the cab signal system was tested on the Indiana Illinois and New Jersey Railroad a non-union Wabash subsidiary which connected South Bend Indiana to the Wabash Railroad about 19 miles south. In the initial test the system failed when the switchman's remote unit could not communicate with the locomotive's cab signal unit with the locomotive was in full sight of the switchman.

Because of the need for a continuous carrier the switchman's unit was transmitting continuously and needed a significicant battery supply. A shoulder strap and belt arrangement supported the remote unit and the batteries. The web carried a monopole antenna mounted at a junction of the shoulder straps behind the head. The antenna and belt furnished by WABCO lacked a ground plane counterpoise.

A counterpoise ground plane was added to the belt by inserting wires down the front and back webbing from the base of the antenna.

This ground plane addition increased the range of communications to over a mile from the initial short range.

The fully developed and tested system was final tested at the Norfolk and Western (Wabash) Landers Yard in Chicago, Illinois.6

These successes led the Union Pacific to provide a better laboratory—"more facilities were requested to devote our whole time to the work." Millener, Dr. Frederick H., Paper "RADIO COMMUNICATION WITH MOVING TRAINS, Presented before the Institute of Radio Engineers, NY, December 5, 1917).

Some of this effort was devoted to develop radio telegraph systems to bridge downed telegraph lines. Because of the distances the Union Pacific Railroad covered, winter storms, heavy winds and icing could cause large scale outages. "We were directed to prepare plans and specifications for such a system, and if possible to make it flexible enough to telegraph to a moving train

The plan developed was to establish radio stations at certain cities to interface the telegraph systems. "Outfit cars were to be fitted with one or two kilowatt sets, which were to be kept at division points. (When a break occurred, they (the train) would be moved to a siding and establish a temporary station either side of the break. Telegraph service would be maintained until such time when the break was to be repaired.

"Various radio systems were considered including those developed by Poulsen, Marconi, Fessenden and others (Paraphrased). "But the least expensive method and the one decided upon was the...[one developed by] Telefunken Company. These stations were to be of sufficient power to be heard night or day, summer or winter, at least as far as the next sending station. We expected the station at Cheyenne to work as far-east as Omaha and an equal distance the other side of the mountains. The other sending stations were to be at Sidney, Grand Island, North Platte, Green River, and Omaha. Experiment taught that we would be able to hear the high pitch note of these stations above the strays, and later developments conclusively proved this to be true. We were then requested to work out a system or radio telegraph and radio telephony, which could be applied to railroad uses where it would have value in protecting human life." The paper goes on to discuss various technical issues including radio buildings and antennae. In addition to the above radio stations, Ogden, Utah was included.

"From the very beginning of the study of radio telegraphy, it has always seemed that the ideal instrument would be a radio telephone; and from the very beginning we hoped to be able to communicate by telegraph and telephone to moving trains. ... It was not till 1909, under rather critical circumstances, that Mr. Harvey Gamer and I devised a successful modulation method."

Dr. Millener developed several radio phones which were by today's standards enormous in size. "Altogether we made four radiophones of the arc type, and the worked very satisfactorily and over considerable distances. They worked very well for radio telegraphy or for any use where they could be maintained in a stationary position, but they were heavy and ungainly and required considerable attention. In fact, they required a skilled operator. Millener, Dr. Frederick H., Paper "RADIO COMMUNICATION WITH MOVING TRAINS, Presented before the Institute of Radio Engineers, NY, December 5, 1917)."Continuing our consideration of the arc radiophone, it was found satisfactory for the continuation of our experimental work in talking to a moving train." Dr. Millener's report proposed to install the radiophone in a baggage car. A telephone system had been developed for communications between cars in the train, which could be connected to the city telephone system when in a station. However, he posited the in-car telephone system could also be connected to the radio telephone system in the baggage car, by an attendant.

"Car 399 was designed as a laboratory to carry on these experiments with the first class trains of the railroad," he wrote. "The war, however, had begun; and in 1916 new men took charge of the railroad and this experimental work was temporarily discontinued."

In fact, the work never continued. Dr. Millener attempted to record radio messages on the phonograph using a Columbia Dictaphone. These early attempts were not entirely successful, and ended with the termination of the experiments.7

The company had put a little money behind the work but regarded Millener as little more than an amiable crank. "The traffic people have felt that this was a good advertisement, and have used him at fairs, carnivals, etc. to good effect," A. L. Mohler (President under Harriman and Judge Lovett) explained to Judge Lovett. But Millener, he added, "is quite a genius in this work." Since 1906 the company had invested $7,179 in the work and received six patents pending. "The invention is perfectly practical," declared Mohler, who viewed the wireless system as a possible alternative when storms knocked out the telegraph system.

While Mohler tolerated the experiments, the railroad saw little value in such a system. Two more years passed before another rash of publicity about Millener's work prompted Judge Lovett to inquire again. The judge didn't want to discourage any worthwhile development, but neither did he care to squander money. "We want the Union Pacific to be in the front rank in every railroad improvement," he stressed, "but we do not wish to persist in anything foolish." Mohler liked the device but was just leaving office; E. E. Calvin (President replacing Mohler in 1916) took a dim view of such nonsense. A test of Millener's system arranged in July 1916 flopped badly and proved to the committee of four observing it "the uselessness of his invention."

There is no doubt that the potential value of such a system escaped the committee entirely. "Even had the experiments been a success," it concluded, "the expense...would not warrant the Railroad Company in adopting the invention of Dr. Millener, due to the excessive cost and infrequent use." Calvin ordered the work terminated at once, and the Union Pacific lost its chance to pioneer in rail radio communications. Ironically, the committee's report was submitted to general manager W. M. Jeffers, who, when he became president, inherited the problem of a railroad that had outgrown its communications system.[8]

11

The Jett Era and Influence

As Mr. Jett approached retirement, he prepared a summary of projects: those which were in progress; those planned for the near future; and those he foresaw a need for in the long-term. This came to be known as Jett's Five Year Plan.

According to the document, from 1937 onward, the growth of business and requirements for better communications necessitated rapid expansion of all forms of communications on the Union Pacific. Expanded communications systems were being pressed by communications managers upon his arrival at the Union Pacific Railroad in 1945. Voice channel communications using carrier systems were installed to meet demand for more direct communications between officials and others. These carrier systems also provided for increased telegraph circuits using voice-carrier telegraph systems. Expansion of traffic and yards to handle this new business led to a need for improved communications between the yardmasters and switchmen. Yard speaker systems in the late Forties answered this need and became popular. Increased demand for communications of voice and data produced installation of microwave systems, and demand for communications to trains resulted in new radio systems.

Early Carrier Systems

Between more important offices, teleprinter facilities were expanded to provide the needed telegraph service facilities for operational and administrative control. The first step was the installation of a number of three-channel voice carrier systems to provide intercity telephone trunks between the major offices. With the advent of voice-carrier techniques and improved business conditions, a Western Electric type CN-4, three-channel carrier system was furnished and installed in the fall of 1937 by the Western Electric Company between Salt Lake City and Los Angeles, and continued in service until 1957. In the early 1950s, it was determined that these low-frequency three-channel carrier systems would, in a very short time, be inadequate to handle the rapidly expanding requirements for intercity telephone service, and, further, that only by utilizing the other carrier techniques could additional facilities be provided.

Around this time,(the early 1950's) the four-channel carrier systems Western Electric OB Carrier became available, which could be superimposed above the existing three-channel carrier systems then in service. A number of these four-channel systems were installed and, again, with the advent of the early data systems, they were found to be inadequate to meet communications service growth and were replaced with 12-channel carrier systems Lenkurt 45A (again above the original three-channel carrier systems). The four-channel carrier systems were moved to locations of lesser importance but which still required improved communications.

Upgrading of telephone carrier systems continued as long as wire lines remained in service. With the advent of microwave, many voice carriers systems were moved for improved service to wire lines serving branch offices needing more voice telephone service, and then for new data services.

By 1960, it was recognized that with the greater use of data and the ever-increasing requirement for telephone service throughout the Railroad in the form of direct distance dialing, the present open-wire circuits on the pole line would require expansion far beyond the pole lines' physical capability. Further, to provide improved service to the many waystations and secondary offices, the intercity direct-distance dialing service would have to be furnished by means other than the presently-used carrier techniques. It was then decided that microwave radio was the most economical means of providing this expansion and would further provide facilities for reasonable expansion as communication requirements grew. In an article in Railway Signaling and Communications, describing the success of direct distance dialing, Mr. Jett reported that direct distance dialing had been used successfully by the Union Pacific for three years, but it became readily apparent that the existing facilities were inadequate, and so the railroad would now embark on a program to install microwave radio on a system-wide basis. The first step would consist of 48 channels between Omaha, NE, and Laramie, WY. A number of these channels would be connected for short-haul operation between Omaha, Grand Island, North Platte, Cheyenne, and Laramie. It was anticipated that the system would expand to at least 120 channels in service westward from Omaha.[1]

Yard Speaker Systems

In the late 1940s, talkback loudspeaker systems became a growing interest to the railroad industry. Railway Signaling and Communications reported "there was a large increase in the number of loudspeakers installed in 1948 – undoubtedly because the roads realized the importance to themselves and to the shippers of getting trains through yards in a minimum of time—and the outlook for the future is good. The Baltimore and Ohio, for example, made an installation in its Barr Yard at Chicago, which includes two control points, 185 two-way speakers and 30 paging speakers; the Elgin Joliet & Eastern at Joliet, IL, including two control points, 96 two-way speakers and 30 paging speakers; and the Union Pacific, at North Platte, NE, including two control points, 110 two-way speakers and 27 paging speakers."[2]

North Platte had a unique location on the Union Pacific Railroad. All trains on Union Pacific from the east to western destinations pass through North Platte. The terrain was flat and available, thus an easy pick for construction of yard facilities and management of car switching.

Hump Yard technology was developing and "train consists," (the list of cars in sequence in a train) to be built for eastern terminals and western terminals, were easily sorted and switched, building outgoing consists. Contracts with Eastern and Western railroads were written to segregate cars to their destinations in a manner to save them additional switching. In timely manner, new technology was being developed to be integrated into the hump yards at North Platte.

A 55-telephone extension PBX was leased from the Bell system.

Talkback and paging speakers were a part of new hump yard classification at North Platte, and there were two separate talk-back speaker systems. The larger one for communication between the yardmaster and men at various places throughout the entire yard area; while the second, the smaller, was used for communication between the tower at the crest of the hump and the men involved in the operations of cars over the crest and certain points in the classification yard.[3]

Two-way radio between eight yard engines and two yard offices were part of the development.

Some Yard loud speaker systems installed on the Union Pacific Railroad were:

Pocatello ID, 1 control point, 60 talk-back speakers, 21 paging speakers.[4]

Council Bluffs IA, 1 CP, 73 TB speakers, 9 paging speakers,[5]

Las Vegas NV, 1 CP, 33 TB speakers, 8 paging speakers, [6]

Denver CO, 1 CP, 78 TB speakers, 7 paging speakers,[7]

Kansas City KS, 1CP, 80 TB speakers, 12 paging speakers,[8]

Nampa ID, 1 CP, 16 TB speakers, 9 paging speakers[9],

Marysville KS, Round Robin system, 10 TB speakers[10],

Ogden UT, 2 CP, 112 TB speakers, 14 paging speakers[11],

Spokane WA, Round Robin system 22 TB speakers,[12]

Cheyenne WY, 1 CP, 63 TB speakers,[13]

Salina KS, Round Robin system, 10 TB speakers,[14]

Salina KS, 1 CP[15], apparently converting the Round Robin system into a standard talk-back system,

Omaha NE, 26 TB speakers,[16]

Hinkle OR, 1CP, 66 TB speakers,[17]

Albina OR, 1 CP, 84 TB speakers, 14 paging speakers,[18]

The Council Bluffs speaker system was described in *Railway Signaling and Communications*' June 1953 issue. It consisted of a console with keys and lamps. "Thus the only audio to the console is in the leads to the console speaker and the microphone," eliminating hum and crosstalk. The audio amplifiers and telephone-type relays were in the ground-floor equipment room; signaling was done by a pushbutton on the speaker, which activated a relay that illuminated a lamp on the yardmaster's console.

> *"Another Union Pacific feature is the use of two amplifiers for the talk-backs. One limiter-type amplifier is used for talking in (to the yardmaster) and another limiter type amplifier plus a 15 watt-power amplifier is used for talking-out. With separate talk-in and talk-out amplifiers, constant level can be maintained. This arrangement permits uniform volume inbound from the person on the ground without regard to his distance from the speaker to the yardmaster, and talk-out to the field regardless of the distance the yardmaster is from his microphone. The loudspeaker system was designed and installed under the direction of C. O. Jett, system telephone and telegraph engineer."*[19]

At the Union Pacific, some yards had yard radios in service before yard talk-back speakers systems were installed. Kansas City terminal was one of them. Discussed in Chapter 11, Early Radio Systems, is the installation of radio installed on 16 locomotives and a yardmaster base radio at Kansas City for communications.

The following is historical accounts of communication construction from Superintendent of Communications C. Otis Jett's Five Year Plan from May of 1973 (Passages not italicized are comments by the author):

> *Construction of the first 240—channel microwave system from Omaha to Laramie was started in 1959. This program was continued with the addition of the Portland-Hinkle, Cheyenne-Salt Lake City, and 600—channel systems Salt Lake City—Los Angeles, Salt Lake City—Pocatello and Pocatello—Hinkle*

systems and the joint system with the Burlington Northern Railroad and the Union Pacific between Portland and Seattle, on which system the Union Pacific has 60 voice channels, Due to the obsolescence of the originally installed 240— channel microwave radio equipment, between Omaha and Cheyenne it was replaced with 600—channel equipment. (A 600 Channel 6 KMC microwave system was being installed between Green River and Cheyenne, WY in 1972[20] Today, all microwave radio facilities on the Main Line have 600—channel capacity. Other microwave radio facilities are the Cheyenne-Denver and the Omaha—Marysville—Salina—Topeka—Kansas City. Of late, a number of low density microwave radio systems have been added, such as the Hinkle-Lewiston, Hinkle—Spokane—Eastport, Los Angeles Riverside Long Beach, (Sierra Peak to Long Beach 2 KMC microwave system was installed in 1972 to serve railroad operations and Union Pacific Natural Resources Department operations and oil fields on Long Beach CA[21] plus side legs, especially for Hot Box detector (A hot box refers to a wheel journal which overheats and failure of which can cause the wheel to burn off, and derail the train) locations, too numerous to list.

So much for the history; now, for a little theory. With a certain amount of poetic license, it can he said that probably the first form of data transmission on a railroad was Morse telegraph, in which the transmitted signal was a series of dots and dashes with spaces in between. Through evolution, voice telephony developed, and with the constant demand for increased speed in transmission, a form of electric teletypewriter was developed, which we now term "Teleprinter." The teleprinter has gone through many modifications and improvements over the years in which it has been in service, until today, it represents a highly developed electro—mechanical device.

With business adopting computers as an industrial tool, a new form of information developed, called "machine language." This information, transmitted from data sets to computers, and vice versa, also resembles Morse code.

Today, Management Information Service (MIS), with computers, data sets and other business machines, provides railroad officers with large volumes of summarized data to guide in the operation and administration of the Railroad, MIS is the largest user of the Railroad's communication facilities next to the intercity and local dial telephone services A very high degree of reliability is required of the communication facilities by MIS in order that their huge volume of data be accurate and timely.

The communication facilities of the Union Pacific Railroad are the most modern of all the railroads in the United States, These facilities have been designed and constructed to provide maximum utilization and expansion capabilities consistent with good engineering practices, economics and compliance with the Rules and Regulations of the Federal Communications Commission., A high percentage of the Railroad's communications, such as telephone service, data (both COIN and teleprinter service), CTC and "hot box" detector reports, are over microwave radio facilities, Only "shorthaul" service on the "main line" and on "branch lines", where railroad open wire pole lines are still maintained, are by physical open wire circuits or by carrier derived techniques on open wire.

The present in-service microwave radio systems have adequate capacity and life expectancy to continue in service until about 1985. However, it is always possible that for one or more reasons this life expectancy can be shortened; especially if any of the following listed conditions should occur prior to 1985:

> *Obsolescence, either by changes in the Rules and Regulations of the Federal Communications Commission or more rapid developments in the "state of the art" that would justify earlier replacement.*
>
> *Expansion in requirements for service far in excess of the anticipated growth indicated by past experience.*
>
> *Electrification of sections of the railroad necessitating placing communication and signal pole line facilities underground. In the event this condition occurs, very definitely a new communication system, and possibly signal system, would have to be engineered to provide adequate facilities for growth beyond the year 1985.*

The railroad conducted several studies of electrification of the track using electric motive power to move trains supplied from overhead catenary conductors, especially the sections between North Platte, NE and Green River, WY. John Kenefick, then President of the UPRR, announced the "UP has just about finished an intensive feasibility study of electrification of our heavy bridge traffic from North Platte to Green River, WY. The costs of such a venture are not as staggering as many people assume…"[22] The plan included use of railroad-owned coal mines and coal on US government land to generate energy, which under the original land grant, permitted the railroad to use this coal for its operations.

However, complications involving changing motive power at the junction of the non-electrified railroad territory and electrified territory presented operational difficulties which defeated the benefits of electrification of the Railroad. In a meeting held in Mr. Kenefick's office on September 4, 1974, electrification was again discussed.

In the meeting Mr. Kenefick said "we'll be rushing to be second." He was assuming a 7% increase in traffic, an increase in electric utility rates, and cautioned that 14.1% ROI gets uncomfortably close to the corporate cost of capital, which would all discourage electrification.

A second electrification study was conducted in 1981. The Reagan Administration offered favorable tax benefits, which caused the

Railroad to reconsider railroad electrification. One issue reviewed was potential interference to AT&T services from an electrified railroad. Management insisted on completion of the review by May 1, 1981. Many of the same issues arose as in the 1970s. However, the decision to not pursue electrification was the same.[23]

> 4. When the use of the microwave radio facilities has expanded to its maximum capacity (600 voice channels or their equivalent), then, a new type of communication system must be designed, engineered and constructed. The Rules and Regulations of the Federal Communications Commission do not, at this time, contemplate any private business being, allotted radio spectrum space in excess of that required for 600 voice channels. (A paralleling 600 Channel 2 GHZ microwave system called by the Union Pacific the "under-build", was licensed in 1976.)
>
> The outside plant-poles, guys, crossarms, open wire and cable (both aerial and buried) have finite life. Careful study has been made of these items from the viewpoint are they now required, and does keeping the plant in service warrant the expense of placing same in good condition and the continuing maintenance expense?
>
> With the approval of the Operating Department (General Managers and Superintendents), the communication facilities (pole lines) on many branch lines have been retired; also, much of the communication pole lines on the main line of the railroad have been reduced in the number of wires retained in service. Those wires and crossarms not required have been removed and retired. Where the cost of rehabilitation of the communication pole line is in excess of the cost to transfer onto the signal pole line, a transfer is made, providing the signal pole line is of adequate size (pole height and class) to carry the additional load. Otherwise, recommendations are made to Management

> to authorize construction of a joint communication/ signal pole line. In either event, the poles, guys, surplus crossarms and wire of the communication pole line is retired and any copper wire sold as salvage by the Purchasing Department. Greater detail on the above items, as well as many others, is provided in the succeeding sections of this five-year plan.[24]

Mr. C. Otis Jett's five-year plan was very insightful in its outlook. Jett's period as Superintendent of Communications was a period of expansion of communications and development of new services. Data services were expanded in speed, accuracy, and to new offices. Union Pacific-owned PBXs were installed at major terminals, and Mr. Jett developed appliqués to expand these services to many wayside locations. Because of his leadership, many of these appliqués were unique to the Union Pacific Railroad. Four Party, 10/20 party Decimonics, and single party appliqués were developed by Jett through his engineering insight and experience.

Superintendent Jett taught his staff to be frugal in expenditures to expand communications services. 8D truck batteries were first used because of economy for microwave sites; second-hand Western Electric rectifiers were used for mainline microwave sites. Likewise, second-hand discarded Western Electric Step-by-Step PBXs were purchased, reconditioned and placed in service across the system. As senior UP management learned to depend upon the Communications Department Facilities, this equipment was later replaced with upgraded and more reliable rectifiers, batteries and electronic PBXs.

When Mr. Jett retired pole lines, he salvaged crossarms and insulators. He retreated the salvaged crossarms with preservatives, and reinstalled them as needed. He gave the old poles to adjacent farmers to remove them saving the railroad the cost of removal. He salvaged and sold copper wire to reduce railroad communications operating costs.

Microwave System Expansion

The communications services expansion successes achieved by Jett led to demands for additional and improved communications, since modern management depended on information and data at high speeds. The new voice and data requirements were initially met by expansion of microwave systems. At the time of Jett's retirement, he listed many improvements to the communications system he thought still necessary: he recommended building a microwave system between Pocatello and Montpelier, both in ID, which was surveyed in February 1974 and completed in 1976 (with extension to Kemmerer, WY), and between Pocatello and Butte, Montana, which was surveyed in November 1974 and completed in September 1976. The extension to Butte from Menan Butte included the system previously constructed from Pocatello to ID Falls via Menan Butte. It replaced fifteen carrier channels—a three-channel and a twelve-channel carrier system—between Pocatello and ID Falls. The Menan Butte M/W repeater site also served to provide radio services trackside.[25]

Not identified in Jett's Five-Year plan but constructed shortly after these systems was a microwave system serving the Provo Subdivision via Lake Mountain, Utah, and several other trackside microwave sites besides Provo, at Payson, County Line, Starr, Nephi, Levan, and Juab, all in Utah, in the summer of 1977.

Union Pacific Microwave Systems: Construction

Mainline microwave systems became the backbone for the Union Pacific Railroad communications network. Because of the length of the Union Pacific Railroad and the importance of communications to its operations for customer service needs, the mainline microwave had a hot-standby microwave-system backup. A singular outage of one site in the chain could deny communication to a large number of railroad offices. A failure of a module at one microwave repeater forces a switchover to an alternate standby module at the repeater site. As the alternate module is in a "hot" standby condition, it is immediately available to furnish continued through-service to the system. An alarm is then transmitted to a major communications maintenance office where a "Wire Chief" dispatches a technician to repair the problem.

Many of the Union Pacific sites were the first microwave installations constructed at their location. Some, however, were adjacent to microwave sites constructed by other companies, such as AT&T.

When a microwave site is the first microwave or radio site built at a location, a number of issues need to be resolved. A legal description of the site is developed by land surveyors, land ownership is established and an easement or permit obtained, and then the site layout requirements are developed. A self-supporting tower uses less footprint than a guyed tower, although in farm land, the area between the base of the tower and the anchors for guys can be farmed. A road is needed for access, and can be relatively short, or difficult to construct, such as the Sloan microwave site west of Las Vegas. This road was constructed up the mountain by blasting a route through the rock with dynamite at a reported cost of $30,000.00. A power line is also required to serve the site. (Some of these issues are also addressed even if the UPRR site is not the first).

The Mt. Emily site near LaGrande, OR was such a site. Located in a coniferous forest in snow country, normal features of site, road, and power were planned as normal. Because of the snow conditions, a helicopter landing pad was constructed adjacent the microwave site, and the power line was constructed using an underground electrical cable from a substation at the bottom of the mountain to the site.

Initially the voltage feeding the cable was 2300 volts, and transformed down to the 120/240 volt service at the microwave site. The electrical cable serving the site was insulated to a much higher voltage, which provided for future upgrade when needed. The US Forest Service subsequently located a radio site nearby and AC power was furnished to them.

In November of 1984, the Pacific Power and Light Company (PP&L) notified the Union Pacific that they desired to build a communications site near the Mt. Emily site. Later, in March 1985, they indicated they "definitely" wanted to build a microwave site at that location, and needed power for their site. A commercial communications company, Racom, later advised a desire to build a communications site there as well. (Exact dates are unknown, however records indicate March 1987). (Still later, Blue Mountain Cellular built a site on Mt. Emily, the summer of 1990.)

As these companies developed their construction plans, PP&L established a non-regulated subsidiary for special power situations. They developed a plan to build an aerial power distribution pole line to serve the communications sites on Mt. Emily and a dual plant, emergency engine-generator system for backup power to replace the Union Pacific buried electrical cable service and emergency engine generator.

Several meetings and discussions were held by a committee of the Mt. Emily site users, wherein the Union Pacific Communication Engineer proposed an alternative: To meet the power demands of the users at Mt. Emily the Union Pacific would upgrade the voltage on the buried cable, individually meter the power to the users at the top of the mountain, and split the power cost between all users, except the Forest Service (which was nominal). Under this plan, each company provided their own emergency generator for backup power. The UPRR proposal was significantly less costly to all users and it was chosen by all, including PP&L.

The asset value of the underground cable was amortized over a number of years against the Union Pacific's investment, should it fail and need to be replaced by the PP&L contractor's proposal. The Union Pacific paid the monthly bills for service and annually split the bill between each user, minimizing the paper work.

To demonstrate the importance of these generators, a story about one failure is presented here. A heavy snowstorm occurred after Christmas, on December 28, 1982, and closed Interstate Highway 80 in central NE. The storm also took out the commercial power to the microwave site at Lexington, NE. Loss of commercial power and failure of the generator to start meant that it was necessary to dispatch a maintainer to the site to start the generator. The microwave equipment relied upon battery backup to maintain microwave service, but loss of controls of the propane gas heater allowed the site to cool. At the time, the Union Pacific had two microwave system operating at the site a 6 GHZ system and a 2 GHZ system. The 6 GHZ system was not as sensitive to the lower voltage as the batteries lost energy and heat as the 2 GHZ system was, which supported the VHF radio systems including the dispatcher's radio.

With loss of commercial power and failure of the emergency generator to start, the wire chief needed to send a maintainer to start the generator to keep all systems working. With Interstate 80 closed due to the snow, the wire chief contacted the

Communications Engineer, as other communication department officers were on vacation. The Engineer contacted the dispatchers and requested the dispatchers put the equipment maintainer on the next east-bound train, which was a coal train to the Lexington Depot.

The dispatcher refused to stop the coal train at Lexington. Not long afterwards, the dispatcher's radio failed and he called the wire chief complaining about the loss of radio service. He was advised the railroad was unable to restore service until it could get a maintainer to the site, and the highway was closed. A caboose special was dispatched to Lexington with the maintainer, where a deputy sheriff, with a Chevrolet Blazer, and a Nebraska Highway Department snowplow, waited for him and took him to the microwave site. Within minutes of arriving, the generator was started and all systems returned to normal.

Shortly afterwards, Jerry Davis, the Vice President of Operations, told the Communications Engineer to call him personally if he needed a caboose hop again.

The example cited above demonstrates some of the conditions found by the Communications Department in support of the microwave system. While the Lexington microwave site is located on the "western plains," many microwave sites on the original Union Pacific System, during the major microwave construction period of the 1960s through the 1980s, were constructed in mountains of the Intermountain and Coastal mountain ranges.

Most Communications Department maintenance centers in this region have a snow cat for maintenance access during winter, when mountains roads are snow covered. The snow cats are equipped with the standard VHF vehicle radios and snowshoes for each occupant. Two technicians are always dispatched when a snow cat is required for access to the microwave site.

Snow cats give more protection to the occupants than a snow mobile and allows the maintenance personnel to bring along test equipment or repair parts when necessary.

Operation of snow cats in winter storms can present challenges during hazardous conditions due to whiteouts. Safety is priority number one on the railroad and that includes dispatching personnel with small vehicles under adverse weather conditions.

Francis Peak, UT

The original microwave system from Omaha to Salt Lake City included a microwave site adjacent the Federal Aviation Agency (FAA) site on Francis Peak in the Wasatch Mountains of Utah. Part of the road to Francis Peak includes a section where the road traverses a side of the mountain where the west side drops precipitously to the valley below. Whiteouts occur on the road reducing the visibility almost to zero. In these conditions, one man walks in front of the snow cat to guide the way, avoiding the chance the driver will steer the snow cat blindly off the road.

Due to the hazard associated with trips to Francis Peak during the winter, the microwave system was rerouted to Big Mountain, Utah, bypassing Francis Peak.

Holiday Hill, CA

In the early days, the Communications Department also gained experience in the design of microwave sites the hard way. One of the first microwave systems constructed was the system between Salt Lake City and Los Angeles. The Holiday Hill microwave site was located near a recreational ski area at the top of a mountain. In the winter, access to the site is served by riding a ski lift up to the site. The exhaust system for the emergency engine generator was simple and exited out the side of the building. There was also an intake vent for oxygen for the engine. The design proved to be tragic.

Due to the snow and wind conditions, the snow piled several feet high off the building but blew clear of the area immediately adjacent the building. A deadly condition arose one winter when the commercial power failed and the generator failed to start remotely.

An equipmentman and communications supervisor were dispatched to the microwave site by the wire chief. Upon arriving at Holiday Hill, the generator was started and observed for a while to verify proper operation. Unnoticed to the men, the exhaust was drawn into the building and resulted in their monoxide poisoning. After attempts to get the men to respond to calls on the service channel, the wire chief found out that the Southern Pacific Railroad had dispatched technicians to their microwave site near UPRR's. The Southern Pacific technicians were sent over and found the two Union Pacific men in distress. They took the unconscious men to their microwave site. The wire chief also alerted the county sheriff of the situation. Emergency medical personnel were dispatched to Holiday Hill; the EMEs took the Union Pacific men to a local hospital. Unfortunately, the equipmentman died, but the supervisor recovered.

Subsequently, the exhaust system was redesigned to improve dispersal and this fix was applied to all microwave sites.

Skamania, WA

In late December 1968, at a microwave site east of Portland on Mount Skamania, the microwave equipment drifted off frequency, requiring constant retuning of the klystrons. No cause could be determined for this condition. Two men, an equipmentman and a supervisor, babysat the equipment twenty-four hours a day. Two teams were established to continually maintain the system continuity. Access to the site was by snow cat. After completing an overnight stay, one team came down the mountain and met the other team for lunch.

The second team would take the snow cat back up to the microwave site, a distance of several snow covered miles. This building was accessed in the winter by a shaft, which extended above the roof with a door for entry. Because of the depth of the snow, the snow cat was parked next to the roof and the men merely stepped out of the snow cat onto the roof.

After several days of being unable to determine the cause of the drifting channel and repeated overnight stays, a Collins technician (representative of the manufacture) was called. He found the problem and made the repair.

Oliver, NE

The Oliver microwave site near Kimball, NE was the location of a tragic occurrence on July 18, 1984. A crop duster airplane hit the guywires of the microwave site and crashed nearby, killing the pilot. A farmer across the road from the microwave site said the pilot "looked into the sun"—he climbed off the field into the noon sun and thus failed to see the microwave tower in his path. He flew into several guy wires, breaking all but one near the top. Construction Engineer Jerry Chatwin was at work in the area and brought several linemen and spare guy wire with him, and immediately started to repair the broken guy wires.

The Communications Engineer, with a communications gang foreman and several linemen, was sent by company jet from Omaha to a nearby airport at Cheyenne to assist in repair of the tower.

However, a thunderstorm with winds up to 60 miles per hour came through the area, causing the jet to be rerouted several times, and requiring the linemen on the tower to leave it for fear of collapse.

Due to twisting of the tower, the 6 GHZ microwave system lost service; luckily, the 2 GHZ under-build microwave remained in service, due to the greater tolerance to antenna deflection. However, the VHF radios on the tower failed due to damage to their transmission lines.

After the thunderstorm left the site, Mr. Chatwin's linemen succeeded in replacing the guywires returning the tower to normal strength, all before arrival of the Omaha crew. Damaged transmission lines were repaired, and the 6 GHZ microwave systems was retuned and restored to service.

The Railroad special agent developed a list of witnesses which were turned over the Federal Aviation Agency inspectors who reported on the crash.

Servicing the Union Pacific microwave system was always a challenge but the communications service it provided were vital to the efficient transportation services furnished by the Union Pacific Railroad.

Parallel Microwave Systems

Jett's Five-Year Plan identified the potential exhaustion of a 6 GHz 600 channel microwave and the need for expansion of communications services. Unlike communications common carriers, the FCC wouldn't allow an additional frequency on a parallel path for railroads and other private microwave systems. However, the need for additional service forced the UP's Communications Department to seek an economical plan to meet the need for new services. Expansion of data services, hotbox channels, centralized traffic control, Automatic Car Identification data channels, and special telemetry services such as a traction motor performance monitoring were all communications services unique to the railroad industry.

To meet these expanded needs, the Communications Department filed for a 2 GHz 600-channel microwave system (identified here as "the under-build") using the same microwave sites and towers as the original Omaha-to-Salt Lake system. The frequency plan was developed on March 9, 1976 after clearing 2 GHZ frequencies in the Grand Island area. A State of Nebraska 2 GHZ microwave system had been planned and the State's system originally prevented the Union Pacific from clearing the 2 GHZ frequencies near the Union Pacific's Grand Island microwave site, and so use of 6 GHZ microwave frequencies were planned instead.

However, before construction started on the UPRR system, the State dropped plans for its system and the 2 GHZ channels reserved for the State became available, allowing the Omaha-Salt Lake under-build system to be entirely 2 GHZ.

Construction started in June of 1977, continuing through the summer. The new system was very economical compared to a completely new route. Use of existing towers, buildings, power plants, antenna reflectors and associated systems made for extremely cost-effective expansion. (Note: nominal 600 channel M/W systems are essentially limited to 432 channels for technical reasons, *i.e.* loading on baseband).

To accomplish this expansion, it was necessary to replace the feed horns on one of the two microwave antennas with a "crossband feed horn." This use of the existing microwave reflector for both the 6 GHZ and the new 2 GHZ microwave systems saved on wind and ice loading on the tower and made for very economical microwave system expansion. The 2 GHz microwave expansion permitted the Communications Department to meet many new demands for service. The new microwave equipment baseband permitted additional branch microwave legs service to trackside for pickup of hotbox detectors, centralized traffic control channels, Automated Car Identification (ACI) channels and other services such as dial telephone for local railroad offices. Additional radio systems such as the Maintenance of Way mobile telephone radios were provided to improve coordination of maintenance activities for track and other railroad facilities.

This parallel microwave system continued in service until fiber optic cable was later installed on the railroad right-of-way. At that time, most long-haul services were transferred to the fiber optic cable, and vital railroad operating services were moved back to the 6 GHZ microwave system. The 2 GHz system was then retired.

With installation of the 2 GHz under-build microwave system and other new systems, the additional relay racks supporting the equipment used up the limited floor space in the microwave buildings. To free up space and provide improved building utilization and to eliminate maintenance problems, a number of facility changes occurred to reduce site maintenance and eliminate avoidable costly travel for technicians.

Most microwave sites were originally heated with propane heaters and window air conditioners. Emergency 5 KW engine generators had been installed inside the mainline microwave sites with automatic power transfer panels. These services depended upon an exterior 500 to 1000 gallon propane tank. Many microwave sites were located at windy sites, many on sides of mountains. One maintenance problem occasionally experienced was the failure of thermocouples on the propane heaters. Between these two problems, it became necessary to send a maintenance technician to relight the propane heater when the pilot light went out, and restart emergency engine generators when necessary.

To avoid pilot light failure, the communication department's management decided to replace these propane heaters with electric heat. At this time, many of the window air conditioners and 5 KW engine generators were original equipment and they were near the end of their life expectancy. At a staff meeting on April 22, 1972, Mr. Jett announced a program to eliminate all propane heaters and replace them with electric heat by the next year. He decided to replace the propane heaters and window air conditioners with an electric furnaces and outdoor mounted Chromalux air conditioner compressor units.

The electric furnaces were 15 KW, consisting of three 5 KW heating elements. These heating elements were wired so that one 5 KW element was wired to the emergency engine generator transfer panel keeping the load on the emergency generator low when operating, and the other two elements were wired directly to the commercial power feed, providing adequate heat under normal conditions. Due to the increased air conditioning and electrical heat load, it became necessary to replace the indoor mounted 5 KW generators with new, higher capacity 12.5 KW generators outdoors, thus providing additional floor space for new equipment additions. With the replacement of mainline 5 KW emergency engine generators with 12.5 KW generators, many rebuilt 5 KW generators became available for use along low density branch line systems.

Jett's Five-Year Plan also called for replacement of storage batteries and rectifiers, and maintenance of towers and buildings:

> *Batteries, storage.* "Many of the batteries were installed in 1959-60 and their storage capacity had been materially reduced by age. Further, at many sites heavy-duty (200 ampere-hour) twelve-volt automobile batteries were used as an economy measure, When the. use of this type of battery was initiated, a life of to 10 years was obtained; however, today this same type of battery, of the same manufacturer as well as others, is providing no more than two years of service. Therefore, the use of automobile batteries should he discontinued and the standard telephone service storage batteries used for replacement, though the initial cost is more.
>
> *Rectifiers, battery charging.* At the time the initial microwave radio system was installed, 23 ampere, 24 volt rectifiers were provided. As later systems were installed, larger rectifiers (50 and 100 ampere, 24 volt) were provided. Today these original rectifiers should be replaced on a scheduled program to provide increased reliability and lower maintenance costs.
>
> *Tower and Building Maintenance,* It has been almost two years since the Western Districts' facilities were maintained, while it has been more than five years since maintenance was performed on the Eastern District. A scheduled maintenance program should be initiated at once on the Eastern District to paint buildings, repair roads, provide drainage, re-tension tower guys, tighten

tower bolts, and perform all necessary maintenance. Also lower parabolic antennas at Olive, Brownson and Chappell sites in view of the added repeaters that have been interspersed between those sites.[26]

M/W Legs – Interface Signal Systems

Above it is reported that "Telephones are being introduced with the automatic block system now being installed,..."[27] The track circuit was invented in 1872 by William Robinson[28] and paved the way for automatic signaling and the automatic block system, both of which were dependent on the track circuit for operation. "Blocks" are defined territories of track to control train movement, and are interconnected to protect a train from opposing trains and following trains. As a result, train movements are under the control of trackside automatic block signals. No attempt is made in this book to address the progress of installation or types of signal systems in service on the Union Pacific Railroad, but, as those systems improved, their usage was expanded and they improved train speed and safety across the board.

As signal systems were improved, advances led to Centralized Traffic Control (CTC). CTC signal systems gave the dispatchers direct control of the trains and monitored their movement in CTC controlled territory. The CTC train dispatcher, using his console buttons or toggle switches, sets signals for "go" or "no go" using the trackside signals to control train movement. In addition to setting the red or green color lamp signal, the dispatcher aligns the switches to speed the movement of trains into sidings or turnouts.

The Union Pacific Railroad made significant use and expansion of CTC during the '40s and '50s. The Union Pacific installed the CTC between the following locations in this period:

Las Vegas NV and Barstow CA in 1943,

La Grande and Reith OR in 1944,

Pocatello ID and LaGrande OR in 1946 and 1947,

Salt Lake City and Las Vegas in 1948,

Los Angeles and San Bernardino in 1949,

Marysville to Topeka in 1951,

Salt Lake City and Provo UT in 1951,

Reith and Hinkle OR in 1952,

Kennewick and Pasco WA in 1953,

Gibbon NE and Marysville KS in 1953,

Lawrence and Kansas City KS in 1954

Granger WY and Pocatello ID in 1956[29]

As with any railroad signal system, "fail safe design" is inherent in its construction. The track circuit protects the movement of trains in its block. Adding CTC to the signal system permits the transmission of information and control between the dispatcher and the block, giving the dispatcher the ability to control train movement by change of signal or switch position, and reporting to the dispatcher the occupancy of the block by the train.

Initially these CTC systems terminated directly in the dispatcher's office and were extended by wire line to the control points along the CTC code line. The speed and performance of code line is dependent upon the number of control points on the code line, and can be improved by splitting the territory into two or more code lines. This is done by using one or more carrier channels superimposed on the code line to split the code line in two, and then using the remote carrier to split off code line to the dispatcher's office. The response of the system to changes in outgoing instructions, or incoming indications from the field, is directly affected by the amount of information transmitted on the code line, in the form of code pulses on the line.

After the mainline microwave systems were installed between Omaha and Salt Lake City and Salt Lake City to Los Angeles, then Salt Lake City to Pocatello and on to Portland and Seattle, the communications network became an opportunity to use microwave capacity to expand performance of the railroad signal systems. During this period (the '60s), the Signal Department also replaced some automatic block systems with Centralized Traffic Control Systems. The microwave system became an opportunity to break up these CTC code lines into shorter blocks.

Besides speeding up system response, failures of the code line were confined to shorter track sections. Extending these limited

CTC systems to the dispatcher via microwave improved overall system performance.

The main line microwave system presented opportunities to improve the communications system overall as well. Communications funding was important, but didn't carry the same priority as expenditures that supported direct railroad operations. However, with impetus of improved signal operations, microwave legs to trackside for improved CTC signal operations became feasible and improved justification for funding of this equipment. Further, installation of hotbox systems and other track-side services aided in the justification for building microwave legs. These microwave legs, funded to support railroad signal operations, additionally allowed for other improved communications services to depots and maintenance offices, eliminating dependence on the congested open-wire lines. Roadmasters, section foremen, special agents, division engineers, engineering supervisors, signal inspectors, signal managers, signal maintainers, communication technicians, agents and other offices were provided dial PBX services which could not always be independently justified without the demand for microwave legs to support CTC services.

A number of microwave legs off the main line system were installed in 1968 and 1969 to trackside offices (*i.e.* Laramie, Rawlins, Rock Springs and Green River, WY), which had sufficient railroad communication needs beyond the signal department. Kansas City, KS and Denver, CO were major railroad operating points and mainline microwave styled systems were built to support their operations and yards.

Other microwave legs were added to support railroad operations as the need developed. In January of 1979, microwave legs were constructed to trackside from the mainline microwave sites at Shoshone ID, Moapa NV and LaSalle CO. A trackside microwave site was installed in the Mojave Desert at Kelso CA to serve a company hotel for train crews and which included a repeater at Cima CA to improve CTC operations.

These minor improvements to communications services were a continuing part of the Communications Department engineering and operations. Top management continued to find needs for improvement best served by expanding these facilities.

Earlier, this book described "Hot Standby Service." A number of other low-density microwave systems were installed to support branch rail lines as mentioned above in the Five-Year Plan. Because of the need for economy when providing service to many of these offices, and the general reliability of transistorized microwave equipment, many "non-protected" microwave systems were constructed. Economies of scale were used to provide service in this manner: Tall "H" pole fixtures for microwave antenna supports were used in place of steel towers; propagation characteristics of Low Band 2 GHZ microwave systems allowed the use of shorter towers to be used for many microwave antennas; a single power system consisting of 24 volt batteries and rectifier were used without installing an emergency engine generator backup plant.

With A/C powered two-way radio systems installed along with the microwave system, a failure of commercial electrical power occurring would result in the failure of the VHF radio systems while the microwave repeater with battery backup would continue in service. (Once a non-protected 2GHZ microwave system, as described, along a mainline railroad track between Grand Island and Marysville, lost commercial electrical power due to an ice storm for about a week. Portable electric generators were quickly brought in to restore the electrical service and A/C powered VHF radios. However, these portable generators required refueling every eight hours around the clock. Because of the impact of lost dispatcher radio service on this important mainline route between North Platte and Kansas City and the continued need to refuel the electric generators, a work order was quickly approved to furnish permanent emergency engine generators and propane tanks for backup A/C power service on this route.)

Two branch line microwave systems of the hot standby system design were built to support Signal Department CTC systems. Salt Lake City to Provo to Leamington UT; and North Platte to South Morrill WY known as the North Platte Branch. The line to Leamington was constructed for train service to support a unit coal haul train from a mine in Coal County UT to a coal fired power plant at Delta UT.

Provo Subdivision Microwave

Emil Krause, Union Pacific Signal Engineer, notified the Communications Department of plans to upgrade the Provo Subdivision in order to support coal service to a new power plant in Delta UT. Steel and Signals were to start September 13, 1982.

A trackside site at Leamington was served off of the existing Salt Lake-Los Angeles microwave system at Lynndyl UT.

The Leamington site required using eminent domain because the tower's anchor would be on adjacent private property. The railroad was reluctant to use the tactic, but it was necessary for the tower's integrity. Union Pacific Construction Engineer Jerry Chatwin and a Communications Engineer met with the Leamington County Council to obtain permission to acquire the encroachment. During a hearing before the council, Jerry Chatwin found old high school friends to be the interrogators. Friendships were renewed, however they determined that they lacked jurisdiction as the microwave site was within the city limits of Leamington, and that the city council needed to give their permission. When approached, the city council gave permission for the eminent domain.

Construction of the microwave system continued into spring of 1984. The first train load of coal was delivered at the UP&L power plant at Delta UT, July 2, 1985.[30]

Project Yellow

The North Platte to South Morrill railroad line known as "Project Yellow" was constructed to service the Powder River WY coal mines. This line provided joint coal-haul rail service by the Union Pacific and the Chicago-and-Northwestern Railroads. Coal is hauled east out of the Powder River mines by the C&NW with the Union Pacific serving as a bridge line from South Morrill to Fremont NE to Omaha NE and Gibbon cutoff to Kansas City; for power plants eastward. The C&NW hauled coal from Fremont, NE east to Chicago with other coal deliveries along the route and other power plants further east of Chicago.

Initially, the Burlington Northern Railroad was the only railroad serving the Powder River coal fields. The Interstate Commerce Commission (ICC), desiring railroad competition for the coal fields, required another railroad to enter and compete with the Burlington Northern. Several years of legal battles resulted in a decision whereby the Union Pacific Railroad and the Chicago and Northwestern were chosen to serve the coal fields.

Along with upgraded rail service, including rail size upgrade and signal upgrade (thanks to implementation of CTC), the Union Pacific constructed a microwave system to provide communications service to support rail operations to South Morrill, and jointly for the Chicago and Northwestern Railroad communications between South Morrill west. The new microwave system eliminated an obsolete pole line with a single open-wire circuit. It consisted of a 6GHZ microwave system which also provided exchange of communications service to the Chicago and Northwestern Railroad in addition to UPRR communications services. The microwave provided voice and data services as well as the usual dispatcher, mobile telephone, and maintenance of way-radio to South Morrill and other railroad offices along the way. This included microwave service to South Oshkosh and Gering.

With approval of Project Yellow, the railroad's Engineering, Signal, and Communications departments were moved into high activity to speed railroad service into the Powder River coal fields. The Engineering Department had previously surveyed the route using surveyors with unmarked vehicles. Advanced work order authority was requested by the Communications Department for more official-style survey work to locate microwave sites along the route. This request made on July 13, 1983, was for $5,000 to $10,000 and approved the same day. With financial approval for the survey, a contract was issued for aerial photographing of the new route to aid in quick selection of microwave sites. By August 1, 1983 the physical layout of the microwave system was designed. Jim Merrick, Asst. VP of Communications, wrote a letter in August 1983 to Guerdon Sines (Vice President, Information and Computer Services), setting a goal of having Project Yellow ready for revenue services of July 1984, just a year later.

A work order for $1,204,580 was issued on September 19, 1983 for the Project Yellow Microwave system between North Platte and South Morrill WY. By November 1983, several towers for these sites were delivered. Power contracts for the electrical service to the microwave sites were in the Law Department by January 3, 1984. Delivery of the microwave equipment was received the end of May 1984, and the system was place in service by the end of June 1984, meeting the goal established earlier.

The Project Yellow microwave system supported train operation including dispatcher radio service, CTC controls, and Hot Box detectors. Maintenance of Way Radio Service supported track and signal maintenance crews along the right of way. It furnished other communications for Union Pacific operations in South Morrill and exchange of services with the Chicago and Northwestern Railroad into the Powder River coal fields for support of their operations.

With the subsequent Union Pacific and C&NW merger in 1995, the entire route was operated as one Union Pacific system.

12

Private Branch Exchanges PBX and the Jett Era Influence Telephone Switchboards (PBXs)

As described previously, the Union Pacific Railroad has a long history with telephone switchboards. Switchboards are telephone exchanges with manual switching of calls by telephone operators. Where automatic switching of calls by relay or electronic means is furnished for an independent business, it is referred to as a Private Branch eXchange (PBXs).

The first switchboard was installed in 1904 and had manual, or human, switching of calls. With a sizable forty individual numbers on the Nebraska Telephone Company exchange at the time, the Union Pacific decided to create its own telephone exchange in Omaha. The Railroad's numbers were converted to the newly installed Union Pacific 200 line exchange (equipped initially with 72 lines and 15 trunks) from the Nebraska Telephone Company.[1]

The 1904 telephone exchange was replaced in 1911 and described thusly by the *Omaha Daily Bee*: "The telephone exchange is on the fourth floor of the building, in close proximity to the telegraph offices, and is a complete exchange in every particular. It has a capacity of 600 individual lines and 170 have already been placed in service. During the day six girls will serve at the switchboards and during the night, while the service will be light, connections be had to every department."[2] In subsequent years, telephone exchanges (PBXs) were added at larger offices. No record has been found which identifies their sequence of installation.

A Union Pacific 50-line PBX owned and installed in the Salt Lake Diesel Shop was reported in *Railway Signaling and Communications*. The phones were distributed throughout the shop and the PBX interfaced an Altec-Lansing paging system. The report also mentioned handie-talkie radios used to communicate from the shop floor to a crane operator in a 275-ton overhead crane and a smaller 35-ton overhead crane. Several other items of shop equipment were radio equipped, including a 25-ton locomotive crane, a 4-ton fork lift truck, two 2-ton crane lift trucks, and four self-propelled platform trucks. A base station radio was remotely controlled from the foremen's office. There was a planned expansion to remotely control the base station radio from the storekeeper's office and install two-way radio in two stores-department delivery trucks.[3]

The Union Pacific Railroad inaugurated intercity dialing over their carrier network between Portland OR, Tacoma WA, and Seattle in 1956. This was the first installation of long-distance dialing on the railroad's private telephone network. To provide circuit capacity for the new long-distance dialing, carrier equipment for four additional voice channels and twelve printer channels was installed on existing line wires.[4] System-wide long distance dialing was complete in 1960 with tie trunks extended to Los Angeles.[5]

Mr. Jett's Five-Year Plan for Switchboards (PBX)

Jett's Five-Year Plan accounts for the number of PBXs in service in the section labeled:

"TELEPHONE SWITCHBOARDS (PBX)."

> *"Today, to meet the needs for voice communications throughout the Railroad, the Communications Department operates 24 dial telephone switchboards (PBX). Five of these switchboards are leased from the local telephone company and the balance are owned by the Railroad. Ten of these PBX installations are attended by operators either on a full or part-time basis."* His report continued as follows as the best

description available (Some liberties are taken here to consolidate like type of comments to avoid repetition:

ATTENDED TELEPHONE SWITCHBOARDS (PBX)

Leased from local telephone company

(a) Chicago - Leased from Illinois Bell and is attended Monday through Saturday from 8:00 AM to 5:00 PM. Unattended at other times, including holidays. When unattended, the Omaha PBX operators handle incoming calls when they originate on the "night number" in Chicago.

(b) Omaha - Leased from Northwestern Bell and is attended 24 hours per day, seven days each week.

(c) Kansas City - Leased from Southwestern Bell ...

(d) Portland (Albina) - Leased from Pacific Northwest Bell ...

(e) Los Angeles - Leased from Pacific Telephone and Telegraph Company ... and are attended five days each week between the hours of 7:00 AM to 9:00 PM, These PBXs are unattended at night, on weekends and holidays.

2. Railroad Owned

(a) Cheyenne ,

(b) Denver ...

(c) North Platte ...

(d) Pocatello ...

Attended five days each week between the hours of 7:00 AM and 9:00 PM. Unattended at night, on weekends and holidays.

(e) Salt Lake City - Attended 24 hours per day, seven days each week.

Note: *When the following listed telephones PBXs are unattended, equipment and circuitry has been provided, whereby all incoming calls from these cities, as well as those calls requiring operator assistance, are handled through the Salt Lake City PBX:*

1. Kansas City

2. Portland (after August 1973)

3. Los Angeles (after early summer 1974)

4. Cheyenne

5. Denver

6. North Platte

7. Pocatello

B. UNATTENDED TELEPHONE SWITCHBOARDS (PBX)

Railroad Owned

1. Grand Island	8. Ogden
2. Marysville	9. Las Vegas
3. Topeka	10. Nampa
4. Salina	11. La Grande
5. Laramie	12. Hinkle
6. Rawlins	13. Spokane
7. Green River	14. Seattle

C. WORK ORDERS"

Jett listed several work orders which added telephone channels to various railroad offices. These channels were to accommodate the 9:00 PM to 7:00 AM closure of operator-manned PBXs. The listing of hours above included planned changes to operator coverage.

"The above four work orders authorize the necessary installation, modifications, rearrangements and such additional equipment as is required at all of the attended telephone PBX locations, except Chicago, to permit eliminating operator attendance at North Platte, Kansas City, Cheyenne, Denver, Los Angeles, Pocatello and Portland during the hours of 9:00 PM to 7:00 AM, weekdays and Saturdays, Sundays and holidays. When the work is completed at the foregoing listed locations, the PBX operators at Salt Lake City will be able to answer any incoming telephone calls from the towns or cities to the PBXs that are unattended and extend service to the desired party or advise the caller as to the reason the call cannot be completed at that time. Further, the Salt Lake City PBX operators will be able to handle any calls requiring operator assistance on any of these unattended telephone PBXs.

Note: It is anticipated this work will be completed by early Fall 1973.

Albina, OR - Install second-hand telephone PBX equipment, including 400 second-hand telephones. Note: This installation should begin about April 2, 1973 and be completed in 120 days (August 1, 1973)."

This installation appears to be timed with the closure of the downtown Portland office in the Pittock Block building. References to attended 24-hour PBX must have been at that location. The Portland Pittock Block PBX office was unique to the Communications Department. In 1966, Pacific Northwest Bell raised the price for termination of tie trunks (Interoffice trunks) in the Pacific Bell owned PBX. To reduce this cost, Mr. Jett arranged for a railroad-owned tandem PBX, which terminated all the PBX tie trunks. Inter-office trunks where installed between the Union Pacific-owned tandem PBX switch and the Pacific Bell-owned operator-maned PBX. Thus, calls between other PBXs (i.e. Spokane-Hinkle calls) were not switched in the Bell-owned PBX, as was done prior to this installation. With the closure of the Pittock Block office and the installation of the new Union Pacific-owned PBX at Albina, the tandem PBX was no longer needed. With closure of the Pittock Block offices on December 20, 1982, the dispatchers also were moved to Albina at the same time.

D. RECOMMENDED ADDITIONS

> 1. "At Los Angeles, replace the telephone switchboard (PBX), presently owned by the telephone company and leased by the Railroad, with Railroad-owned equipment. This leased PBX has provisions for 600 lines with 352 in service. Inasmuch as a 400-line PBX would not provide sufficient lines for growth and a 500-line switchboard will cost almost as much as a 600—line PBX, the larger unit should be installed.
>
> This project was approved in the 1973 Budget and should be progressed for early approval in order that all material can be ordered and be on hand so that installation can be started about August 15 1973 (on completion of similar project at Albina).
>
> "System - Design, assemble and wire a transportable Communication Center for 400 telephone lines, central office trunks (connections to the local telephone company) and 48 company intercity dial long lines, Further, this unit should provide facilities for attendance by two PBX operators. This transportable Communication Center should be constructed in two (2) truck-trailers to permit ready movement over the entire railroad system to a point of required use. (The second truck-trailer van was never used. Space in the

switching equipment van was modified, walled off, and environmentally controlled for switchboard operators; and all equipment including the switchboards were installed in a single van.)

"Recognizing that the Railroad will, by early 1974, own and operate 22 telephone switchboards (PBX), eight attended and 14 unattended, it is almost mandatory that some form of standby protection be provided. It is always possible that fire, floods, earthquakes, as well as sabotage, could remove one of these telephone switchboards from service. With this transportable Communication Center, service could be restored within 24 hours after arrival of the trailer,

"The Communications Department already has on hand a second-hand trailer that could be used for this purpose and would require one additional trailer, which could be an obsolete unit from the Union Pacific Motor Freight. Second-hand switching equipment should be used for this transportable Communication Center and much of the required equipment is already on hand.

"The first application of this transportable Communication Center would be to install same at Kansas City adjacent to the 7th Street Yard Office, permitting removal of the telephone company owned equipment and the installation of Railroad-owned equipment in space presently occupied by the telephone company. This concept will avoid the expense of remodeling part of the yard office to provide room for the installation of Railroad owned attended PBX. The savings should be more than adequate to pay the cost of construction of the transportable Communication Center.

3. "At Kansas City, Kansas, replace the telephone switchboard (PBX), presently owned by the telephone company and leased by the Railroad, with Railroad owned equipment. This leased PBX has provisions for 400 lines and the Railroad owned PBX should have the same capacity. This project should he planned and approved to begin upon completion of the installation of the Los Angeles PBX, which should be early March 1974.

(Note: Space in the communications office was made available and the transportable PBX in the van was not needed. As electronic PBX's were installed, the manufacturers of electronic PBX's advised they could quickly provide a replacement electronic PBX.)

4. "At Omaha replace the telephone switchboard (PBX), presently owned by the telephone company and leased by the Railroad, with Railroad owned equipment. This leased PBX has a capacity for 1500 lines with 1445 lines in service. To permit future growth, a 2000-line crossbar unit that permits use of touch tone dialing and other features should he provided. The suppliers who have been contacted advise it will take 12 to l8 months to furnish after receipt of order. It will require six months to install the new PBX, Therefore, the new telephone PBX could not be placed in service for l to 24 months after receipt of work order approval.

(A 2000 line crossbar PBX (state-of-the art in Mr. Jett's time) was not installed. An electronic GTD-4600 PBX was installed in Omaha as one of the last major office PBX's installed.)

5. "At Chicago, in August 1973, at the time Assistant Manager of Communications Office Mr. Henry Doles retires and Assistant Chief PBX Operator Mrs. Irene Tranke also retires, it is recommended that a review of the operation of the telephone switchboard he made. It should be feasible to provide attendance of this telephone switchboard (PBX) only from Monday through Friday, hours 8:00 AM to 5:00 PM, The Manager or Assistant Manager of the Communications Office could provide relief for the PBX operator between the hours of 12:00 Noon and 1:00 PM,

6. "During the fall and winter of 1974-75, a review of the operations of the various attended telephone PBXs should be made. A careful analysis of these operations should show that an operator can be eliminated at several of the locations, as railroad personnel, by that time; will have accepted telephone service without operator assistance and no longer will expect the telephone operators to act as secretaries.

7. "Hinkle OR - In the event a retarder yard is built in this area, the present unattended telephone PBX will be inadequate. A new attended telephone PBX should be planned for installation in the Communications Department building. This telephone PBX should have a capacity of not less than 200 lines, Further, since this PBX will have part-time attendance, several city (Hermiston) trunks to the local telephone company central office should be provided. Also, additional Railroad—owned intercity dial trunks will be required due to the increased activity in this yard.

8. "Las Vegas NV, - Due to the increased activity in this area requiring additional Railroad-furnished intercity dial telephone circuits, the present single digit prefix used to select the intercity dial telephone circuits should be converted to two digits at the time of the issuance of the next Railroad telephone directory.

9. "The issuance of a new Railroad telephone directory should be planned and issued in the Spring of 1974 and at two-year intervals after that date. During a two—year period, a large number of the entries are out of date due to promotions, retirements and other changes,

10. "At Spokane, Washington, replace telephone key systems leased from the local telephone company with

Railroad-owned units. The savings in rental should pay for Railroad—owned equipment in one year or less and provide improved service.

11. "At Seattle Washington, when the Communications Office is moved from the Union Station to an enlarged yard office, a new unattended telephone PBX of 200-line capacity should be installed. Further, at that time, Railroad-owned telephone key equipment should he installed and the lease with the local telephone company for similar equipment canceled,

"The presently used temporary PBX installed in a trailer can be retired in favor of the proposed 400-line transportable Communication Center.

12. "At Omaha, NE-Council Bluffs, Iowa - In the event a new division office is constructed in the Council Bluffs yard area, this building should be provided with a 200-line unattended telephone PBX, A recent count of the number of telephones that would be served by this PBX is in excess of 100. Service to this PBX would be by microwave radio from the roof of the Headquarters Building.

13. "Salt Lake Utah - The present 50-1ine isolated and unattended telephone PBX located in the diesel shop should be replaced with a similar unit of 100-line capacity to service the one—spot car repair facility, the present diesel shop and to provide for the proposed expansion of the present diesel shop. The 50-line telephone PBX replaced should be overhauled and used at some one—spot car repair facility.

14. "Pocatello, ID - The present centrally-controlled inter communication system in the diesel shop should be replaced with l00-line telephone PBX that is isolated and unattended. This new 100-line telephone PBX will also serve the Maintenance of Way (M/W) heavy

equipment repair shop and the one—spot car repair facility. The l8-1ine isolated unattended telephone PBX released from the M/W heavy equipment repair shop can then be used for a one-spot car repair facility.

15. "Ogden Utah - Inasmuch as the Southern Pacific is constructing a microwave radio system into Ogden, it is obvious they will desire to terminate additional intercity dial telephone lines on the jointly— owned (UP 55% - SP 45%) unattended telephone PBX. Implementation of this item will depend upon the Southern Pacific's plans.

16. "Replace all Telephone Company 507 switchboards, terminating foreign exchange (FX) lines on the system, with voice connecting arrangements. Conversion will represent approximately 33-1/3% saving on present Telephone Company billing at each location. Voice Connecting Arrangements (VCA) were permitted after the 1968 Carterfone decision.

"From time to time it may become necessary to add additional FX connections are in the next to last section of the railroad's Telephone Book Section titled, "City Numbers." Technique for providing this service has been approved by the local telephone companies and can be economically provided. This service is provided in lieu of wide area telephone service (WATS) if the Telephone Company and is very much less expensive than WATS."[6]

Many of Jett's recommendations were made as he envisioned, though the actual date of the changes has been difficult to identify.

Several of the telephone company owned PBXs were replaced more than once with Union Pacific owned. The telephone company's PBXs were initially replaced with Union Pacific's second-hand Western Electric step-by-step PBXs, then later by electronic ones. The Portland-Albina PBX and the Los Angeles PBX were installed under the 1973 work order, identified in the Five-Year Plan.

The transportable PBX (identified under the Communications Shop work above) was built but not used as described above.

At Hinkle the retarder yard was built and a new company-owned PBX was installed as planned.

At Las Vegas, as planned by Mr. Jett, a Union Pacific-owned WE 740 PBX was installed in a prefabricated building due to demolition of the Union Pacific Depot and replacement with construction of the Union Plaza Hotel and Casino on the same location.

Mr. Jett was seen by many as a tough-minded, no-nonsense boss. And indeed, he was a strong-minded supervisor. But he was fair. His concern for employees was no better demonstrated then his concern for the Communications manager and switchboard operator at Chicago as seen above.

Jack Baird Era

With the employment of Jack Baird in June of 1972, Jett revealed that it was his plan to transition every PBX on the Union Pacific Railroad from AT&T to proprietary systems within five years, and that it would be Baird's role to achieve that goal. Jack Baird was a good choice, because he had formerly worked for Pacific Northwest Bell as a telephone equipment technician. When hired by Jett, he became responsible for overseeing all PBX installations on the Union Pacific, and ultimately retired as a communications department director. He subsequently served as a consultant to telephone equipment installation companies. Mr. Baird lives on an Ashton ID ranch in the shadow of the Teton Mountains.

However, electronic PBXs were not part of the original Five-Year Plan. Jett's scheme was to replace the AT&T-owned PBXs (as represented by the Bell Operating company for each location) with second-hand Western Electric equipment. During Baird's first years, he proceeded to install many railroad-owned 740 and 701 PBXs across the railroad, replacing similar Bell Operating Company owned equipment.

(Note: The terms PBX and PABX are industry terminology referencing Private Branch Exchange (PBX) and Private Branch Automatic Exchange (PABX), which was the local telephone switching equipment for businesses for their internal telephone service.

The term PBX indicates switching equipment attended by a local telephone operator, while PABX indicates switching equipment without a local telephone operator, aka automated. The term PBX in this context is used interchangeably here without regard to the presence of a telephone operator or not; as many PBXs originally installed with a local telephone operator were later changed, either removing the telephone operator or removing the operator's services off-premise.)

The first electronic PBXs were installed after Mr. Bob Brenneman became Director of Communications. The first electronic PBX installed on the Union Pacific Railroad was a GTD-120 Digital PBX at LaGrande OR on September 12, 1976.

Other electronic PBXs installed on the Union Pacific Railroad were:

Rawlins, WY	GTD-120, January 1977
Hinkle, OR	GTD-1000, June 1977
Kansas City, KS	GTD-1000, February 1978
Los Angeles, CA	GTD-1000, July 1978
Pocatello, ID	GTD-1000
Omaha, NE	GTD-4600, October 1982
Salt Lake UT	GTD-1000 , Omni SII
Portland, OR,	

Installed first Direct Inward Dialing (DID) (whereby incoming calls to an individual station bypassed the switchboard operator and went directly to the station on the PBX) into a Customer Owned and Maintained (COAM) PBX (WE 701B). The PBX was installed April 1973 at the Albina Yard Office. The CD-9 Interface DID GTE Voice Connecting Arrangement (C22VCA) installed September 1977 after the Carterfone Decision in 1968. Prior to this installation of DID service, only the Omaha Northwestern Bell PBX had DID service.[7]

Omaha GTD-4600 PBX Installation

The Omaha PBX was one of the last major offices to receive a company-owned electronic PBX. The establishment of a division office at Council Bluffs in 1981 required an increased number of PBX stations working off the Omaha PBX, so a decision was made to defer expansion or replacement of the Omaha PBX to accommodate the increase in lines needed for the Council Bluffs office by installing a Railroad-owned electronic GTD 120 PBX in Council Bluffs itself. Installation of the Council Bluffs PBX released 91 PBX numbers from the Omaha PBX. The Communications Engineer met with Mr. John L. Jorgensen on June 4, 1981 to evaluate the relative costs of using a Northwestern Bell Telephone Company leased PBX, or a Union Pacific owned PBX. The economics of the decision favored purchase of a company-owned and maintained system.

The installation of a Council Bluffs PBX post-phoned installation of a new Omaha PBX by about one year.

When it was decided to submit a **R**equest **F**or **P**roposal (RFP) for the replacement of the Omaha PBX, the RFP was also submitted to Northwestern Bell for their proposal in addition to other PBX equipment manufacturers.

When the bids were returned, Mr. John L. Jorgenson required that all bids for a Union Pacific-owned PBX include all the services provided by Northwestern Bell (NWB). The company-owned version had to include the cost of Union Pacific telephone installation, maintenance, and training personnel, since these services were provided by NWB. The initial review of the bids appeared to indicate the NWB bid to be the low bid due Mr. Jorgensen's requirement that Union Pacific had to include a telephone feature trainer because the NWB bid included one for the new electronic features. The addition of Union Pacific maintenance and installation personnel also increased the cost.

The bid originally was reviewed by Mr. Jorgensen with further review by Communications Engineering; both questioned the low bid. Since the Union Pacific-owned plan was required by Mr. Jorgensen to include the maintenance and installation personnel, comparable cost of telephone "moves and changes" installations paid to NWB had not been included. Review of the past year's "moves and changes" independent charges were researched and when the charges for the past year were added to the NWB proposal, the balance of costs was changed, swinging the cost benefit in favor of PBX ownership by Union Pacific. In time, the new Union Pacific electronic GTD-4600 PBX was installed by Union Pacific technicians.

Since the Union Pacific had on-staff trainers, who trained company personnel in use of computer terminals, these trainers were given the added responsibility of training office personnel in the new electronic telephone features, and no new telephone trainer was ever added. The Communications Shop personnel were brought over to assist in the installation of the PBX, however, several technicians were retained and added as required to make the telephone moves and changes. In addition to making the telephone moves and changes in the headquarters building, their workload also included wiring the Union Pacific Headquarters building for installation of computer terminals when required, and to assist communication shop projects when necessary, providing a great deal of workload balancing between communications projects.

The GTD 4600 PBX was cutover to service on October 1, 1982. Installation of the GTD 4600 permitted recording of all long distance calls' incoming and outgoing numbers. These records were sent to the head of each department for oversite. At a 1986 staff meeting, it was reported that the new equipment reduced the telephone bill $100,000 per month, including $40,000 per month in leased PBXs. At the April 2, 1987 staff meeting in Las Vegas, it was reported that the GTD 4600 PBX was handling one million call records per month.

Union Pacific Universal Numbering Plan

With the flexibility ingrained in the electronic PBXs, improved efficiency of the switched telephone network had operational potential not imagined or capable in the old, mechanical-switch PBX network. The United States national telephone network went to direct distance dialing using a Universal Numbering Plan in the mid-1950s; the Union Pacific Switched Telephone Network previously used unique city trunk codes for each PBX to route calls from one PBX to another. Calls could be routed beyond the adjacent PBX, if a direct route was busy, but the originator of the call needed to know the trunking codes of each PBX through which the call was to be routed.

The electronic PBXs had a trunking plan embedded in computer memory. Mr. Baird developed a Universal Numbering Plan for the Railroad which was implemented April 13, 1984, but the plan paralleled AT&T's Nationwide Universal Numbering Plan so that if a Union Pacific network failure occurred, routing of calls could be seamlessly switched over to the Nation-wide network.

Prior to implementing the Universal Number Plan, many more mechanical PBXs were converted to electronic. The critical tandem switching nodes were required to be electronic PBXs. The tandem nodes were:

Omaha, NE

Salt Lake City, UT

Portland, OR

Cheyenne, WY

Pocatello, ID

Los Angeles, CA

Oakland, CA

St. Louis, MO

Tandem PBX offices all had direct trunks from Omaha (trunks are direct telephone circuits between PBX's as opposed to stations which were telephone lines appearing on the PBX to a telephone instrument), and most had trunks between adjacent tandem PBX offices. Salt Lake had trunks to all other tandem offices except St. Louis.

One of the side benefits of the nationwide telephone plan was the ability to track all off-network toll calls and identify the originator's phone. Thus, charged calls were referred to the responsible supervisor to determine if the call was necessary, or if it could have been routed internally on-network.

The Union Pacific Universal Numbering Plan was expanded to the Missouri Pacific and Western Pacific Railroads, providing one of the Nation's largest and most modern private telephone networks.

Dispatcher Office Consolidations

With the expanded communications services available with the 600-channel microwave across most of the railroad, projects which were once inconceivable were now possible. Thus, management decided to consolidate dispatchers. Many dispatcher offices had reduced activity in the evening and at night because of the reduced number of local trains operating at night, so dispatchers' responsibilities could be consolidated by expanding their territories at night. However, balancing the load where there are few or only a single dispatcher console in an office did limit rebalancing the workload during off-hours.

It was decided to move certain dispatcher offices (and consoles) to other locations. One of the first dispatcher's offices to be moved was the move of the Las Vegas dispatcher's office to Salt Lake City in 1967, and the Laramie dispatcher's office to Cheyenne. Many dispatchers' responsibilities were moved from the old location to the new office.

The critical services supporting a dispatcher was the CTC controls and the dispatcher's voice circuit. These are the most important services the dispatcher needs. These services were remoted* to the new locations using the microwave system. Additionally, the dispatcher had a telephone number listed in the old office, and in some cases the chief dispatcher's number was listed. Most times these same single party lines were remoted on the microwave to the new office for ease of communicating with the dispatcher without potential blocking of calls to the dispatcher because of busy tie trunks.

Remoting of a dispatcher to another location meant that all communications and signal services that supported the function were extended by communications services to the new location. Generally new microwave channels had to be provided and telemetry circuits for signal controls and hot box equipment, and voice circuits for dispatcher radio channels voice circuits installed.

Reliable operation of the dispatcher was a must and provisions were provided for protection of this function should the microwave fail. In most dispatch-office moves, a wire-line carrier system provided for alternate protection for dispatcher services. As well, a switch-over system panel was installed at the new and old communications offices in the event that a microwave system outage occurred. In those instances, these panels transferred the CTC code line circuits on **Voice Frequency Carrier Telegraph** channels (VFCT) and the dispatcher's voice circuit from the microwave system to the wire-line carrier system automatically. The switchover equipment used a single VFCT carrier on the wire-line carrier-channel to monitor itself to avoid switching into a dead channel. Another VFCT receiver also monitored a channel for a high level of noise, also to avoid switching into a defective channel. As dispatchers' offices were consolidated, this protection pattern was expanded to other locations.

Dispatchers' radios on the mainline microwave system are located at the individual microwave site. The controlling radio voice-channel is inserted directly on the baseband between the microwave site and the dispatcher's associated communications office. With the move of the dispatcher to the new office, many times the base band was continuous between the microwave radio and new office. To move the dispatcher's radio controlling voice-channel, only a new channel module needed to be installed at the new dispatcher's office location to interface with the dispatcher at the new office. Other times, a new channel pairing was needed for the change in channel assignment.

With the early successes, management chose to further consolidate dispatchers. Nampa dispatchers were moved to Pocatello, Hinkle dispatchers moved to Portland. Later in 1974, the Los Angeles dispatchers were moved to Salt Lake City. Due to the distance and lack of availability of line wire-carrier systems, the move of the Los Angeles office presented some unique solutions. However, the Southern Pacific Railroad had recently completed a microwave system into Ogden, from San Francisco.

The Union Pacific Railroad had an Exchange of Service Agreement (See section on Exchange of Services Agreements (EOS) later in book) with the Southern Pacific; in fact, the Union Pacific had previously furnished channels from Los Angeles to Ogden over its microwave system for the backup of Southern Pacific Railroad CTC service.

With the move of the Los Angeles dispatchers, the Union Pacific routed its dispatcher's backup service via our microwave system to the Southern Pacific's microwave via Holiday Hill (The

Southern Pacific Railroad and the Union Pacific Railroad each had microwave buildings at Holiday Hill in close proximity, and a pair of coaxial cables were laid between the two buildings for the exchange of services. Initially, two groups of twelve channels each were installed for the transfer; later additional groups were added). From Holiday Hill, the Southern Pacific routed the backup service from San Francisco to Ogden via Los Angeles onto the Union Pacific microwave system at Salt Lake City. As new communications services were developed, more services were moved with the dispatcher's office, such as the hotbox and other services discussed below.

In December of 1981, the Denver Machine at Cheyenne and the Kansas City Dispatcher were both moved to North Platte.

Dispatcher consolidation continued as opportunities developed. The Portland dispatch office became a test site of technologies which led to the ultimate consolidation of the entire system into the Omaha Harriman Dispatcher Center in 1984 (covered below).

Installation of Hotbox systems, other trackside services, and additional CTC expansion forced the installation of many "Microwave Legs" between mainline microwave sites and trackside locations. These microwave legs additionally allowed other improved services to depots and maintenance offices.

During the mid-1960s, the railroads, experiencing journal bearing failures which caused many accidents, requested suppliers to develop technology to detect hot bearing before they burned off and caused derailments. Hot box detectors were installed at trackside. Some railroads tied these systems directly to the trackside signals to stop trains for inspection.

The Union Pacific Railroad System, with its extensive communications network, elected to remote these services over wire lines and voice channels to the associated dispatch centers, where the degree of a hot box problem could be evaluated and train crew advised.

Next up, the book will discuss how the new communications network allowed the Union Pacific Railroad to develop many other communication services using in-house engineering experience and knowledge.

13

Radio Systems in the Jett Era and Influence Early Radio Systems

At the end of World War II, the railroad industry was intensively investigating the advantages of radios in railroad service. Inductive radio (described below) and "space radio" presented opportunities for increasing the efficiency of railroad service. The technology was developing from wartime research into a tool to speed up communications between railroad workers.

The FCC was in the process of rulemaking and dividing up radio spectrum to satisfy new petitioners. Mr. Jett's paper below describes some of the issues and discussions.

"The Railroad Radio Service was established by the FCC December 1945. From the beginning the railroad industry recommended an increase in the number of channels assigned the service as being inadequate. Mr. L. J. Prendergast of the B&O Railroad as chairman of the "Association of American Railroads Committee on Radio and Allied Communications as Applied to Railroad Operations" recommended 85 channels. He referred to the results of a questionnaire circulated by the AAR to ascertain the Railroads' plans for utilization of radio in the coming three-year period, particularly in congested areas where heavy yard and terminal operations are carried on. The survey indicated, he told the F.C.C., that 77 railroads representing 90.1 per cent of Class I mileage on the United States and 19 of the smaller roads are "now using or expect to use radio communications within the next three years." Such a program, he added, will entail and expenditure of approximately $15,000,000."[1]

(The Federal Communications Commission granted the Denver and Rio Grande Western a construction permit for 32 new units as mobile train (end-to-end) stations. This was announced on February 27, 1946, pursuant to the first application submitted under the Rules and Regulations Governing Railroad Radio Service Part 16 of the FCC.[2]

While the D&RGW received the first FCC license in February 1946 for thirty-two end-to-end mobile units, they were initially only able to equip four locomotives, four cabooses and ten wayside stations due to lack of conduit and fittings. The Chicago Burlington and Quincy Railway actually equipped twenty-two locomotives and eight cabooses in 1946 with "space radios" for operation on 386 miles between Hastings, NE and Denver, CO. The balance of the D&RGW radio equipment was installed later.[3]

(The Union Pacific's dispatcher radio system used a radio channel officially identified by the Association of American Railroad's Frequency Assignment Plan (FAP) as Point to Train. Other channels were designated as End-to-End (meaning locomotive to caboose) for yard service.)

Mr. C. Otis Jett presented a paper to the Chicago Section of the Institute of Radio Engineers on November 18, 1949. In the paper, he outlined some of the issues of two-way radio use in the railroad environment. The title of the paper was "FROM PONY EXPRESS TO MILE LONG TRAINS." He made no specific reference to Dr. Millener's experiments, but reported that the Union Pacific Railroad made an experimental installation in the early 1920s. He said it operated, but was not practical. This author has not found any other reference to Dr. Millener's experiments in Mr. Jett's papers.

He acknowledged that World War II brought tremendous progress in radio art and also acknowledge that it is possible to design two-way radio for the use of railroads that operate successfully and is also practical.

He described the railroad environment with mile-long freight trains and 18- to 24-car passenger trains operating at 80 to 100 miles per hour. *"Reliability,"* he stressed, is vital; *"nothing can be left to chance." "Therefore, each and every piece of equipment and component thereof must be the very best money can buy. For that reason, the railroads have hesitated to adopt radio as a standard means of communications."*

He went on to describe the need for the radio to be as reliable as the existing modern wire communications circuits and associated equipment. *"The present communication and signal circuits are the wire line type and have been tried and proven over years of use. The engineers designing this type of equipment are also striving constantly to improve their type of facilities. These wire line facilities are of the utmost reliability except for Acts of Gods, such as severe sleet storms, landslides, earthquakes, and similar catastrophes such as man with his puny efforts cannot prevent. Radio, to be a useful tool to the railroad, must be of the same reliability. I do not intend to infer that radio today does not serve a purpose, but when its reliability is on a par with our wire line facilities it will become a far more useful tool since it will provide us with communications beyond the capabilities of our present facilities as well as be less affected by Acts of God."*

In "train order" territory—that is, railroad territory which is not protected by color light signals and associated track circuits—train orders are given to the train crew on written instructions passed to the crew by a train order clerk (or telegrapher). The train order clerk receives the order via telegraph or telephone from the dispatcher, and repeats the order back to the dispatcher word for word. Other train order clerks, monitoring the circuit, must also copy the order for additional accuracy and reliability.

"In early 1945, the railroads met with the Federal Communications Commission and requested an allocation of a band of frequencies in the 158-162 megacycle portion of the spectrum. The railroads were assigned 60 channels with 60 kilocycle separation between each channel."

He goes on to say that, *"In 1949... they reduced the number of channels to 39, however, keeping the same 60 kilocycle spacing between channels. These channels were then allocated to the various railroads throughout the nation on an area basis. The Union Pacific was allocated a number of these channels. On consulting the several leading manufacturers of radio equipment for use in this portion of the radio frequency spectrum, we decided that it would be much to our advantage to arrange to secure our frequencies in the middle of the band, spaced on alternate frequencies or channels."*

The further describes the various channels allocated and the uses for each channel. He postulated that, *"In the not too distant future there is an excellent possibility, if facsimile equipment is developed sufficiently, that instructions on how the train is to be operated will be given direct to the conductor and engineer."* (The article said, "The Union Pacific Railroad is investigating the use of facsimile for rapid transmission of orders." Mr. Jett made the announcement before the Engineers Club of Omaha[4], where he said, *"Certain operations require written orders, we have a saying you cannot operate a railroad by jawbone."* The identical words were quoted in the IRE paper.)

In consultation with a number of radio manufacturers, the Union Pacific secured five channels in the middle of the band separated by 120 kilocycle separation between adjacent channels on a system-wide basis, *"The first channel being 159.93 megacycles, followed by channels on 160.05, 160.17, 160.29 and 160.41 megacycles."* The first and third channels are used from train to wayside station. Two channels were… *"Not selected for duplex operation, but for an alternate to provide additional reliability.*

"Channel no. 2 is used for communications for end to end on the train, i.e. from the locomotive engineer to the conductor in the caboose.

"Channel no. 4 and no. 5 are used in yard and terminal operations. Channel No. 4 being the primary frequency used in yards and terminals, for example, from a fixed location under the control of a yardmaster to a switch foreman in a diesel locomotive switching car. The fifth channel is used primarily for safety purposes in our retarder yard. This is used by the yardmaster in charge of the "hump" to direct the operation of the switch engine, pushing cars over the "hump"."

Jett also said that, *"To date, (November 1949) the Union Pacific Railroad has spent approximately $350,000 investigating and determining whether or not radio can be adapted to railroad operation. As a result, we now have a coherent and comprehensive operating plan. Radio equipment in use on our railroad system can also be utilized on any part of it. Locomotives and rolling stock equipped with radio can be sent from one portion of the system to another portion as the need for equipment develops, depending upon the time of year and type of traffic to be moved, without regard to frequency assignments."*

The IRE paper described the introduction of radios on the railroad by testing them in a *"proving ground"* in various railroad yards throughout the Union Pacific System. He reasoned that, *"A failure or improper operation of the equipment would not be of serious consequences: That is, impairing the safety of the traveling public, employees of the railroad, or railroad equipment or freight in our hands for transportation."* He noted, *"We have a number of installations...now in service."*

"The Union Pacific, in early 1945 conducted a series of tests in the Kansas City area using standard mobile 30 to 40 megacycle equipment, which equipment was all that was available at that time, to determine the practicability of radio. (While not discussed in the paper, the 30 to 40 MHZ band transmitted the radio signal for great distances and resulted in considerable interference between railroad operations in other areas).

"In early 1946 further test comparing radio versus inductive equipment were conducted in Eastern OR." (Inductive radio was tested in the railroad industry. The Pennsylvania Railroad reported on an extensive use of inductive radio on their system between Pittsburg, PA and Harrisburg, PA, a distance of 1025 miles of main line track for 300 locomotives and 100 cabin cars and 16 wayside stations.[5] Inductive radio to operate successively required open wire lines adjacent the track to transmit an induced signal from the locomotive to the caboose. The radios on the locomotive and caboose each had a long inductive loop to couple the signal to the wire line. The system had limited capabilities and lost to current VHF two-way radio systems because of these limitations.)

"As a result of these tests a complete radio installation was made in 1946 for yard operations in the Kansas City area. This original installation consisted of 16 mobile stations on diesel switch locomotives and one fixed station remote controlled over approximately seven miles of telephone line from three separate locations. Since this initial installation in 1946, we have expanded our radio system until it numbers more than 100 sets in all types of railroad service."

In conclusion, Mr. Jett recommended that *"Radio manufacturers canvas the railroad industry for all the ways of using radio that have been discovered to date, and these ideas be placed in book form and distributed…to the railroad industry for their guidance and assistance in applying radio to their work. I hope that this suggestion bears fruit at an early date, as it will I feel materially aid in the expanded use of radio on railroads."*[6]

Several articles in *Railway Signaling & Communications* supported the report in Mr. Jett's paper, and described the expanded new radio installations and some of the success the Union Pacific achieved.

The call letters of the Kansas City fixed station* were KRUP (**K**ansas **R**adio **U**nion **P**acific). The fixed station was a 50-watt FM transmitter with the antenna mounted on a 100-foot floodlight tower in the Fairfax yard. The principal control point was the Armstrong yardmaster's office and two other control points in the Fairfax north (Fairfax) and south (Central District) yard offices. All fixed and mobile radio equipment were provided by Motorola Inc.**

*(The term "Fixed Station" is the FCC approved term of a licensed radio station located at a fixed location; the term "Base Station" is term describing a fixed radio station in vernacular commonly used in the industry. The term "Wayside Station" is a term used in the railroad industry describing fixed radio stations commonly located along the railroad normally used to communications to trains. The terms fixed and base are used interchangeably in this book).

16 Diesel-electric switch engines are equipped with radios powered by 64 DCV to 115 volt AC rotary converters, a practice the Union Pacific continued for all locomotive units.[7] The paper also identified the communications system was planned and installed by Union Pacific forces under the jurisdiction of G. R. Van Eaton, Superintendent of Telegraph and under the supervision of C. O. Jett, System Telephone and Telegraph Engineer.

(**Early reports in *Railway Signaling* referred to Motorola as the Galvin Manufacturing Corp.)

Successful results with the initial Kansas City radio system led to expansion of yard radio systems across the railroad. A $125,000 program of yard radio communications improvement provided installation of yard radios at Denver, Omaha, Salt Lake City, Seattle, Los Angeles, Portland, and Pocatello ID. The program also included a trial installation of radios on four road locomotives and four cabooses for operation between Kansas City and Marysville KS, and five fixed radio stations on that route.[8] This installation of radios on locomotives and cabooses is the first reported installation of road radios on the Union Pacific Railroad.

With this expansion of system-wide two-way FM radio program in 1948, Bob Brenneman was promoted to Equipment Supervisor to oversee the program.

Yard radio installations were expanded in 1949 to include the new hump classification yard at North Platte, NE. Two fixed stations were installed to provide radio coverage. One fixed station served yard operations and one served the Hump operation. Eight locomotives were provided with two channel radios; a two-frequency transmitter and two receivers for use in whichever service they were assigned to for operation.[9]

The results of improved radio service in the North Platte yard were phenomenal. "The Union Pacific terminal at North Platte, NE has reported a 98 percent record of delivery promises since installation of two-way radio, as against 70 percent before. Other advantages were that eight engines were now doing the work of nine, no time is lost in picking up orders, and during severe winter conditions radio has permitted the yard to remain open constantly. While initial cost of complete railroad radio equipment may seem high," Mr. Galvin (President of Motorola) noted, "it is significant that in the case of this Union Pacific yard alone the system amortized itself in six months"[10]

FCC reported authorization of new radio licenses in 1951, at the following locations:

Yard and Terminal Green River WY, 1 fixed station Motorola,

Yard and Terminal Kansas City KS, 1 fixed station Motorola,

Yard and Terminal Council Bluffs, IA, 1 fixed station Motorola,

Yard and Terminal Denver, WY, 1 fixed station Motorola,

Yard and Terminal Cheyenne WY, 1 fixed station Motorola,

Yard and Terminal Cheyenne WY, 1 fixed station Bendix[11] Other new FCC reports of a new license: Yard and Terminal Las

Vegas NV, 1 fixed station Motorola; and modification of the Yard and terminal mobile license for 47 Motorola radios.[12]

As railroad technology improved, new installations were made for unique situations. Two new radio systems were planned and installed at Council Bluffs and Kansas City by Bob Brenneman, assistant system telephone and telegraph engineer as described in several articles in *Railway Signaling and Communications*.

An article in the September 1951 issue of *Railway Signaling and Communications* described an installation in the Union Pacific Yard in Council Bluffs, IA for a car inspector's radio system. The system described the use of portable Motorola radios carried by car inspectors and carmen; the radio repeater system consisted of a radio receiver located on a 100-foot floodlight tower in the west end of the yard and a transmitter on another flood light tower about out one-half mile away in the east end of the yard. The lead car inspector's office was served by a control console to monitor and supervise the operation. The installation not only sped up inspections operations, but improved the safety for the car inspectors.[13]

During 1953, a 43-mile railroad track cut-off was constructed on Sherman Hill, a high point on the Union Pacific Railroad, to increase train operations on this grade bottleneck. Installation of a radio repeater system similar to the car inspector radio system reported above but expanded over a larger area, aided the construction of the cut-off. Handie talkie radios aided the surveyors in layout of the route and grade. Mobile units in vehicles permitted field engineers and supervisors to communicate with the construction headquarters in Cheyenne.

This system greatly aided engineering and construction work on the new route: work progress-reporting improved construction plans as well as the scheduling of men and equipment. A second system, using train-to-wayside channels, permitted communication to the work train, which delivered construction materials to the work site. Radio coordination minimized interference between freight and passenger train operations.[14]

By 1955, the Kansas City terminal radio system was expanded to three fixed radio stations and twenty-eight switch engines and three automobiles all equipped with radios. A car inspector radio repeater system was added along with equipping the car inspectors with quarter-watt handie-talkie radios. The expansion was engineered and supervised by Bob Brenneman.[15]

The Union Pacific Railroad expanded the use of two-way radio to a subsidiary, Union Pacific Motor Freight, in the Omaha–Council Bluffs area by installing radios in all pick-up and delivery trucks. The trucks were assigned specific routes and the dispatcher directed the trucks for servicing customers in the area. The base station radio, controlled by the motor-freight dispatcher, was located atop the Blackstone Hotel in Omaha.[16]

By the mid-1960s, locomotives, cabooses, and other equipment such as automobiles were equipped with two-way radios.

Initially, radio equipment available for railroad mobile units were designed to operate on common automotive voltage of 12 volts. Radios using locomotive voltages of 64 volts DC required a vibrator to convert input voltages to standard radio voltages. These vibrators were troublesome maintenance problems. (Electrical contacts in the vibrators experienced considerable high voltage arcing causing burnout and failure.)

As transistorized equipment became available, many railroads installed two-way railroad-approved standard mobile radios which had power supply switchable between 12 Volt DC (automotive standard voltage) and 64 Volt DC, the power available on locomotives. Switchable power for railroad standard radios allowed the industry to use a single style radio for both locomotive and cabooses. Additionally, stand-alone AC power supplies allowed the same radio to be used for base stations.

The locomotive power was subject to many transient voltages of several thousands of volts. Prior to transistorization, such "transients" had not been a problem. However, with transistorization of the power supply, these transients caused frequent radio failures. The radio manufacturing industry developed "brute force transient suppressors" to eliminate the locomotive radio failures, but, through Mr. Jett's leadership, a dynamotor was installed on locomotives which converted the 64 Volt locomotive power source to 12 Volts. The dynamotor was more tolerant of the transients and provided clean transient-free DC power to the radios. The Union Pacific thus chose to use a relatively inexpensive mobile vehicle radio (a Motorola Business Dispatcher) as the Union Pacific standard train radio, compared to a more costly industry standard railroad radio with its switchable power supply (which was about three times higher in cost). The UP Standard permitted the radio to be used in locomotives, cabooses, automobiles, trucks and various types of track maintenance equipment, and wayside base stations in depots.

Compared to many installations of road locomotives and cabooses on other railroads, installations on the Union Pacific Railroad progressed slowly. Mr. Jett's paper stressed the importance of reliability in use of radios on trains and his concerns slowed implementation on the Union Pacific. His paper stressed the reliability of wire lines. Tube radios were subject to vibration on locomotives and track equipment with resultant failures not experienced in automobiles.

After the Kansas City-to-Marysville trial in 1948, in 1964, the Union Pacific made its initial installation of road locomotive and caboose radios. It was a small but significant endeavor: Twenty-four locomotives and four cabooses were equipped with radios along with two fixed-base stations.

The following years saw rapid expansion of radios on locomotives and cabooses, along with installation of supporting base stations. Note the imbalance between installation of base stations and microwave sites in the later years.

   1965, 150 locomotive radios, 32 microwave (M/W) sites

   1967, 150 locomotive radios, 250 caboose radios, 5 base station (BS) radios, 2 M/W sites

   1968, 110 locomotive radios, 120 caboose radios, 13 BS radios, 13 M/W sites

   1969, 105 locomotive radios, 12 base station radios, 24 M/W sites

   1970, 90 locomotive radios, 17 base station radios, 30 M/W sites

   1971, 360 locomotive radios, 36 base station radios, 8 M/W sites

   1972, 192 locomotive radios, 28 base station radios, 17 M/W sites

   1973, 302 locomotive radios, 31 base station radios, 7 M/W sites

   1974, 523 locomotive radios, 30 base station radios, 1 M/W sites.[17]

Initial base station radios were installed to communicate with train crews, controlled by nearby waystation operators. The Union Pacific also developed a wire-line interface to the wayside radio stations for direct communications between the train dispatcher and the train crew. The dispatcher had the capability to selectively connect the radio base station to monitor or operate the radio station on the dispatcher's voice wire line.

Two-way VHF radio base stations were initially installed along with construction of microwave sites along the main line of the railroad. The first one installed, the dispatcher's radio system, permitted communications with train crews in locomotives and cabooses, and where radio coverage permitted, to crews at trackside through use of vehicle and handie-talkie radios.

A second radio system was also installed at the microwave sites. A supervisor's radio service (identified within Union Pacific as "Mobile Telephone Radio") was also installed for the purpose of communicating with supervisory personnel to avoid interference with train crew operations. Both systems were remoted via the microwave channels to terminals. The dispatcher's radio system used a radio channel officially identified by the Association of American Railroad's Frequency Assignment Plan (FAP) Point to Train. This radio channel terminated on the dispatcher's radio control counsel and the chief dispatcher's counsel. Mobile telephone service terminated on PBX operators' switchboards. When the mobile radio call was made, it illuminated a lamp on the PBX; the PBX operator then patched the call to the PBX station requested by the caller.

An added feature of the mobile telephone service was its design as a radio repeater. This permitted two radio users, in the field, to communicate directly via the base station radio repeater when both users were within the coverage area of the base station. While the dispatcher's radio used a single radio channel for "simplex" communication, (radio operation in this mode required each user to advise the other party when to respond by saying *"over."* When the user had completed communication they said *"over and out"*), the mobile telephone radio system was a duplex radio system and each party could hear the other as in standard telephone communications. It was necessary for mobile telephone service to use two widely separated spectrum radio channels.

One of the great advantages of the "mobile telephone" radio service on the Union Pacific Railroad was permitting local supervisory personnel (i.e. division superintendents, trainmasters, division engineers, roadmasters) to leave their desks and observe operations in the field first-hand. This greatly improved efficiency of operations because issues or problems that were observed in the field by the division superintendents, division engineer, roadmaster, trainmaster or other field personnel could be relayed by the mobile telephone system directly to their office, subordinate, or superior for handling. Similarly, other railroad officials were able to reach these officials for reporting, consolation, or advice. The ability to communicate from the field by radio sped up decision making and contributed greatly to the Union Pacific earnings' bottom line. This system preceded the use of cell phones for the same purpose; even today there still is little or no cell phone coverage in many areas the railroad operates.

In later years, another mobile telephone service was added for exclusive use of the Maintenance of Way (MOW) Department to aid trackside workers to efficiently communicate their needs. "Track and Time" permits from the dispatcher are easily given to these workers as required. Need for materials to support trackside work were requested and quickly delivered to the field or workers' HQ. This "Maintenance of Way mobile telephone" improved the performance of the Maintenance of Way personnel because of the efficiency which improved their operations. With this capability more vehicle radios were installed in their MOW trucks, and more handie talkie radios given to MOW workers. This expansion of radio use allowed track-side workers to communicate directly to the locomotive engineer on the "end-to-end" radio channel, or to the dispatcher should they observe an equipment problem during a "roll-by inspection" of trains they regularly, made thus improving safe operations. ("Roll by inspection" of trains, looking for train defects, was a requirement for all trackside personnel).

Radio Equipment Configuration

The standard Union Pacific package of radio systems installed at the microwave radio sites separated their transmitters and receivers between antennas. The receiver antenna generally was installed at the top of the microwave tower, and the transmitter antenna a minimum of twenty feet lower on the tower. The coaxial location of the two antennas on the same tower (one directly beneath the other), avoided interference and desensitization of the receivers from the other transmitters. The receiver antenna was located at the top of the tower to provide improved reception of low-powered portable radios, and other lower powered mobile radios (compared to the higher powered output of base station transmitters).

The two mobile telephone radio systems were later converted to dial operations and terminated on the PBX switching equipment, as many PBX switchboard operators were eliminated in the late 1970s and early 1980s.

Locotrol Tests

In late 1969, the railroad industry was investigating the use of remote-controlled locomotives at the end of train, or perhaps two-thirds back from the lead locomotives. They would be controlled by a radio link to the lead locomotive to extend the length of trains without losing train dexterity. This system was known as "Locotrol." The industry had to decide on the radio band to be used for this radio link.

The VHF (Hi-band) available to the railroad industry was fully assigned, and clearing allotted Railroad VHF Band frequencies for nation-wide Locotrol service was a problem. The Union Pacific had a member (Robert H. Brenneman) on the AAR Communications and Signals Committee "B"—Radio and Microwave. It was decided to conduct a test across the railroad to determine which band of radio frequencies best served locotrol service, VHF (Hi-band) or UHF.

What followed was a radio frequency survey conducted by the Union Pacific. The test consisted of two radio links one VHF and one UHF. A radio transmitter on each band was installed on a locomotive, and a radio receiver on the UPRR test car BC210. The receivers on the test car had signal strength recorders monitoring the Automatic Gain Control (AGC), which measured the received signal strength of each radio.

The BC210 test car was placed at the end of a train, usually of 100 cars or more, in front of the caboose. The recorders were installed in the cupula of the test car and an observer recorded the passing trackside Mile Post on the recorder's tape throughout the test run, day and night.

The test runs were from North Platte, NE to Portland, OR and back again. The first run started on October 24, 1969. The second run was from North Platte, NE to Los Angeles, CA, where the test ended.

The results concluded that the VHF test provided more continuous signal strength. However, in the Railroad Radio Service UHF band, separation of frequencies pairs were better suited for radio repeaters where their use was necessary because of coverage problems, particularity in mountainous territory. As a direct result of these tests, the availability of channels for radio repeaters factored into the decision to ultimately use UHF channels for Locotrol Service.

Interface UPRR Communications with Bell Telephone System

Because of FCC Rules, many private communication systems were prevented from interfacing the Bell Telephone System network. Railroads were permitted to interface the Bell System network as long as the communications pertained to official railroad business and were handled by a live switchboard operator. This changed when the Bell System was required to interface other telephone networks with a voice connecting arrangement (VCA) due to the 1977 Carterfone decision. After that date, the Bell System required interface standards governed by FCC Part 68 Rules and Regulations. The UPPR had many railroad-owned PBXs and a number of leased Bell PBXs (both generally at major railroad terminals). Traditionally, certain PBXs were manned by switchboard operators during daytime hours but closed in the evening; at night, the operators' duties were remoted to a more distant PBX switchboard which remained manned throughout the night.

As railroad operations were consolidated and depots closed, it became necessary to extend local Bell Telephone service to distant switchboard operators. Some PBXs were operated on night connection full time to interface the local telephone network. Mr. Jett determined the UPRR could order installation of a small PBX from the Bell System. These small PBXs could only handle a very limited number of stations manually. These PBXs, identified as a 507 PBXs, were ordered with a single station which was put on night connection and extended via a UPRR microwave channel to a manned switchboard. Thus Union Pacific complied with the requirement to interface the local Bell System telephone network with a switchboard operator. After the June 26, 1968 Carterfone decision, the FCC Part 68 rules permitted a new legal Voice Connecting Arrangement (VCA) interface which eliminated the need for a PBX interface between railroad telephone circuits and the Bell Telephone voice network.

14

Communications Shop and the Jett Era and Influence Communications Shop

The Union Pacific Communications Shop (CS) was a great asset to the railroad and the Communications Department to which it provided great support. The CS consisted of a Shop Foreman and approximately nine technicians (called groundmen an archaic position title from telegraph days). The exact number varied through the years. The CS provided maintenance and repair of the communications which passed through and was stored in the shop awaiting some need.

The cost of the shop operations was very economical considering the service provided. Equipment maintenance cost such as radio repair consisted of the technician's labor, parts and labor charges such as Railroad Retirement, along with test equipment, facilities and building expense of climate control and power.

While the shop had a number of technicians for continuing shop operations, new hires recruited for assignment across the railroad, while already having an FCC radio license, needed to learn repair of equipment unique to the railroad industry were trained in the shop. The shop provided on-the-job- training (OJT) for equipment unique to the UPRR. In response to a question raised by *Railway Signaling and Communications*, Van Eaton wrote on how the Communications Shop repaired and refurbished communications equipment for installation across the railroad:

> "The Union Pacific operates one system repair shop at Omaha, where all major construction, repairs, and maintenance are performed on communications equipment. This shop, under the supervision of a foreman, has a normal force of six to ten men [The Union Pacific bought the "Biscuit Building" (and later known as "the Union Pacific Annex") in 1942 at 13th Street and Capitol Street for records storage, as well as a signal and telegraph repair shop.[1]]
>
> "In addition to the main repair shop at Omaha, we have a small shop in each of the four districts where minor repairs to equipment are performed. The personnel utilizing these shops is normally assigned to that district, being in the shop only a part of the time. Further, it is at these district shops that a major part of the radio maintenance is performed."[2]

Expansion of the communications system under Jett kept the shop busy with many projects. It hired many skilled electronic technicians to maintain its equipment, and as the communications system expanded, shop activities expanded to meet new needs. Priority was given to annual FCC-required frequency checks and the repair of two-way VHF radios used on locomotives and base stations, as well as the repair of other electronic equipment. The FCC-required frequency checks were performed and noted on a service card included within the radio housing.

Repair of locomotive VHF radios was one of the most important activities of the communication's shop. This repair was centralized in Omaha "at the Annex" and later in Council Bluffs' "ice house" when the shop was relocated. Repaired radios were placed in a rugged shipping box and returned to the originator by Union Pacific baggage car service until passenger service was discontinued. Later, most radios were shipped by bus and still later by UPS or FedEx. "End of Train" devices (EOT) consisted of two parts: The locomotive, unit installed in the cab of a locomotive, and the stand-alone unit, installed on the coupler of the last car in the train. The EOTs were added and removed by yard workers, frequently being dropped or damaged. Service and repair of the EOTs was assigned to the Communications

Shop, as it used radio technology to communicate with the locomotive mating unit.

Interestingly, on October 30, 1982, an agreement with the UTU (United Transportation Union) was reached to eliminate cabooses on trains. The idea was to improve train efficiency and safety (personnel injuries caused by slack run-in, jarring trainmen in the caboose). Efficiency is improved by "not handling cabooses in and through terminals". An additional benefit was stated as "better crew relations" by moving the conductor to the locomotive: "We've always said the conductor is in charge of the train, but he's never been in a position to really be in charge[3]."

End of Train devices made the removal of cabooses possible. These devices check the brake line pressure and transmit this information to the locomotive engineer up front. Several versions of the EOTs also provided additional information such as "direction of movement" and "that the end of train is moving." The EOT also included a rear marker light.[80] Communications department personnel also handled the installation of new microwave systems purchased from manufacturers. Local technical personnel (designated equipmentmen and radiomen) were used for these installations, augmented by communications shop personnel (technical personnel designated "groundmen," a hand-me-down title from telegraph days), while the installations served as on-the-job training for both. Microwave systems in service couldn't be easily interrupted for training, but during installation, there was an opportunity for these installers to flip switches, make adjustments, and test the new equipment before it was placed in service.

With the expansion of the communications network, new equipment replaced older equipment and the replaced equipment was returned to the shop for refurbishing. Frequently, this meant tuning radio and microwave equipment to a new frequency and verifying the equipment met manufacturer's original factory standards. The refurbished equipment would be used for expanding service to another location.

Talent of these shop technicians seemed at times to be unlimited. Steel was cut and welded and structural equipment manufactured for projects. For instance, microwave antennae might be purchased from suppliers, but the structural supports for them were built by the shop, and generally exceeded the strength of those available for purchase. Severe environmental conditions such as heavy ice loading at many microwave sites dictated greater strength for antenna support.

Working with steel wasn't their only special talent. A carpentry shop cut wood and shaped products as needed. As the microwave system expanded, low-density microwave routes needed low-cost solutions to justify their existence.

A number of obsolete shipping containers also became available to the Communications Department. They didn't meet current container standards for international shipping and were thus retired from service, but these containers were ideal for use as low-cost microwave repeater buildings on low density microwave routes. The Communications Shop in Council Bluffs reconditioned many of them for this purpose.

The containers were lined with studs and plywood walls with insulation. Doors were cut in the side for entry. The buildings were wired with breaker panels, conduit, lights, wire entry goosenecks, ventilation ducts, and electrical meter socket. Electric wall heaters were installed for heat, and a window air conditioner or a recreational vehicle roof-type air conditioner was installed for cooling. An interior wall was also installed, separating the equipment room from a small generator room. The normal double-door end of the container was walled off from the equipment room with sufficient room for a reused and rebuilt 5 KW engine generator. Modifications of the generator room included an air intake vent and an engine exhaust system with muffler. The container was painted with a color selected for its final location, for instance forest green for woodlands and sandy shades for deserts.

Several of these containers were modified for use for PBX equipment rooms. As previously mentioned, a retired van was modified in the communications shop for use as an emergency PBX equipment room, including the PBX equipment. It ended up never being used for their intended purpose.

Several of the planned microwave systems required passive reflectors at locations where a microwave repeater would have been expensive and or lacked commercial power. Three systems were planned, one for Caliente NV, one for Kemmerer WY, and one for Butte MT.

Two passive reflectors were constructed. The Caliente passive reflector was a 12-foot by 18-foot device installed on a mountainside in September of 1978. The Kemmerer passive reflector was a 28-foot by 36-foot reflector installed on nearby Oyster Ridge Mountain above the town. The Butte passive was to be installed outside of Butte near Silver Bow MT, to serve Butte. It was planned to be a 32-foot by 48-foot passive reflector, but was cancelled when an alternate microwave site location was discovered which permitted a direct transmission path to Butte.

These passive reflectors were massive construction projects for the shop (they were equivalent to a billboard in size). They consisted of structural steel and 4'x8' sheets of aluminum with aluminum "H" beam structural backing. The Caliente Reflector was preassembled in the shop. The Oyster Ridge passive reflector was only assembled once on-site.

A reflector's path design, including tilt angles and positioning angles, was designed by the communications department office engineer Paul McKiernan. Field construction was done by a communications construction gang under the supervision of construction engineer, Jerry Chatwin.

Major yards had talk-back speaker systems with speakers distributed to strategic locations in the yard, so that yardmasters could give instructions to switchmen on the ground while handling car switching. Speakers which failed were rehabilitated in the communications shop. Some new speakers were assembled in the shop as well. A local foundry manufactured castings for the speaker housing; the speaker, wiring, and shop-manufactured pushbutton switches were all assembled in the shop as well.

Early telephones installed on the Union Pacific were wood-box local-battery telephones (the batteries were inside the telephone), some with hand-crank generators and some without. When Mr. Jett redesigned the multiparty conversation lines (telephone circuits which dropped into each waystation and phone booth) (called message phone lines on other railroads) to a Bell Telephone standard battery-fed circuit with dial capability, these old phones were returned to the shop for modification. As the new standard was extended across the system, the rebuilt telephones were reused on these lines, saving the cost of purchase.

C. Otis Jett's design of the conversation phone system for the Union Pacific also used several ringing systems for station selection. He also designed single-party, four-party, and decimonic ringing systems. (Operation of which is described in a nearby sidebar). He also designed applique panels to control radio base stations. These relay-designed panels were sometimes built in the shop, but many were contracted out to local manufacturers. These panels were repaired or refurbished in the shop as needed.

Workings of Telephone Dial Appliques

A common railroad industry communications standard on main lines was to have two voice circuits: A dispatcher's voice circuit, whereby the dispatcher gave train orders and receive reports of passing trains, and a conversation phone circuit for other railroad business.

Naturally, the dispatcher's phone circuit terminated on one end at his position. The conversation phone circuit's other end was usually a switchboard for the operator to select the appropriate wayside station to relay to.

The dispatcher could select a wayside office by a selector system. The selector had a wheel with strategically placed pins. At the circuit head, a selector system placed positive 160 volts to one wire and negative 160 volts to the other wire.

The reversal of the voltage from one wire to the other produced a stepping on the selector wheel. With five reversals of the voltage, the selector would step five times. If the selector had a pin in position five, the selector wheel would hold at that location. All other selectors without a pin in the fifth location would return to normal. A second series of pulses would perform in a similar fashion. At the end, on the third series of pulses, only the desired selector would be in a position to ring a bell to alert the trainorder operator.

Most railroads used the above described dispatcher station selection method for the conversation phone.

C. Otis Jett used his experience with the Bell System to use the common battery telephone circuit Bell technology for the Union Pacific Railroad. He designed applique equipment for single-parties, four-parties, and deciomonic circuits.

These "conversation phone" telephone circuits were extended to a PBX, many over dedicated microwave channels. Using standard common battery circuit design simplified the interface to the dial switching network **Common Battery** in the telephone industry is normally 48 volt DC. Because of the length of many Union Pacific wire line services, especially the decimonic services, the common battery is replaced with a 120 volt DC power supply. Jett designed a current-regulator to limit the current to a nominal 23 milliamps.

Single Party appliques were used to extend a microwave channel to a single location and the ringing occurred by placing a ringing voltage across the line (Technically) identified one wire as "Tip" and the other wire identified as "Ring" (This term comes for the cord on a switchboard to patch the lines, where the plug has one wire connected to the brass tip of the plug and the other insulated back from the tip which is a ring of brass).

The **four-party** applique generally worked directly off of the PBX, and each station on the PBX interfaced a relay on the applique. At the wire line interface of the applique, a ring voltage was placed between the "tip" and ground or the "ring" and ground. The selection allowed only the telephone with the "ringer" in the phone connected in that manner, (between tip and ground or ring and ground) to "ring." This allowed two stations to be selected independently. The choice of the ringing voltage, usually 60 cycles per second (cps) or 20 cps, allowed two additional choices for the four-parties. (20 cps tip, 20 cps ring, 60 cps tip, 60 cps ring)

The **decimonic** applique was similar in its operation, but ten stations could be selected. The applique was connected to the PBX, but not the PBX lines. The decimonic applique was connected to a trunk circuit, similar to circuits used to route the PBX to another PBX in a remote city. When a station number was dialed, it was accessed as if it was a small PBX. The number dialed was converted to the ringing voltage of the station desired.

Decimonic circuits usually had five different ringing voltages available. Like the four-party ringing described above, ten parties could be selected. The ringers of the individual station phones needed ringers tuned to the selected ringing voltage.

This shop is also used to train personnel as communications technicians for use all over the railroad. There was a great deal of flexibility in work assignment, and vocational teaching. Certain individuals provided leadership in a certain skills such as carpentry or welding. One individual Charlie Brombaugh a former lineman, would have been separated from the railroad for disability, but was instead retained in the shop in a productive capacity. Most people in the shop were FCC-licensed technicians who serviced the radios, microwave equipment and repaired or rehabilitated the department's equipment.

Frequently, the shop technicians were sent across the system to install new equipment or assist in other moves and changes.

Equipment returned from the field was salvaged, repaired, reconditioned, and restored to like-new condition. As new work orders were issued, this refurbished equipment was shipped to the project and installed as needed, billing at the rehabilitated value. Microwave equipment returned from the field was refurbished when necessary. Occasionally, the microwave equipment was needed at a new site or for temporary installation to aid a relocation of equipment. Don Allison, a communications engineer assigned to the communications shop, oversaw this work. Don also assisted the shop technicians when his technological knowledge was needed.

The shop printed and assembled a circuit board that changed a mobile telephone call from being handled manually by a telephone operator, to permitting the radio user to dial up telephone numbers across the Railroad. The dial-up mobile telephone panel was designated a "4800" panel and was initially designed and built in early 1978. Later, the panels were also installed on the Maintenance of Way Radio system, permitting signalmen and section men to dial over the Union Pacific dial telephone network.

When the North Platte dispatchers were moved to a new building, the shop built a modern pushbutton communications console for the dispatchers to access their radios and other telephone lines in late 1978. Performing this work in the shop proved to be very cost effective.

The shop manufactured other items like structural antenna mounts, equipment appliques, and these items were appropriately charged to the work orders at production costs. The cost of shop labor and materials that went into these items were controlled to the benefit of the department and the railroad.

15

The Rise of Computers and Real Time Reporting in the Jett Era and Influence Data Transmission Systems

The history of data transmission systems has been one of movement of information from one point to another. Volume of information, speed of transmission, and accuracy have been limited by the technology. However, as new technology develops, the Union Pacific has been at the leading edge of the industry, so the history of data transmission on the Union Pacific Railroad has paralleled the history of data transmission.

Morse telegraph was the first data system in service on the Union Pacific. The code developed by Samuel Morse was designed to use the telegraphy efficiently, conveying letters, and therefore whole messages, over a series of dots and dashes. The most frequently used letters were the shortest: The letter "e" used a single dot for transmission, "a" a dot and a dash.

While the initial transcontinental telegraph permitted messages to be transmitted across the nation, many technical issues limited message throughput of the telegraph technology. First of all was the human side: Telegraph used a key and a sounder operated by hand for transmission of messages because hand-driven transmission of messages didn't stress the technology. Hand-keying limited the throughput to the operator's ability.

Capacity of early telegraph systems was limited by the number of wires available. To overcome some limitations without stringing additional wires, various experiments were conducted to increase message traffic capacity. An early system was developed called "duplex telegraph," which allowed a message to be transmitted in each direction simultaneously on a single wire. Later, a system called "quadruplex telegraph" permitted two messages to be transmitted in each direction simultaneously on a single wire. A combination of telephony and telegraph called "Phonoplex" was used on the Union Pacific Railroad.

> "Prior to April 1917, when our first Morkrum printer circuit was set up between Omaha and Chicago, our communications were handled chiefly by Morse. Late in 1920, three additional printing telegraph circuits were added. These extended from Omaha to Cheyenne, Omaha to Denver, and Omaha to Kansas City. All of these circuits were duplexed to permit simultaneous transmission in both directions. This equipment soon proved itself. In 1924, the Chicago circuit was multiplexed to provide added message capacity, and in 1926, the Cheyenne, Denver, and Kansas City circuits were multiplexed, thus doubling the printing telegraph facilities for a considerable portion of the road's communications." [1]

Early mechanisms used telegraph technology to automate the speed of transmission. As telegraphy evolved into mechanical transmission, teletype machines were developed which combined telegraphy with the typewriter. Jett's Five-Year Plan identified that, "*Various types of printing telegraph machines were installed on the Railroad as early as 1918.*"

The Union Pacific reported completing three telegraph circuits for printing in 1920 and having three printer circuits under construction in 1921.[2] (Two units of the Union Pacific System, the Oregon Short Line and the Oregon-Washington Railroad & Navigation Co., completed 495.1 miles, and 398.9 miles respectively of multiplex printing telegraph circuits (in 1925).[3]

> "The four-channel Morkrum multiplex teleprinters were used as late as 1946, at which time all the teleprinter facilities were replaced with modern teleprinter equipment.[4] The Union Pacific Railroad,

> *Pennsylvania Railroad and others installed equipment replacing Morse circuits with Morkum equipment at the outbreak of World War I and subsequent entry by the United States due to a shortage of skilled Morse telegraphers.*[5]

Early teletype equipment operated at 30 to 60 words per minute and was later improved in 1939 to 75 words per minute and in 1944, 100 wpm. These machines continued to use telegraph type circuitry.

It is not the intent of this book to show development of teletype machines, but merely to acknowledge their existence and use on the Union Pacific Railroad. Paper tape printers were favored early because they operated without carriage return function, which delayed throughput.

The Teletype Story reported that a production reperforator was introduced in 1928: *"Principal users were the railroads. [...] The reperforator expedited retransmission of messages using the "torn-tape method" to switch the individual tapes (messages) between circuits without retyping the message."*[6]

With the introduction of wire-line carrier systems, the telegraph system was expanded greatly by dedicating one voice channel of a three-channel carrier system (like the Western Electric "C" Carrier system) to telegraph service. By converting a telegraph circuit to a carrier signal in the voice spectrum, up to 16 telegraph circuits could be superimposed on a single voice channel. This technology was called "Voice Frequency Carrier Telegraph" (VFCT) channel.

Mr. Jett also described the technology in a 1950 paper whereby *"Each carrier telephone circuit can be easily made to serve a dual purpose of telephone voice and VFCT service by 'clipping out' a narrow band of frequencies. ...a band of about 450 cycles is provided for VFCT service...called "speech-plus-duplex."*[7] His paper describes various choices and number of VFCT channels, dependent upon the frequency and bandwidth, whereby up to 4 VFCT channels could be imposed. His paper also discussed the benefits of Amplitude Modulation (AM) (On-Off) versus Frequency Modulation (FM). This technology was extremely beneficial where a singular voice carrier such as an "H" carrier served as the communications backbone.

> "One reason for the heavy volume of Teletype communications on the Union Pacific is that we have found it advantageous to handle not only our general message traffic but practically all reporting information for the road through this medium. This includes our block reports, manifest reports, set-out and pickup reports, and passing reports—which constitute the main source of our Trace Bureau information. Then of course, we handle the diversion reports, which sometimes run as high as 1200 per day in and out of the Omaha office. Thousands of space reservations messages also are handled by our various offices—as are numerous miscellaneous reports pertaining to general operations."[8]

With hundreds of trains moving thousands of cars on the Union Pacific Railroad, customers needed to know where their shipment was and when it would arrive at its destination. Early hand accounting of cars led to computerization of the information as the technology developed.

The Union Pacific first use electric punch cards in 1909 was in Omaha. In 1928, a paper card with holes cut in it was developed by IBM, called the "IBM card." The cards permitted the sorting of the data contained in the card at each office, to assist in switching cars and build a departing train. By the end of World War II, the UPRR succeeded in getting all its car movements on punch cards.[9]

As transmission of data expanded, the demand for greater throughput capacity was needed. To meet this demand, a new transmission technology was developed by IBM: The transmission of data requiring a card-reader at one point and conversion of the data to paper tape for telegraph transmission and/or reconversion at the receiving end to IBM cards, was slow and inefficient. Instead, IBM developed a data transmission system called an IBM 1050 transceiver which operated at 134 baud and outputted one of four frequencies which could be transmitted on a single voice channel, expanding not only the throughput of the individual transceiver circuit, but multiplying the number of channels transmitted over a single voice channel. Mr. Jett described the "...extensive installations of IBM transceivers in converting the yard-to-yard car reporting system from IBM-Teletype to an all-punch card operation." In a paper entitled "UP Upgrades Car Reporting" he described the Union Pacific carrier network involving 17 yard locations with various "C" Carrier systems interconnecting these communication centers.[10]

The IBM transceivers used four 500 cycle bands superimposed on a single "C" Carrier voice channel which moved data between the adjacent yards directly to Omaha transportation and accounting departments. "There being four bands used by the IBM machines operated on frequencies of 800, 1300, 1800, and 2300 cycles in a 200-2800 cycle voice channel." He described how some bands terminated at one office, while others were patched through to an office further down the line. For example, he described that:

> "A three-carrier system operates between Omaha, North Platte and Cheyenne. Channel 1 is used for conversation service. Channel 2 is split into four IBM transceiver bands for service to Cheyenne and west. Channel 3 is also split into four IBM transceiver bands:
>
> Band 1 provides facilities for data transmission between yard office at North Platte and Council Bluffs.
>
> Band 2 provides for data transmission between North Platte yard office, and the transportation office at Omaha.
>
> Band 3 is idle except when required for overflow business from North Platte.
>
> Band 4 is connected to Band 4 on the three channel carrier system between Kansas City and Omaha. This interconnection permits establishing an IBM transceiver band between the North Platte and Kansas City yard offices."

Jett also recommended the use of speech-plus-duplex on a single "H-1" carrier system between Green River and Pocatello.[11]

The cards were sorted by mechanical IBM card sorters and later by digital computers. The railroad sorted these cards at the Omaha transportation office and then transmitted the results to yard offices and traffic offices across the railroad once a day, a processing system known as batch procession. (See "real-time processing" below). The system was an improvement over early record keeping and reporting, but the delay in reporting meant the information on car location was always obsolete with continued movement inherent in railroad operations.

Initially, the direct transmission of "IBM" cards between terminals meant that car waybills and train location were readily available for processing at headquarters, and in advance of train arrival at destination yards for car switching. The "C" carrier systems described above provided the initial backbone of data transmission. Expansion of the backbone communications network with introduction of microwave radio systems and later fiber optic cable network to support this expansion is described elsewhere in this book.

The development of the Computer Department on the Union Pacific Railroad and the demands of railroad service meant that new systems were developed to meet requests by customers to know when their car would arrive at their business or factory.

Maury Klein, in his book *Union Pacific, The Rebirth 1894-1969*, described the computerization of the Union Pacific, which will only be partially presented here: One morning in 1954, President Stoddard got on the elevator and spied Jett, a bright electrical engineer who had come to the Union Pacific from Bell Systems. "Mr. Jett," he asked. "What's a computer? I hear that we could use one profitably."

The book describes much of the development of communications and computers on the Union Pacific in a few pages, describing how Mr. Jett and Mr. Van Eaton traveled to Minneapolis to visit Univac, only to be told the railroad was no place for a computer. An IBM man subsequently called on them, which led to the beginning of the history of computers on the Union Pacific.[12]

In the late '50s, IBM introduced System 360 and its operating system OS/360.[13] The computer processing system on the Union Pacific Railroad was developed in 1965, known as "COIN" - Complete Operating Information Network system, operated on the IBM System 360 and successor IBM System 370. This system permitted "Real Time Processing" of data transmitted across its network.

Real-Time Reporting and Processing

"Real Time" reporting meant a computer terminal or a teletype machine could be located remotely from the computer, and a "data channel" be established to connect them. A query could be entered into the computer to determine the location of a customer's car or other question with an immediate response. Thus, "Real Time" reporting became the new standard for information handling.

Implementation of this computer system required expansion of the communications network to accommodate the goals of the data system. The first phase of COIN went online in April of 1969. It consisted of fifty-three IBM 1050 computers terminals located in thirty-eight yard offices for data input. The teletype network of Model 28-KSR and 35-ASR teleprinters were re-terminated to interface with the Omaha computer for message switching, and also had the capability to make real-time inquires of car and train movements through direct interface to the Union Pacific computer network.

Response time was almost immediate. A New York Central traffic man visited our Lewiston ID traffic office shortly after installation of a network-connected Teletype 35ASR and was very impressed that an office in a highly remote location in the country had a faster response time than his own company's. The New York Central had what was then considered one of the best real-time systems in the railroad industry.

The initial COIN system was upgraded in late 1972 and 1973 and fully online by January 1974. It was called COIN II.[14] Expansion of the COIN II network required further expansion of the communications network as a whole; work orders of the time covered installation of communications equipment at major and minor communications sites across the railroad.

The installation of COIN II increased the number of data interface lines to the Omaha computer from 176 to 356 lines. Besides the increase in lines at some locations, new data reporting points were also installed. Some existing teleprinter sites were changed to IBM 1050 equipment, and a few sites saw a minor but significant change from model 28-KSR teleprinter to a model 35-ASR for improved speed of transmission and reliability.[15]

New data channels were created and installed on voice channels across the railroads. With the new microwave systems, major offices had capacity for many voice circuits terminating in the communications offices, which allowed for easy expansion of the data network. Three- to twelve-channel voice carrier systems released from offices served by the new microwave systems became available and were used for expanded COIN I and COIN II data input terminals to offices not served by the microwave system. Meeting the demand for data service to these lesser offices provided added communications equipment to serve other communications needs for these offices, such as dial access voice telephone lines to nearby PBXs.

As carrier systems were replaced by microwave systems and expanded voice channel capability, the data transmission system was upgraded and expanded. The near-simultaneous development of the central processor IBM system 360 (and 370) and microwave system expansion permitted replacement of the IBM 1050 terminal-to-terminal system, transmitting at 134 baud, with IBM 3270 display terminal system directly connected to the mainframe computers in the early 1970s via the IBM 3704/5 communications controller using higher data rate speeds.

Smaller agencies across the railroad also needed the "Real Time" data access to serve their customers. Data circuits for these small agencies were established by installing a wire-line carrier systems. A special filtering of the voice channel on a carrier systems to small telegraph offices used a filter described above called "speech plus duplex" filter, which filtered off the upper portion of the voice band (channel) for COIN data circuits. This filter allowed a VFCT to establish a data or telegraph circuit to serve the small office as well as providing a voice channel to handle other voice needs.[16]

Data Transmission System Progress

Data transmissions progressed rapidly between 1960 and 1990. Introduction of the IBM 1050 system using 134 baud was the beginning of rapid increase in data transmission speeds from the highest teletype speed of 100 wpm. Commercial 300-baud data systems were placed in service, most of which were asynchronous data systems, and designed for operation over dial-up telephone channels. IBM provided research and leadership in these systems, and in 1957, the Union Pacific converted their car reporting system from printers to IBM 1050 transceiver operation.[17] In the end, the Union Pacific Railroad computer systems were wedded to the IBM systems.

As describe in an IBM publication "*IBM Data Communications: A Quarter Century of Evolution and Progress*, Authors David R. Jarema, Edward H. Susenguth)", *"In 1960, IBM announced Synchronous Transmitter Receiver (STR), a new form of synchronous line control which was used in a new family of terminals.*

"Heretofore, with asynchronous transmission, additional bits had to be transmitted with each character to define the character boundaries for synchronization. Maximum line efficiency is a function of the number of bits representing a character and the additional start/stop bits for each character. With STR, character synchronization was achieved by sending a synchronization check once per block of characters rather than for each individual character, thus increasing the line efficiency."[18]

With STR, synchronous transmission over dial up telephone facilities at 1200 bits per second (bps) was possible, though it was generally unnecessary to use dial up data transmission systems on the Union Pacific since most systems used dedicated circuits. With the introduction of the IBM 3270 display terminal system, 2400 bps data modems were commonly used between the computer center and the major offices across the railroad on this equipment.

AAS/TIS

New computer operating systems called "Agency Accounting System (AAS)" and the "Terminal Information System (TIS)" were installed across the railroad using Digital Equipment Company (DEC) computers. Remote terminals were connected to these computers throughout the yards and nearby railroad offices. These distributed DEC computers were connected to the Omaha host computer by 2400 bps data circuits. (The first of these distributed computers was installed in Omaha for the Terminal Information System in January 1973.[19] The majority of these distributed computers were installed later.) Initial plans for AAS installations began in 1974 for 7 major locations. Ogden, Salt Lake, and Los Angeles were planned for DEC installations in 1977 and Pocatello in 1975. Green River was to follow.

The use of distributed DEC Computers was a learning and growing experience for the Management Information Systems (MIS) Department. Many changes occurred in the strategy for using the DEC computers. They served as a data concentrators, changing the design of the communications network to support them. It was basically a plan to replace the 1050s.

Some processing and reporting was moved from the Omaha central computer to these DEC computers. Generally, yards slated for the DEC computers were prioritized based on the number of 1050 circuits they were using. High-volume yards with three or four 1050s were priority one; medium-volume yards with one to two 1050s were priority two; and low-volume yards with one 1050 or a multi-pointed 1050 were priority three. The action plan was to replace high volume offices and look at medium and low volume offices. The goal was to handle five times the line capacity of the 1050s. Changes in the priority two and three offices were put off for at least 18 months but were looked at on a cost and volume basis.

Throughout the following years—1974 to 1982—AAS and TIS systems were installed across the Railroad. Input/output (I/O) terminals were remoted to nearby offices on microwave or carrier systems as available, to blanket the Railroad.

In these services, the data protocol consisted of the clerk filling information in formatted screens. Downstream data consisted of a form presented to the terminal and displayed on the monitor. The clerk filled in the required data in the blanks. This data was limited to the typing speed of the clerk. Experiments with various data modems demonstrated when a 2400 bps modem was used the downstream data filled the screen in a couple of seconds. When first tested with a 9600 bps modem, a formatted report was flashed on the screen. Yard clerks filled in the blanks of the report, saving time in filing. Costs differences between the data modems was minimal.

I/O terminals directly connected to the DEC computer use an economical 9600 bps modem as their standard, other yards connected to the AAS/TIS computer via microwave or wire line carrier continued to use the 2400 bps modem as standard modem.

In the above local tests, physical observation of the differences between 2400 bps and 9600 bps transmission speeds led to consideration of upgrading the entire data network to increase the data speed. 4800 bps modems were being offered as an upgrade to the data network. However, if the system could handle the new data transmission speed, the decision was made to skip introducing the 4800 bps modem upgrade, jumping technology in favor using newer 9600 bps modems.

9600 BPS

Early attempts to transmit 9600 bps data across the Union Pacific microwave system were not very successful. The original tests were conducted between Omaha and Portland, and Omaha and Los Angeles. A relatively high incidence of "hits" were observed during these tests. Hits usually caused errors in the data, and the data error-checking protocol required retransmission of the data. These errors produced a slowdown of the data throughput.

Questions arose about the technology. In the Bell System, some data circuits required equalization of the channel to achieve quality data throughput. Comparing Union Pacific microwave voice channels with standards established for the Bell Network, equalization should not have been necessary. Most times, the Bell Network required many microwave channel modems in a single data circuit due to routing between the AT&T Long Lines Department and local Bell Telephone Operating Companies. The local Bell end circuit frequently used load coils, which affected band width and spectrum delay characteristics. Each voice modem introduced a slight delay in the signal across the frequency band, whereas the Union Pacific channels usually had few modems and little delay. The Union Pacific microwave system did not encounter these network limitations. The direct channel interface to the cable plant of most UP data circuits and lack of load coils avoided channel spectrum delay parameters.

To shorten the length of the data circuit, a test channel was established between Omaha and Kansas City. During these tests, it was discovered that few hits occurred during the data transmission. Through observation of channel activity, it was proven that these hits occurred during radio transmissions by the dispatchers' radios.

When the dispatcher keyed the radio to transmit, it was found that transients from the dispatcher radio transmitter relay was inducted into the microwave base band. With this discovery, we found a solution to eliminate these transient spikes by installing transient suppressors on all microwave site radio equipment. The communication shop was instructed to quickly build a number of transient suppressors, which consisted of a capacitor and a resistor.

These transient suppressors were installed on all radios and other relay equipment in service between Omaha and Kansas City. New data channel tests using the 9600 bps modems were made, and transmission errors were eliminated.

Having discovered the source of the hits to the data transmissions, all radios on the microwave systems or carrier systems had transient suppressors installed, thereby eliminating these hits and permitted successful operation of 9600 bps modems as the standard Union Pacific data modem, bypassing the potential upgrade to 4800 bps data modems. New data transmission test were conducted between Omaha and Portland and Los Angeles confirming the anticipated successful results. Later, as newer solid-state radios were installed at microwave sites, the older tube-type radios were replaced by transistorized radios, which didn't produce transients.

Data transmission improved and 9600 bps data was extended across the railroad to the major communications offices. New data circuits now used the 9600 bps modems as the Union Pacific standard.

Later experiments with 56/64 Kilobit modems were tested, however, they required a full base group channel, which was the equivalent of and replaced 12 voice channels. They were of limited value to the Union Pacific at the time as they had limited flexibility in data services, and reduced voice channel capacity. Data speeds of 56/64 Kilobit were not required by the railroad between any two points, and by the time they were needed, fiber optic services were available. The standard voice channel in the fiber optic data hierarchy used 64 kbps. Thus, a 64kbps data circuit required only one voice channel. With the Missouri Pacific Railroad merger, the system now had two major computer centers, Omaha and St. Louis, and the higher data speeds were used.

The Omaha data center was established to principally serve train operation (TCS) and the St. Louis center principle served yard inventory. Data was passed between the two data centers for operational needs. Data transmission between the two centers required high data speeds, which were available by using the fiber optic network. Each data center also served as a backup data center for the other system.

16

Expansion of Communications Systems and Jett Era and Influence

The communications network allowed the Union Pacific Railroad to develop many other communication services using in house engineering experience and knowledge. Many of these services are described in the following pages.

Exchange of Service Agreements

Under the Rules and Regulations of the Federal Communications Commission 47CFR94, companies operating private microwave systems are permitted to exchange communications services with like companies licensed under these rules. Billing for communications services allowed under these exchanges of services agreements was not permitted.

The Union Pacific Railroad used agreements with various companies to extend communications beyond its right-of-way, e.g. Agreement with Western Union Telegraph for a wire, Omaha to Chicago on the Western Union Telegraph pole line, for a wire on the Union Pacific pole line from Omaha to Ogden. The Union Pacific continued to have an agreement with Western Union Telegraph Company to exchange facilities. The Railroad used this agreement to route cables through Western Union conduits to offices off the UP right-of-way, including fiber optic cables in later years.

The Railroad made extensive use of these rules to exchange service with other railroads, permitting the Union Pacific to establish voice and data services to offices off the right-of-way. These off right-of-way communications services were very cost effective. Incremental cost to The Union Pacific to reciprocate to serve the other railroads needs were marginal. Generally, they required the Union Pacific to add minor microwave equipment to provide the service.

Cities like New York, Philadelphia, Chicago, San Francisco, and Minneapolis-St. Paul where the Union Pacific has executive and traffic offices, were serviced through these exchange-of-service agreements, as well as headquarters of other railroads.

The Union Pacific had Exchange-of-Service Agreements with these railroads:

Burlington Northern Railroad

Pennsylvania Railroad

Conrail-Consolidated Rail Corporation

CSX Railroad

Illinois Central Railroad

Norfolk Southern Corp

Santa Fe (Atchison, Topeka and Santa Fe Railway Company)

Southern Pacific Transportation Co.

The Union Pacific Railroad had a long-standing agreement with the Southern Pacific, which gave the Southern Pacific service to Ogden UT for their communication needs in Ogden, including backup Southern Pacific CTC service west out of Ogden for their signal department. In exchange, the Union Pacific received service to its San Francisco traffic offices. This agreement dates back to the initial construction of the Los Angeles – Salt Lake City microwave system. The agreement was of particular value to the Union Pacific Railroad operations for backup services when the Los Angeles dispatchers' office was moved to Salt Lake City.

The Union Pacific had an early agreement with the Pennsylvania Railroad (later to be changed to Conrail) for voice and printer services to New York executive and traffic offices. The Union Pacific provided communications and printer services to Pennsylvania Railroad traffic offices throughout the west. The move of the

Union Pacific Executive Offices to Bethlehem, PA necessitated modification of the subsequent agreement with Conrail.

Another early Exchange of Service Agreement was with the Burlington Northern Railroad (BN) (at that time the Chicago Burlington and Quincy Railroad) for communications service into St. Paul and Minneapolis. It would service the Union Pacific traffic office and interface with BN headquarters and their own communications network. Communication services were also provided to Union Pacific Chicago Traffic Offices. This agreement included an early agreement with the Northern Pacific Railroad (merged into the BN), which provided the Union Pacific Railroad joint trackage and communications agreements between Portland and Seattle.

The BN exchange-of-services agreement was expanded after the merger to include services to the Missouri Pacific Railroad on a jointly owned microwave system between Tulsa OK and Ft. Worth TX. The Missouri Pacific subsidiary required a two-foot microwave antenna on the BN tower at Tulsa and the BN needed a four-foot antenna on the Union Pacific microwave site at Rocky Point, OR. The Union Pacific also required radio services at BN sites in Washington. To expand these radio sites, the Union Pacific installed a building adjacent to the BN M/W site at Moyie Springs, WA, because of insufficient space in the BN building. The Union Pacific also used Southern Pacific microwave sites in southeast Missouri for a Union Pacific microwave system between St. Louis and Poplar Bluff, MO.

An upgrade to Union Pacific Railroad operations consisting of introduction of CTC in Illinois on the Missouri Pacific's eastern subsidiary Chicago and Eastern Illinois Railroad (C&EI), developed a need for an exchange-of-service agreement with the Illinois Central Railroad (ICRR). Illinois Central had a microwave system which served their operating needs, which was also located near the C&EI route. Agreement was reached to install antennas on their microwave towers to link to C&EI communications sites, and provide channels on their system to serve the C&EI needs. The Union Pacific paid for structural analysis of the microwave towers to support the additional antennas and strengthening of towers when necessary.

The Union Pacific also provided communications services for the Illinois Central Railroad between Chicago and Memphis.

The ICRR subsequently signed an agreement with Union Pacific Technologies for computer support using the Union Pacific Host Computer. The agreement provided for PBX tie trunks, and several 56KBS data circuits between Chicago and St. Louis for this support.

The Union Pacific Railroad also had an exchange-of-service agreement with the Norfolk and Southern Railroad to provide similar communication services in Southern Illinois, between St. Louis and Salem IL, which supported the C&EI rail service in southern Illinois with the standard Union Pacific communications package, namely dispatcher radio, mobile telephone, and maintenance of way-radios and multipoint access radio (MAS) for support of CTC signal control systems.

The railroads are in great competition for service to their customers, but each railroad highly values their bottom line and are very cost conscience. These exchanges started before the Staggers Act but continue to save operating costs for each railroad in a way that is roughly balanced between them. The added costs for providing the service is marginal and usually identical to the marginal costs of equipment added to their own system, passing these savings on through cost avoidance of off-way service and infrastructure leases.

The above references to Exchange-of-Service agreements include only a partial listing of agreements and services rendered through them. The inclusion of this section in the book reflects the benefits to each railroad provided by these agreements.

Inductive Coordination

When the Union Pacific Railroad first constructed its telegraph lines and later the signal pole lines, commercial power along the right-of-way was non-existent. Edison developed the light bulb, while Westinghouse developed alternating current, transformers, and improved transmission techniques. People liked these services; in the 1800s, electric lights replaced gaslights and coal oil lamps. In the 1900s, Refrigerators replaced iceboxes.

Over time, the demand for electric power service expanded exponentially, and power companies were formed to satisfy electrical service needs for homes, manufacturing, and business. Local power generation expanded service outward from these cities to adjacent towns and farms, many times paralleling the railroad.

Power lines built to support these commercial and industrial needs were built throughout the nation. Hydroelectric dams such as Boulder Dam and the Grand Coulee Dam brought power to the major cities of Los Angeles, Portland, Seattle and many others. As power lines encroached on railroad rights of way, inductive interference occurred, inducing, at minimum, noise into the railroad's lines and at worst, dangerous voltages. Many major power transmission lines were widely separated from the railroad, however, some came near enough to create problems. Additional power distribution lines were built to serve local needs.

Mr. Jett was educated as an electrical engineer, and thus, he was able to recognize the problem and provide leadership in protecting the railroad communication and signal-wire lines from receiving harmful interference from these nearby power lines. In fact, prior to his education as an electrical engineer, he was educated as a lawyer as well, so he was able to protect UPRR interest from harm in various facets.

Jett demonstrated to the power companies that power company transmission and distribution lines had the potential to and indeed cause damage to the Union Pacific wire lines, endangering train operations at a substantial cost to the railroad. He influenced state legislatures to pass laws protecting the railroad by requiring the power companies to notify the railroad of plans for power line construction and their design. Notification to the railroad of planned power line construction permitted the railroad to evaluate the impact on the safety of linemen and train operations, and consider what changes could be made to mitigate any negative effects.

When feasible, he convinced the power companies to construct their line at a sufficient distance from the UPRR lines to avoid interference. Where it was more economical to eliminate the UPRR communications line, agreement was reached with the power company to replace the pole line with alternate communication facilities.

The power company planned on building a new 110,000-volt power transmission in the vicinity of the Union Pacific pole line on the Joseph Branch. Because of the proximity and parallel of the power line to the railroad's dispatcher communications circuit, the electrical induction into the line would have rendered it inoperable.

An agreement was reached between the railroad and the power company for the railroad to use dispatcher radio to cover the Joseph Branch in place of the wire line. To provide radio coverage of the branch, a VHF radio base station was constructed at Minam OR with a radio repeater control link via UHF radio to the Mt. Emily OR microwave site. Because of the remote location of the radio site, the power company furnished power for the radio site. To power the radio repeater, the power company installed a substation to convert the 110,000-volt power to 120 volts. The power company was able to service their customers and the railroad was able to provide interference free communications operation.

Power generated by the Grand Coulee Dam, and later by other dams constructed on the Columbia River, transmitted power to eastern Oregon and Washington including Portland and Seattle. To avoid inductive interference between the Bonneville Power Association (BPA) transmission lines and the railroad communication lines in this region, a settlement was reached between the BPA and the Union Pacific Railroad whereby the Union Pacific would transfer its communication services from its wire lines to microwave, thus avoiding damage to the Union Pacific wire lines and creating hazardous voltages to linemen. (See "microwave system was constructed between Hinkle OR and Spokane WA, to serve intermediate stations at Walla Walla, Yakima," below.)

Hydro Electric Power Transmission Pacific Northwest to Lower California

During 1966 the Bonneville Power Administration and the Los Angeles Department of Water and Power developed plans to transmit hydro power from the Pacific Northwest Columbia River Dams to Southern California. The plan was to transmit the electricity by using a High Voltage Direct Current Power (HVDC) transmission line. Transmission of large blocks of electrical energy long distances using direct current transmission avoid line reactance losses; by using direct current power transmission for equal power capacity versus alternating current, the peak voltage of AC transmission is avoided and the insulators required for DC are limited to the nominal design voltage. The DC line requires expensive AC to DC and DC to AC converters at each end, but permits over-all lower cost due to the use of shorter insulators, and needing only two conductors. The saving of weight of a third conductor, and larger and more insulators as in A/C transmission, permits use of a structurally smaller tower, saving overall costs of construction of the DC transmission line.

Construction of a HVDC line from The Dalles OR to Sylmar CA was monitored by the Union Pacific from beginning of the proposed project, due to the proximity of the converter station at Celilo, and the parallel of the HVDC line to the Union Pacific Bend branch in central Oregon.

The AAR Communications and Signal Section held a seminar in November 1966 to educate the industry and study the various problems associated with this HVDC line.

The High Voltage Direct Current line was a two-conductor bipolar D.C. transmission line operating at +400,000 volts on one conductor, and -400,000 volts on the other conductor, transmitting 1800 amps of current 853 miles from the Pacific Northwest to Southern California. The converters are center-tapped for a reference voltage, and to permit emergency operation with ground return should one conductor fault. (In January 1985 the voltage on the Pacific Intertie was increased to plus and minus 500,000 volts).

During building of the converter station, a number of tests were conducted by the Bonneville Power Administration (BPA) with interested parties, including the Union Pacific, during the first half of 1967. The D.C. converter tests included monitoring of pipe-to-soil tests on pipe lines and Union Pacific track/trackside equipment, and harmonic interference to Union Pacific communication line facilities. Most of the harmonic tests were made in the voice frequency band.

While most power line interference usually consists of odd harmonic frequencies, the back-feed harmonics from the test converter revealed significant even number harmonics being developed. DC lines generally are not expected to cause inductive interference, particularly when the DC line runs parallel to the Union Pacific wire lines in Bend, OR. The Pacific Northwest has many high voltage transmission lines collecting hydropower to serve the power needs of the Northwest as well as those high voltage transmission lines feeding the converter station at Celilo.

Interference in the carrier frequency band of 3 KC to 150 KC was not tested and was unanticipated. It was only after the energizing and placement in service of the HVDC line that interference in the carrier frequency band was discovered. The frequency band was used by the Union Pacific for carrier systems transmitting in that spectrum for railroad long distance voice and data channels, including lines in the Celilo vicinity.

Later a series of tests were conducted in May 1969 by the Los Angeles Department of Water and Power (LADWP) using a 5 KW tone generator operating between 360 HZ to 5040 HZ with the output impressed on the recently complete HVDC conductors at predetermined frequencies and measured on LADWP test lines. The LADWP and BPA determined that they should install filtering on the DC line as well as the AC lines feeding the converter station at Sylmar. A Faraday screen was installed on the entire converter station due to Radio Frequency Interference (RFI) emanating from the converters. No Faraday screen was installed at Celilo Converter Station due to the isolated area where it is located.

During March 1970, BPA and LADWP performed acceptance tests on the equipment.

Harmonic test were conducted by the Union Pacific and the Burlington Northern between May 31 and June 7, 1970. Significant carrier frequency interference was noted on the Union Pacific, and a formal report was written and presented by Hugh M. Robertson, Assistant to Superintendent Communications, to the September 1970 Communications And Signal Section AAR meeting in San Francisco, CA September 17, 1970.[1]

The interference to the Union Pacific facilities led to a financial settlement between the Union Pacific and the Bonneville Power

Administration. The funds were used to build low-density 2 KMC microwave system from The Dalles OR (Haystack Microwave Site WA) to Madras OR between Hinkle OR and Spokane Washington, and between Mica Peak WA and Bonners Ferry ID.[2]

Another HVDC line was constructed paralleling the Union Pacific in the mid-'80s. Utah Power Company and several Los Angeles area power utilities led by LADWP formed a corporation known as the Intermountain Power Agency to operate what is known as the Intermountain Power Project (IPP). They constructed a 500 KV HVDC power line running from Delta, UT to Victorville, CA. A converter station was constructed adjacent the coal fired power plant near Delta UT and a converter station near Adelanto CA.

Coal from Utah coal mines in Carbon, Emery, and Sevier counties served the power plant near Delta, feeding electrical power to the Southern California power grid. The line was energized October 1, 1985. This line required the Union Pacific Railroad to make several changes to communication facilities along the route, and a settlement was reached between and the Union Pacific and the IPP.

A coal haul rail line was constructed to serve the coal-fired power plant at Delta. To serve the CTC controls on this line and other railroad operational communications and data needs of the railroad, a 2 KMC microwave system was constructed from Lake Mountain, UT to Juab, UT via Provo. The last microwave site on the route at Leamington UT was served off of the Salt Lake City-to-Los Angeles microwave system. The first train delivering coal to the IPP plant near Delta took place with a ceremony attended by over 300 people on July 2, 1985.[3]

Other Interference Issues

The Sacramento Municipal Utilities District (SMUD) approached the Union Pacific Railroad in March 1984 about using its right-of-way to construct a 500KV high voltage power line. The railroad not only refused to permit usage of its right-of-way, but objected to construction anywhere near where the inductive influence would harm its communications and signal services.

A number of meetings were held about the issue. At one with SMUD on March 5, 1984, SMUD "has sympathy for our problem" but they had difficulties and scheduled another meeting for March 13, 1984. Over some elapsed time, MCI plowed a fiber optic cable between Sacramento and Stockton, CA.

With agreement and a settlement from SMUD, the Union Pacific obtained dark fibers in the MCI cable, and install drop and insert (**drop** voice channels **and insert** communications services at specific locations along the fiber optic cable route, what is known as a drop and insert (D&I) fiber optic cable system.) communications circuits to operate dispatcher radios, CTC data for signal control points, signal maintenance voice and communications service channels, between Sacramento and Stockton at Phillips and Pollock, and removed the pole line in October of 1986. SMUD started construction on September of 1987.

Railroad Relocation Projects

One of the early projects requiring relocation of the communications facilities was due to construction of the John Day dam along the Columbia River between Hermiston and The Dalles, Oregon. The John Day Dam was started in 1958 and completed in 1971. Due to heights of the dam and reservoir of water behind the dam on the Columbia River, the United States Government paid to move the rail facilities to higher ground. Besides the track, the railroad had two pole lines, the signal pole line which not only controlled signals, but had a 2,300 volt power line on the top crossarm; and the communications pole line, with its various communications services, including several wire-line carrier systems serving the northwest. Negotiation with the federal government produced a cash settlement to eliminate the communications pole line. With the cash settlement, the communications department built a microwave system in 1961, described earlier, between Hinkle and Portland. One wireline circuit was moved to the signal pole line for local services.

Dam construction along the Upper Snake River for the Little Goose and the Lower Granite Dam projects in Washington also required the railroad and its communications lines to be moved to higher ground. The Little Goose dam started in in 1963 and was completed in 1970, the Lower Granite started in 1965 and was completed in 1975. During 1969, by eliminating and avoiding relocation of the communications pole line, a settlement with the federal government was reached; moneys were used to pay for extension of the Union Pacific microwave system to Lewiston ID for communications services to the Union Pacific and Camas Prairie Railroad's joint offices.

The Camas Prairie Railroad was a joint subsidiary of the UPRR and the then Burlington Northern Railroad to replace the dispatchers' service and carrier systems along the Snake River. Two-way dispatcher's radio coverage was furnished via a radio repeater system into the Snake River canyon also with the savings from the forgone pole line relocation project.

Other "Projects and Future Recommendations" identified in Jett's Five-Year Plan are included in Appendix B.

Jett Era Commercial Investigations and Planning

A plan to leverage Union Pacific right-of-way assets and expand other railroad assets was developed in 1966 by Mr. C. Otis Jett and the communication department to provide commercial communication services across the country. Common carriers, including AT&T and General Telephone, were using coaxial cables to expand their systems. The AT&T Long Lines division was plowing and trenching coaxial cable to expand services using existing pole line right-of-way. Coaxial cable systems also required right-of-way; the cost of right-of-way increases were added to the communication facility costs per route and was distributed across the many telephone channels in the cable.

The railroads, with their continuous and fully-owned right-of-ways, potentially had a favorable cost advantage compared to common carrier companies. Com-Net, a Nevada corporation, developed a highly extensive plan for a project entitled "COAXIAL COMMUNICATIONS NETWORK" in conjunction with ITT World Communications, Inc. At a meeting in International Telephone and Telegraph Company's (ITT), New York offices on December 2, 1968, with representatives of IT&T, Union Pacific Railroad Company (represented by Mr. Jett), Com-Net Inc., and Utah Construction Company, IT&T made a tentative computation on the costs of installing a coaxial cable along railroad rights-of-way and were of the opinion that, if the arrangement could be put together, there would be a ready market for communication services provided by the cable. IT&T further developed an economic study to determine the feasibility of the plan.[4]

The Union Pacific proceeded cautiously with interest in the project by commissioning Page Communications Engineers, Inc. to prepare a preliminary report. For the plan to succeed, the inclusion of the Southern Pacific Railroad or the Santa Fe Railroad was needed to expand the network to the west coast. Other railroads would be needed to expand to the gulf coast. The Page Communication Engineers report was included in the overall plan. As the meetings and plans expanded, it was determined that the Santa Fe Railroad lacked interest in participating, but the Southern Pacific became extremely interested.

During the period that followed, concerns of financial stability of the Penn Central Railroad (the eastern railroad partner) developed. Additionally, cost benefit to the UPRR and other financial and organizational considerations were developed. However, bankruptcy of the Penn Central led to consideration of bringing in the C&O/B&O and N&W in its place, but interest in the plan declined. While the commercial plan died, the concept of expanding the asset value of railroad right-of-way to other opportunities remained alive. Discussed below, the later development of fiber optic cable systems presented a new opportunity. These early plans for the coaxial cable project and comments were later reviewed by the Law Department, and were again referenced in the later study when the fiber optic issue was under consideration. Similar agreement was reached that the Union Pacific had the right to use the right-of-way to leverage this asset for railroad financial reasons.

The Southern Pacific Railroad continued interest in being a provider of alternate commercial communication services. Mr. John Albertson, Superintendent of Communications, formed a subsidiary of the SPRR called Southern Pacific Communications Company (SPCC). Initially, the SPRR Communications microwave sites in the West were used to expand the new company. Buildings were added adjacent the SPRR microwave sites and equipment installed. SPRR microwave towers and other facilities served this system.

The system was expanded to the east coast and was ultimately sold to United Telephone Company. The SPCC system ultimately became the US Sprint subsidiary of United Telephone Company. (The acronym **S**print was derived from **S**outhern **P**acific **R**ailroad **I**nternal **N**etworking **T**elephony according to an interview with Brijet Neff, a former Southern Pacific communications control wire chief, with Melissa Block, host of an NPR program on October 15, 2012.) Subsequent corporate changes reversed the organizational relationships.

Other companies saw new opportunities to enter the alternate-communications provider-services business. One company saw this era as an opportunity to build a commercial microwave system between Chicago and St. Louis. The company called itself Microwave Communications Incorporated (MCI).

Mr. Albertson continued interest in the common carrier market and leveraged the Southern Pacific Railroad assets. He formed a new corporation known as SP Communications Company. Using the Southern Pacific Railroad Right of Way, SP Communications plowed in a fiber optic cable. This corporation was later sold and reorganized as Qwest Communications. Qwest was later purchased by US West for its fiber optic cable services. Ultimately US West was renamed Qwest, and was followed by takeover from Century-Link.

17

MoPac WP and UPRR Merger

Completion of the Interstate Highway System and improvement in air transportation resulted in most railroads petitioning to abandon passenger rail travel. Amtrack was created to absorb rail passenger service from the railroads. The Staggers Act eliminated the ICC rate structure permitting the railroads to split off non-profitable routes, reorganizing the railroads into a more competitive structure and setting competitive rates to attract new business. In this environment, more merger flexibility was permitted.

The Union Pacific Railroad filed an applications for merger with the Missouri Pacific Railroad and the Western Pacific Railroad before the Interstate Commerce Commission on September 15, 1980.

On December 22, 1982 the Union Pacific Railroad, the Missouri Pacific Railroad, and the Western Pacific Railroad merged into one railroad system. The new Union Pacific Company was formed and became the parent of the three railroads.

The Merger Handbook issued by the three railroads noted:

> *"The proposed consolidation of Missouri Pacific, Western Pacific and Union Pacific into a single system will yield a long-term strengthening of each railroad as well as immediate and direct benefits to shippers located in the 21 states served by the three carriers.*

> *As a by-product, the consolidation will intensify rail competition in the western half of the United States; and, importantly, will have no negative impact on public interests. And for the nation this represents a recommitment of Union Pacific Corporation to the railroad business. This is important because it comes at a time when some segments of the railroad industry are facing liquidation and reduction of plant and service.*
>
> *This commitment by Union Pacific Corporation reflects a recognition of the need to preserve and strengthen Union Pacific Railroad to avoid erosion of its competitive position and financial strength in the face of rapidly changing competitive and regulatory conditions. And it also is indicative of a confidence in the future of the rail industry and anticipated growth in the demand for rail services in the American West.*"[1]

The railroad industry was changing. Eastern railroads, namely the Pennsylvania Railroad and the New York Central Railroad, had merged. The Norfolk and Western Railroad merged with the Nickel Plate Railroad and leased the Wabash Railroad, then merged the Wabash Railroad into one corporation. The Baltimore and Ohio Railroad merged with the Chesapeake and Ohio Railroad to become the CSX Railroad. The Norfolk and Western merged with the Southern Railroad to become the Norfolk and Southern Railroad.

Earlier, the Union Pacific Railroad attempted to merge with the Rock Island Railroad. The Interstate Commerce Commission reviewed the proposal and took ten years to approve a merger. Believing the merger and takeover of the Rock Island by the Union Pacific Railroad was inevitable, management of the Rock Island Railroad bled the Railroad of assets by failure to maintain the infrastructure, resulting "slow orders" (Train orders issued by the dispatcher to operate at slow speeds, usually because of weak track) equipment failures and poor service to customers. By failing to maintain the Rock Island, the management maximized income which was distributed as dividends to stockholders. At the end of ten years, the ICC approved the merger with the Union Pacific. In reviewing the merger plan after the ICC approval and determining the costs to restore the Rock Island into profitable shape, the Union Pacific decided the merger was no longer economical. The Union Pacific therefore chose to not merge with the Rock Island Railroad. Failure to meet customer demands for service through slow orders, delays and other slow train movements, the Rock Island lost their customer base and income, and it resulted in the eventual bankruptcy of the company.

Size and poor management decisions by the Penn Central merger led to government takeover and creation of Consolidated Railroad known as Conrail. Difficulties in operation of Conrail by the government led to it being split into two between the Norfolk and Southern, and CSX Railroads.

In the West, the Burlington Railroad merged with the Northern Pacific; the Great Northern; and the Seattle, Spokane, and Pacific Railroad; and the Frisco Railway to become the Burlington Northern Railroad (BN). Later the BN merged with the Atchison Topeka and the Santa Fe Railroad (Santa Fe) to become the Burlington and Santa Fe Railroad.

Merging Communications Systems

With merger of the UP, MP, and WP railroads, it became critical that the three communications systems be quickly merged to form an efficient network. Several office consolidations made rearrangements of communications facilities to support these changes.

Several Missouri Pacific offices were moved to Omaha, forcing the relocation of Omaha offices. The Brandis Department Store business closed around this time, leaving space available for rent in downtown Omaha. The Union Pacific, needing space in Omaha for the incoming personnel, decided in February 1983 to lease several floors of the Brandis building in order that the entire expanded Accounting Department could be relocated. To facilitate the move and minimize communications expense from leased telephone company services, the Communications Department developed a plan to lease a cable duct from Western Union, which had an extensive cable duct system in Omaha. (The Union Pacific already used Western Union cable duct for communications cable between the headquarters building and Council Bluffs yard.)

A 600-pair copper cable was installed along with a CCTV cable and several RG-62 coaxial cables. 3M Company had developed a high-speed data system using standard stackable TV signals modem on the CCTV cable. Thus, data services normally used by the Accounting Department were established between the new offices and the headquarters building without loss of functionality. The 600-pair telephone cable was used for off-premise telephone service and for several other voice and data services.

The merger of the Union Pacific with the Missouri Pacific and Western Pacific created a need for new microwave systems as well. The Missouri Pacific and Western Pacific each had microwave systems over parts of their systems; the merger forced their expansion and interconnection.

Merger of Union Pacific Communications with Western Pacific's began by initially installing a printer in the Western Pacific Depot in Salt Lake City to permit the WP to get information from the UPRR on rail traffic headed for the WP. The Union Pacific had an exchange of communications service agreement with the Southern Pacific Railroad (discussed above), so communication services between Union Pacific and Western Pacific headquarters were routed from UPRR communications offices in Salt Lake City via microwave to the UPRR microwave site at Holiday Hill, and on SPRR microwave to San Francisco. Communications to the Union Pacific San Francisco offices were rerouted to the Western Pacific Railroad communications offices via this route and quickly used for service between the Union Pacific and the Western Pacific Railroad communications networks.

Union Pacific Railroad had microwave services into its Kansas City Armstrong Yard. The Missouri Pacific Railroad had a microwave system into its Kansas City Neff Yard. A microwave link between the UPRR Barber Microwave site and the MPRR Independence microwave site was established to link communications services between the two railroads. Dial PBX tie trunks were established, permitting the two railroads to dial into each other's communication's systems. In addition, an ATT Bell T-1 lease was established initially to link the computer centers of the two railroads.

The preliminary linkage of the communications services of the two railroads continued to expand. The Missouri Pacific Railroad communications services originally left the headquarters building in St. Louis via Southwestern Bell leased services. The Bell leases were transferred to microwave when this lease segment was converted to Missouri Pacific Railroad microwave.

The Western Pacific microwave system originated in San Francisco and went only as far as its depot at Portola CA via the Claremont CA microwave site. With the merger, it was decided to interconnect the Western Pacific microwave system to the Union Pacific Network. The Western Pacific Railroad headquarters office was downsized and moved from San Francisco to the Western Pacific Oakland yard, where a new headquarters office was built. As a first step, the microwave system was rerouted to the Oakland office.

The Union Pacific microwave system was extended west out of Salt Lake City, paralleling the Western Pacific Railroad.

Prior to this construction, the Great Salt Lake was at the highest level in hundreds of years. Because of the increase in lake level, the Union Pacific tracks were continually raised to avoid flooding between MP 895 and 911.20. The pole line became submerged and the wire line was floated using crossarms lashed to 50 gallon barrels to keep wire line circuit continuity between MP 904+35 through 905+16 and MP 909+12 through 909+34.

Initially, a 6 GHZ microwave system was installed in 1984 from Salt Lake City thirty-one miles west to Cedar Mountain, and a 2 GHZ microwave leg was established from Cedar Mountain to trackside at Burmester Utah, at the west side of the lake, where the wire lines were terminated to interface the microwave leg, thus eliminating the floating barrels.[2]

Later, the Cedar Mountain microwave system was continued to Elko, NV for 244 miles involving seven locations for $778,000.[3] The railroad microwave channels were extended to Winnemucca NV by installing a drop and insert (D&I) lightwave communications buildings adjacent the MCI regenerator sites to provide standard Union Pacific track side radio coverage. MCI built a fiber optic cable west out of Salt Lake City and the Communications Department elected to interface the Salt Lake – Elko microwave with the light wave system at Elko. The principle problem associated with this MCI route was that MCI left the Union Pacific right-of-way at

Wesco, Nevada, and it was necessary for the Union Pacific to install its own fiber optic cable into Winnemucca, a distance of 3.27 miles.

From Winnemucca Depot the Union Pacific installed a 2GHZ Microwave leg to Winnemucca Mountain and followed the Western Pacific Railroad across Nevada to interface the Western Pacific microwave system at Claremont CA via a new microwave site at Pevine NV (north of Reno). This system initially was left with a gap between Gerlach NV and Sand Pass NV. Two-way radio coverage covered the entire route, and it was believed it was unnecessary to complete the base band services over the entire system. However, an outage in 1993 at Black Mountain CA (an intermediate microwave site) took out considerable radio coverage without the ability to reverse feed the radios using recently installed fiber optic cable services. A missing microwave repeater site at Bronte, NV was quickly installed, completing the missing link, which allowed radio control channels to be reverse-fed in case of a failure.

The Communications Engineer inspected potential microwave sites to support the construction of the Western Pacific microwave system between Salt Lake City and Portola CA. Site planning west of Salt Lake City was relatively simple to Elko NV. AT&T had earlier constructed a system which mostly paralleled the Western Pacific Railroad and locating our microwave sites adjacent the AT&T sites served our system well. The only real challenge was selecting a site near their site at Barro UT.

AT&T and Mountain Bell had sites adjacent each other. However, the salt flats on each side of the microwave repeater at the Barro site presented propagation problems due to thermal heating and potential interference to the individual microwave beams from reflections due to thermal layering.

An AT&T engineer had written a report for the AIEE Transactions (or Bell System Technical Journal, neither found) describing the problem and their method to correct. Years earlier, the Communication Engineer read the report and was familiar with the issue.

Microwave reflections from the salt flats, and the thermal layering, interfered with the primary beam, producing an out-of-phase signal, which cancelled the primary signal. AT&T

microwave engineers installed three RFI barriers at about ¼ mile intervals each side of the Barro site to attenuate these interfering beams. Mountain Bell located their microwave antennas and building close to the AT&T site to benefit from these RF Barriers. In turn, the Union Pacific placed its microwave site adjacent these two sites to enjoy the protection they provided.

Layout of the microwave system from Winnemucca NV to Black Mountain (A PGE microwave site the Bureau of Land Management required the Union Pacific to share) was over Black Rock Desert, an isolated desert. The logical microwave site starting west of Winnemucca was an abandoned FAA radar site above the Winnemucca Station. The next adjacent potential site was at Floka NV, 54 miles west adjacent the Hycroft Gold Mine's microwave site, which was powered by solar panels. While the gold mine had a power substation adjacent the mine, the manager initially would not let the Union Pacific obtain power from it. Because of the proximity of commercial power roughly one quarter mile away, the microwave site power line was laid out to the commercial line. However, just prior to constructing the line, the manager relented and permitted the Union Pacific to tap the mine's power substation. In the agreement, the Union Pacific also fed the Hycroft microwave site with A/C service, allowing Hycroft to eliminate their solar panel.

The next site west was a site called Trego, which was logical as it had power, road access, and adjacent the railroad. Further west, the town of Gerlach NV was an important station on the railroad and a natural for the microwave site.

Expanding the Western Pacific Railroad microwave system east of Claremont (north of Portola), a microwave site at Pevine NV (north of Reno) was selected and served as the repeater site between Claremont and Black Mountain, CA. The Black Mountain site (called Herlong, the nearest railroad station) was operated by Pacific Gas and Electric. Since the Bureau of Land Management (BLM) controlled access, they required that the Union Pacific collocate its microwave equipment in the PGE building.

The South Sand Pass microwave site was selected but it presented a problem with powering the site. The nearest power was the Union Pacific Signal Department 2,300 volt battery-charging power line atop the pole line several miles away. Considering the power load, including air conditioning, communications equipment, and other needs of the microwave site, the added facilities would add significantly to the signal power load. The load would greatly reduce the voltage due to line losses, adversely reducing the voltage to the signal equipment it served.

It was determined that a large solar power plant was necessary for equipment power, and the equipment needed to buried in a vault for environmental conditions. The Engineering Department estimated that a vault covered by three feet of dirt would experience an overall temperature maximum of 76°F and minimum of 50° F, because of the ambient earth temperature, absorbing heat in the summer, and providing heat in winter.

A reinforced concrete vault with interior dimension of 8' x 10' x 8' high with three feet of earth covering was placed in the excavation. The personal and equipment opening was about a three-and-one-half foot deep entrance from the surface, extending about six inches above the surface. The vault had sleeves for the microwave and radio transmission lines and solar power entrance. A removable hoist was installed to lift equipment into the building and a dual-lighting systems using the 12-volt solar power and 120-volt lighting from a portable power generator when needed. 12-volt and 24-volt rectifiers were provided should the solar power batteries needed recharging. The 24-volt and 12-volt dual-battery systems were also buried for the same environmental reasons.

During the survey, the team needed to visit two adjacent proposed microwave sites in the Black Rock Desert.

The Communications Engineer and Ken Moss, a retired Union Pacific communications manager rented a four wheel drive Subaru out of Las Vegas. It was late spring and the normal rental agencies had eliminated their normal stock of four wheel drive vehicles. The Subaru was rented from a small agency as it was felt we would be traveling in rough terrain. In traveling between the two sites, it was decided to drive on the dry lake bed rather than the roundabout dusty road between the two sites. However, during the drive, it turned out that the dry lakebed wasn't as dry as the caked surfaced appeared. With four-wheel drive, and continuing to drive as fast as the Subaru could maintain, the forward motion kept the car from sinking in the mud and ultimately returned to the road. Without radio coverage and 50 to 100 miles to get help, the team mopped their brows appreciating its luck.

Other Microwave Systems Provided to Support the Merger

With increased rail traffic from the merger, several Missouri Pacific Railroad routes needed improved communications services. The Missouri Pacific previously used a number of dial up radio sites for dispatcher radio coverage, which limited their service operations to train movement and minimized usage for maintenance-of-way support.

A microwave system serving Missouri Pacific's Iron Mountain lines in Southern Illinois and Southeast Missouri was designed in 1988, which took advantage of the exchange of services (EOS) between Union Pacific and the Southern Pacific. The Union Pacific needed an upgrade of radio services in Southeast Missouri. The Southern Pacific met this need for service south of St. Louis along the Mississippi River to Dexter, and with extensions to Gorham, Bush, and Benton Illinois, and Poplar Bluff, Missouri.

Microwave services between St. Louis and Chicago Heights, IL were also developed by negotiating a plan to use Norfolk and Southern Railroad and the Illinois Central Gulf Railroad microwave sites for communications and radio services to the Missouri Pacific's Chicago and Eastern Illinois (C&EI) route. Between St. Louis and Champaign, IL the Union Pacific took advantage of EOS agreements with the Norfolk and Southern and their microwave sites with legs to Hillsboro, Findley Junction, Villa Grove, and Ellis, all in Illinois. North of Champaign, Union Pacific used ICRR sites to Chicago Heights yard for communications and radio services. These services were provided during 1990.

18

Fiber Optic Cable Planning and Construction

Initial interest in fiber optic communications by the Union Pacific Railroad began with Roger Sullivan (a Communications Engineer in the Communications Engineering Group)s comments to the Communication Engineer which alerted him to the potential to use glass fibers for communication service. In subsequent years The Communications Engineer continued further observation of this technology through its infancy and development. Multimode glass fiber technology demonstrated it was possible to use glass fibers as a communication medium for limited distance and limited capacity. The Union Pacific Railroad took advantage of this technology for several early communications needs.

Denver Fiber Optic Cable (First use of fiber optic cable for communications in the railroad industry)

In September 1978, a closed-circuit TV (CCTV) optical link was engineered by General Cable Company for the Union Pacific Railroad in Denver, employing a multimode optical fiber cable as the transmission medium. The closed-circuit TV optical fiber system was used for car identification (previously, the Union Pacific used coaxial cable in a similar application). This was the first use of fiber optic cable in the railroad industry.

A test experiment of fiber optic cable as a transmission medium was desired by both the railroad and General Cable Corporation. The railroad wanted to see if the cable could be used between the video monitor at their offices at 14th and Dodge and the trackside video camera for high-speed data transmissions and examine this new media for future communications services. Among other things, General Cable was interested in the survivability and performance of fiber optic strands in aerial cable service in varying weather conditions.

In a joint effort, the prime contractor for this system, General Cable, supplied the figure-eight cable (a figure-eight cable has a support wire included in the sheath for structural support along with the communications conductors or fiber optic strands as in this use); Video Masters, a Kansas City based CCTV company, provided the electronics; while the UP Communications Department developed a service and installation plan. The Union Pacific selected the Denver Yard for the trial and the Communications Department provided the construction labor, a bucket truck, and additional engineering support.

The second use of fiber optic cable on the Union Pacific Railroad was to accommodate a move of several groups of the MIS Department to nearby offices. The Electronic Research and Development group of the Communications Engineering staff along with MIS programmers, on a separate project, were relocated from the headquarters building to the "Creighton Building", a building formerly owned by the "Ballantyne Corporation" one block north of the 14th and Dodge Street UP headquarters in the fall of 1982.

This installation consisted of two cables: one a multimode fiber optic cable, and one of standard copper wire. The Communications Department used the multimode glass fibers for communications services to off-premise offices to handle high-speed data transmission.

The test was a success. Multimode fibers demonstrated their capacity for use as a communications medium, and the copper cable was relegated to plain old telephone lines for the office.

Fiber Optic Technology Development

In the late '70s, Nippon Electric Corporation reported producing a single-mode fiber optic strand with the capability of transmitting a laser light 50 KM. With this development, use of a fiber optic cable installed along the right-of-way showed promise in railroad service. 50 KM spacing of repeaters with drop and insert capability gave the railroad a way to provide needed trackside services. In such a lightwave system, VHF Railroad Radios, with proper antenna design, could be spaced appropriately for trackside radio services. Other existing and unforeseen services could easily be provided from such a system as well; an unpublished internal paper developed for UP Communications management outlined that a typical 100-mile segment of railroad right-of-way, using lightwave repeaters with 25 mile spacing and drop-and-insert capability, could be used for VHF radio and other trackside services.

Interest in fiber optic communications was further aroused when a paper published by Mr. Paul S. Gardiner, "A Multi-Billion Dollar Bonanza for the Railroads: Fiber Optic Communications over Rights-of-Way" came to our attention; it demonstrated the feasibility of using fiber optic cables on the right-of-way for railroad communication service and as an asset multiplier. This paper was published in the *Interstate Commerce Commission Practitioners' Journal*, Volume 47, March-April 1980. Mr. Gardiner was a Senior Traffic Management Specialist, Military Traffic Management Command, Department of the Army. Gardiner made reference to the Union Pacific's first use of the fiber optic cable CCTV system a few years earlier in his paper.

Needless to say, railroad communications management stayed alert to the potential of fiber optic systems and their possible applications for future railroad needs.

Many communications companies started to investigate the benefits of a fiber optic communications network and developed plans to implement fiber optic cables in their networks. Among them were United Telephone Company, AT&T, MCI, General Telephone Co. Western Union Telegraph Co., Southern Pacific Telecommunications, LDX (later merged into Wil-Tel (a new entry into communications industry)), and others. Several railroads investigated the feasibility of entry into business as private telephone companies. The Norfolk Southern Railway, Southern Pacific Transportation Co., and the Santa Fe Railroad formed a joint venture to build a fiber optic cable network for installation of an 8,000 mile system which would link fifty-three cities coast to coast. Their network would offer wholesale communications capacity to telecommunication carrier. Fibertrack was the name of the proposed carrier's network.[1]

As discussed here and outlined in chapter one, one of the first fiber optic cable installation plans for a railroad right-of-way was an agreement between Amtrak and MCI. The plan was to install a 225-mile cable in existing Amtrak ducts in the Amtrak trackage corridor between Washington and New York, NY, which allowed Amtrak to receive communication service in the MCI cable. Since the agreement was non-exclusive, Amtrak was permitted to lease service to other communications companies, such as Cable and Wireless. Amtrak initially was granted 9DS-3 services. They used one DS-3 for internal communications use and had 8 DS-3 available for lease.

Other agreements quickly followed: MCI with CSX, 4,000 mile for service in Florida and New York to Chicago; GTE/Sprint for 960 miles of Southern Pacific Transportation Co. in California and Texas. Lightnet was formed as a joint venture between Southern New England Bell and CSX.

Paul Gardiner periodically updated the Union Pacific Communications Engineering of current issues concerning the subject of his paper. One such item was that the Department of Defense had an interest in seeing redundancy in the "National Communications Network," believing that railroad rights-of way were an attractive route and could quickly be used for fiber optic cables. It was a strategic plan to protect the nation's communications network.

Between August 28, 1981 and September 1, 1982, Gardiner had about eleven verbal contacts with the Union Pacific Communications engineering group. It is believed he was no longer with the U. S. Army and for a time he represented Cable and Wireless.

During these communications, Gardiner presented information on a number of potential and ongoing projects concerning fiber optic cable projects on railroad rights-of-way. Principle of which was Cable and Wireless work on the British Railway "Project Mercury," and on CSX's and the Florida East Coast Railway's (FEC) fiber optic cable route from Miami to Chicago via St. Louis.

In a communique on December 1, 1981, he advised that the National Communication Office of the military may have funds for a study which would allow for planning for a fiber optic cable installation between 1982 and 1984, with construction to begin in 1985.

On January 14, 1982, he discussed a possibility that the Bell Operating Companies may increase rates (as a result of the break-up of the Bell System). He thought there would be many changes to the communications industry, including CATV operators' desire to get into data services and a need to link these cable TV operators with each other along "CATV Long Lines."

He advised there to be "15 to 20 major users" interested in a study to determine the market and costs. Gardiner pointed to the "explosion" of Local Area Networks and asked "Who will provide trunk line capacity?" (From the author's personal logbook notes)

He frequently mentioned the interest of the Department of Defense and the ability to develop financing (sometime mentioning the insurance and banking industries). Mr. Gardiner, through contacts with Page Communication Engineering Inc., was aware of earlier interest in 1966 of the Union Pacific under Superintendent Jett in the national coaxial cable study they performed for the Railroad.

Gardiner made a presentation to the CSX on April 6, 1982, in Richmond VA supported by Hugh M. Robertson, then retired. In retirement, he worked part-time as a communications consultant.

September 1, 1982, Gardner advised the Union Pacific Communication Engineer of his employment by the CSX in their Washington, DC office. He reported progress was slow and it included the (Kansas- Texas Railroad) KATY conclusion that "Money may not be a problem."

Gardiner's approach of the Union Pacific was interesting; however, it came at a time when the Railroad was undergoing a major change in operations with the pending Missouri Pacific and Western Pacific merger. After consolations of the three railroads were behind, other opportunities were investigated.

The Union Pacific Railroad, under the leadership of John L. Jorgenson, VP of Management Information Systems, initiated several studies of fiber optic cable services. These studies were designed to consider various options for the Union Pacific to benefit from using the right-of-way for fiber optic cables:

- Operate a communications network as a communications service provider similar to the earlier coaxial cable plans of C. Otis Jett;
- Lease the right-of-way to the various communications companies maximizing the value of a continuous rights-of-way presented to these companies, dealing with one owner versus their need to assemble right-of-way from many different owners (this option allowed the cable company to deal with a single property owner aiding speedy installation of their fiber optic cable. Early provision of service was a distinct competitive advantage as LDX proved in its system design); and
- Package an agreement to lease the right-of-way and obtain communications services as part of the agreement.

The studies (one by A. D. Little, the other by Carruthers, Deutsch, Garrison & Williams Inc.), compared the pros and cons of the various options. Operating a commercial telecommunication system would result in the company entering into a new unrelated business. This involved working under new 1984 Bell System Settlement, Federal and State laws, establishing a communications-oriented business staff that would have to develop new customers, and competing with existing communications companies in their area of expertise.

Leasing the right-of-way was an area where the UPRR Real-Estate Department had experience and could maximize the property value from past experience and future projections. (Indeed, one of the early proposals was an investigation by Western Union with the Real-Estate Department; the Union Pacific already had a long term agreement with Western Union for the placement of pole, wires, and cables on the right-of-way and railroad use of Western Union Ducts and other facilities off the right-of-way. Use of Western Union ducts was beneficial when extending railroad cables of off right-of-way to offices, especially in Omaha and St. Louis).

Under the guidance of Mr. Jorgenson, and discussion with senior Railroad Officials, Plan 3 was chosen. Under it, the Union Pacific permitted the fiber optic cables to be place on the right-of-way under the UP supervision for a one-time payment of $5,000 per mile cash and telecommunication services consisting of 3DS-3s, the equivalent of 2,016 voice channels per cable. Each study proved that this plan was the most beneficial to the railroad, contending that the communications services may well be more beneficial to the railroad in the long run than the cash received in the initial settlement.

Indeed, the communications service value of these agreements has provided the UPRR with great economic benefit when considering the costs to lease these equivalent services or to build them using alternatives. Reflecting on this choice, it was found that the communications service benefits greatly exceeded any cash benefit the railroad derived from its contract.

However, many of these fiber optic cables placed on UPRR right-of-way have been disputed to be a violation of railroad easement rights, where the railroad operates on an easement right-of-way versus ownership of the right-of-way in fee simple title. Where Union Pacific communication services are in cables and the railroad has an easement for railroad services, a clear right for the cables to be on the right-of-way has long been established. Historically, commercial communications services have been operated on the railroad right-of-way with the railroad receiving communications on these facilities. Western Union poles or other commercial telegraph companies lines were placed on the right-of-way along with construction of the railroad. From the earliest days of construction of the railroad, commercial communications services and railroad communications were constructed jointly and operated jointly. Fiber Optic cable on railroad easement and land grant property were the latest enjoyment of this cooperation with the new technology.

Installation of Fiber Optic Cables and UPRR Construction Support Services

Contracts with MCI, Sprint, and LDX were signed between June 27 and July 3, 1984. The first fiber optic contract was signed on June 27, 1984 with United Telephone Company (UTCI) (now Sprint). Thus began a flurry of activity; the cable companies each developed plans, released construction contracts, and quickly implemented their projects. For them, this was an extremely competitive activity and time was money. Cable routes were selected, engineering plans were made, and organizations were formed and staffed. While they did that, the Communications Department began coordination of the alternate and expanded Union Pacific communication services to be held within the cables.

Some of the early activity recorded included plans for UTCI to Hi-Rail (any type of highway vehicle equipped with retractable rail wheels normally use to inspect track) several routes, including: St. Louis-to-Kansas City and Stockton CA-to-Winnemucca NV, and a decision to use the Feather River Canyon, of California, was considered the only route to use August 31, 1984. MCI said they were "hot to move" cable between Niles Junction, CA and Sacramento August 29, 1984. LDX submitted plans for Shreveport-to-Dallas August 28, 1984, which proved to be the first fiber optic service activated on the Union Pacific Railroad.

This was an exciting time for the Fiber Optic Companies and the Union Pacific Railroad. Many routes were discussed and the Railroad quickly reviewed and approved plans, assisting with HI-Rail trips and surveys. The Railroad was fully cognizant of the competition between the Fiber Optic Companies and cooperated to aid their construction.

For the two weeks between November 5 and November 27, 1984, Fiber Optic Companies selected routes, plans were approved, and issues were resolved—including crossing irrigation canals in Colorado and rock cutting near Pacific, Missouri. The Fiber Optic Companies were hitting the Union Pacific Railroad with many issues with blazing speed, which were being addressed and mostly satisfied, resulting in more Railroad routes being chosen.

It is further believed that quick response to the Fiber Optic Companies requests and problem resolutions satisfied any apprehension their managements may have had about locating on the Union Pacific. Their choice turned out to be the right decision for them, influencing future choice for additional routes.

Fiber Optic Group (SAFT)

To protect the Union Pacific Railroad from any adverse impact of installing fiber cables on the right-of-way and to speed the placement of cables, the Union Pacific developed an organization within the Communication Department that advised the cable companies to place their wire in appropriate locations and to avoid placing their them where they may by damaged in the future. Mr. Jorgenson, VP of MIS, likely arranged the initiative.

Jim Farrell was selected as Director Fiber Optics and Asset Utilization of the group informally known as the Fiber Optic Group and later as the **Safety, Asset Utilization and Fiber Optic Technology (SAFT) Group**. After Farrell's retirement, Craig Johnston became Director of the group. The fiber optic group consisted of the Director, numerous right-of-way inspectors, a legal representative, and a communications engineer.

The railroad engineering inspectors coordinated the construction work of the cable companies with the railroad field personnel. Problems were quickly reviewed and alternative suggestions made to avoid delays in cable construction. Safety issues were discussed and when conditions required, additional railroad personnel such as pilots were added to protect workers when they were in proximity to the track.

While leadership of the SAFT group met with the fiber optic companies' executive, administrative, and technical leaders, the heart of the SAFT group were the on-the-ground right-of-way engineering inspectors, who, through their personal relationships with the fiber optic company field representatives and contractors, made possible for smooth, safe, and quick progress installing fiber optic cable, and keeping projects on schedule. "As Built" plans were transmitted to the Union Pacific Engineering Department to document the location of the fiber optic cables on the right-of-way. As Built plans were digitized and stored in a data base.

A **Call Before YoU Dig (CBUD)** Group was established in the Communications Department Customer Service Center. The CBUD group used a digitized database to record any planned work and advised on fiber optic cable locations. Any party planning to work on the right-of-way needed to phone into the CBUD group to verify the location of any fiber optic cables near their work, and railroad workers themselves were required to. They were also required to be alert of outside parties working near the right-of-way and advise them of the CBUD phone number, recommending they call.

Warning signs placed along the right-of-way included a 1-800 number to call prior to digging on the right-of-way. The CBUD also received calls from and coordinated with other CBUD groups across the twenty-one states the Union Pacific serves, to avoid disruption to utilities on or near the right-of-way.

Safety Issues

The Union Pacific conducts an extensive safety program throughout the company.

Each department is charged to conduct an effective safety program, and to strive to continually improve safety performance. Each employee is requested to buy into the safety program, and point out unsafe practices or actions they observe.

Before any contractor's employees can gain entry to the railroad right-of-way, they must go through a railroad sponsored safety training program. Upon completion of the program, they receive a certification of completion and a sticker to apply to their safety helmet so railroad personnel can quickly identify their right to have access to the right-of-way.

Safety training does not always produce desired results, but the Union Pacific Railroad has a goal of perfection in keeping personnel on the right-of-way safe from harm.

On July 6, 1985 a contractor violated safe procedures, resulting in damage to equipment but thankfully avoiding injury to the contractors, railroad employees, or the public.

The incident was the result of Amtrack train #33 traveling from St. Louis to Kansas City hitting a Kiewit backhoe. No damage to the contractors or train crew occurred, only the machinery. Mr. R. K. Davidson, Missouri Pacific VPO, told the contractor "stay off railroad until we get safety people out," clearly putting people first. Later, on July 8, 1985, Davidson added that the contractors would "…not working nor will they be allowed to work." They will need a flagman and a Form "Y" train order to continue work and apply 48 hours in advance.

The absence of a flagman during this construction was due to fact the contractors' work order only allowed them to work well clear of track, but the fact the backhoe was hit by the train demonstrated that they apparently tried to cross from one side of the right-of-way to the other in violation to their work permit. The accident was caused by a contractor exceeding its contractual rights. Safety training for the fiber optic company personnel and their contractors was subsequently required before entry to the right-of-way, in order to protect these individuals from harm and the railroad from liability.

Safety training of the fiber optic company personnel and their contractor's employees had always been required and necessary before entry to the right-of-way to protect these individuals and protect the railroad from harm and document safety training of these individuals. The accident limited the contractor and its freedom of construction activity adversely impacting their productivity.

Implementation of the Fiber Optic Cable Program

The UPRR Fiber Optic Group conducted a morning conference call between field personnel and office personnel to monitor progress of existing projects and discuss new ones. The office staff included admin, right-of-way engineering, communications engineering, CBUD representative, and legal. These conference calls proved to be vital to expediting the cable companies' plans and satisfying their sense of partnership. It was in the interest of both the railroad and the fiber optic cable company to quickly develop staking plans for the route.

At times, legal issues developed which were referred to the law department representative on the team. One such issue concerned Sprint construction on the former Western Pacific right-of-way through the Plumas National Forest. The government attorneys representing the Department of Agriculture were prepared to present an injunction restraining construction on the railroad right-of-way through the forest. Our legal team met with the government attorneys and satisfied them we had the legal right to allow the cable construction to continue. The UP attorney pointed out to the government attorneys that the railroad had been constructed before the National Forest had been created, and that the right-of-way didn't impinge on the National Forest. The government attorneys returned their injunction documents to their briefcases and left.

The Union Pacific had a "Chaining Trailer" used to document construction on the right-of-way. The chaining trailer was offered to the fiber optic companies as a device to assist their route planning. The chaining trailer was replaced with a Hi-Rail Suburban developed by Perly Scoville, a track engineer, loaned to the Communications Department from the Engineering Department. The Suburban, a Hi-Rail vehicle, was equipped with considerable electronics, including sensors to identify facilities along the right-of-way. Through the years, as new sensors, optics, and software were developed, they were added to the "Precision Measuring Vehicle" (PMV). The PMV documented all facilities, lengths of track, and sidings, poles, signals, signal equipment houses and other buildings, as well as road crossings. In later years, these objects were identified not only as mileage distance and separation from center line of track but also latitude and longitude by GPS equipment.

(The PMV was also contracted to the Ferrocariles National de Mexico to aid in placement of fiber optic cables on their rights-of-way.)

The merger between Union Pacific, Missouri Pacific, and Western Pacific Railroads greatly expanded communications needs of the merged railroads. The fiber optic cable contracts enabled the Communications Department to meet these needs and greatly expanded the capacity and quality of Union Pacific communications services. Many new developments in the Railroad Industry were accommodated through the fiber optic digital services. Moving long-distance communications services to the lightwave from microwave opened up microwave capacity for the new drop-and-insert communication service requirements, and allowed for new technologies such as channels for multiple access systems radio (MAS) for CTC controls, ATCS, and later, Positive Train Control (PTC).

Cooperation between the Union Pacific and the fiber optic cable companies was very amicable, since their goals were highly compatible. The cable companies needed Union Pacific support when relocation of the cable became necessary. The SAFT group provided assistance to the fiber optic companies to gain right-of-way access to inspect or repair the cable and to deal, with other organizations occupying railroad right-of-way such as irrigation companies and utilities. The need of the railroad for reliable and uninterrupted communication services dictated close cooperation between the companies. For example, in Wyoming, a situation arose wherein the commercial power failed at a Sprint regenerator site west of Cheyenne during a heavy snowstorm on March 14, 1988, and their 35 KW diesel backup emergency generator failed to start—as did their snowcat. Sprint notified the Union Pacific that they had 80 DS3s in service and could only reroute twelve, requesting any assistance the Union Pacific could provide in accessing the regenerator site. The Communications Department had a snowcat at Cheyenne and used it to take a Sprint crew to their regenerator. A day or so later, the Communications Department's snowcat also died. The Railroad then brought a front-end loader from the sand pit at Granite, WY to remove the snow from the road and opened it to the Sprint regenerator site.

Extra ordinary cooperation between Fiber Optic Companies and the Railroad occurred many times through the years, including occasions where their trackside workers aided the Railroad by identifying safety issues on trains such as hotboxes.

LDX

LDX was a small communications company that had determined that to be successful as a new entry in the industry, they had to be ahead of the giants. So, they designed their cable, the cable plow, their choice of route, and implement plan to maximize their early entry into the field. In the end, LDX was the first fiber optic company to plow a cable on Union Pacific holdings. Our first service in this new technology was a telephone circuit between our Shreveport LA office and Dallas TX offices. It was placed in service April 1, 1986.

Other than the direct route between Houston and New Orleans, LDX chose routes which were on and off the right-of-way in such a manner that the DS3s were of limited value for a continuous Railroad communications network. In order for the contract to be of mutual benefit, the contract was modified to convert the route miles of DS3 services to route miles of DS1 (T-1) services across the LDX network. One DS3 mile was equivalent to twenty-eight DS1 (T-1) miles.

The significant advantage of having T-1 services between major Railroad operating offices was a benefit to provide alternate routing of dispatcher services, should a fault occur on the basic route.

Constructing last few miles of fiber between LDX and Union Pacific communications offices under this arrangement could be very costly and uneconomic. As a result, many LDX services were extended to the Union Pacific communications offices using digital microwave, or leased Bell Telephone services. One major exception to this arrangement was in St. Louis. Union Pacific installed a 46-fiber cable from the right-of-way at the entrance to the Eighth Street tunnel, where the Railroad's fibers interfaced MCI and Sprints fibers. The FO cable was installed in Western Union's duct system and was routed past the LDX communications office in the Valley Building (old Hoffman Printing building) in downtown. A lateral cable was installed into the LDX site, giving the Union Pacific lightwave interface a bulk interface between the networks. Among the first T-1 services established were those between St. Louis and Houston, and St. Louis and New Orleans.

At Houston and New Orleans, the LDX communications office were in highrise buildings downtown. These locations permitted the installation of 18 GHZ microwave systems between the LDX and the Union Pacific communications networks.

In Houston, the LDX communications office was in the Allied Bank building. The 18 GHZ microwave link was originally transmitted to the Settegest yard, a path which proved unreliable, but provided the alternate T-1 service desired. Later, when fiber optic service was established to Houston Belt Junction, the 18 GHZ path was rerouted to Belt Junction and a reliable backup service established. A similar 18 GHZ microwave link was established in New Orleans between the LDX communications office in the First Bank and Trust Building and the Union Pacific yard at Avondale.

As LDX/Wiltel expanded their network, the Union Pacific turned on T-1 services in and between Los Angeles, Salt Lake City, Cheyenne, Denver, Kansas City and Omaha in April 1987.

MCI

MCI, a long-distance telephone company, originally provided much of their services on a national microwave system. Initially, MCI opted to provide fiber optic cable services between cities in California and Texas needing high-volume commercial communication services. The California route was initially of limited benefit to the UP communications network, but with later expansion of MCI fiber optic cable routes, this route greatly benefitted the railroad. The Texas route between Houston and New Orleans showed early promise over an area east of Beaumont where the Union Pacific Railroad plans were being made for an extension of an existing microwave system to New Orleans to improve radio coverage on the route. MCI originally developed detailed planning for this route by hi-railing the week of August 19, 1985, and placing the system in service in December 1988 and January 1989.

MCI was extremely flexible in interpretation and/or modification of these contracts. A modification of communications services, as specified in the agreement, permitted the Railroad to exchange digital communications services as required under the standard agreement (3 DS3s), for a pair of dark fibers. The Communications Department could use the dark fibers to install its lightwave equipment, which would **drop** voice channels **and insert** communications services at specific locations.

With this exchange, the Communications Department could provide the standard UPRR VHF radio systems (Dispatcher, Mobile-tel and Maintenance-of-way radio services) along with other railroad trackside services such as CTC and hot-box detector services and other data and voice services. The Union Pacific installed a small equipment building adjacent the MCI regenerator building, extended the dark fiber (dark fibers are glass fibers which have not been interfaced to the lightwave equipment which transmits the signal for communications, dark fibers permitted the railroad great flexibility in assignment of the communications services needed at that location) pairs into the UP building and installing fiber optic electronics to illuminate the dark fibers. The electronics allowed the Union Pacific to install the radio equipment and other channelizing electronics.

A radio tower was installed adjacent the UP Communications building for the VHF antennae. This communications system eliminated the need and costs for the planned microwave system on this route. A microwave tower and transceiver was constructed at Lavonia in order to back feed the VHF radios and Signal Department CTC control circuit. The Lavonia microwave terminal was installed to connect the new fiber optic communications circuits to the existing Missouri Pacific microwave tower at Morigolin, LA. The Lavonia lightwave site also provided communications service to the newly constructed railroad yard at Lavonia.

Interestingly, just prior to construction of the Houston to Lavonia light wave system, flooding along the Gulf Coast identified L/W sites subject to flooding. As a result, the Lavonia building was raised three to four feet prior to construction to avoid future flooding.

MCI originally developed planning for this route by hi-railing between Houston and Lavonia the week of August 19, 1985, and placed the system in service in January 1989.

While MCI's early goals were limited to the Gulf Coast and California, as their comfort level with the Union Pacific contract and the Railroad's response to MCI desires improved, their goals expanded. With MCI's selection of additional routes, the Union Pacific recognized an opportunity to improve communications service between offices and along routes

MCI selected to build a fiber optic cable system from Longview TX to Little Rock AR. The UP/MCI relationship improved to the point that MCI gave the Union Pacific a separate room in their building protected power for the Union Pacific equipment, avoiding the need for the Union Pacific to set up its own equipment building, as was previously done. The costs for the UPRR's equipment room were balance against MCI expenses, such as Union Pacific flagging personnel. The agreement allowed MCI to install its telephone maintenance radio antenna on the Union Pacific tower.

North Little Rock (location of the Union Pacific yard and MCI's FOP) became a hot spot in the Fall of 1988. The Little Rock to Longview and the Little Rock to Memphis Drop-and-Insert systems and DS3 services to Houston, Bald Knob AR and Memphis TN were placed in service. Also, the isolated Missouri

Pacific microwave system between McGehee AR and Wynne AR was integrated into the overall communications network.

Sprint DS3 service between Tulsa OK, Van Buren AR, Little Rock AR, and Memphis TN was also placed in service at the same time.

MCI elected to build from Houston to Los Angeles via the Southern Pacific Railroad and onto Stockton CA. The Union Pacific negotiated an alternate route for communications service into Los Angeles. On July 21, 1986 MCI said it was okay for the Union Pacific to take service at their FOP at 1 Wilshire Place, Los Angeles. This location became an important location for Union Pacific to interconnect some of their service with LDX, which also had a FOP and with the Southern Pacific.

SPRINT

Note: Over the early years, Sprint's name changed several times, including UTCI, US Telcom, and US Sprint. References, notes, and correspondence changed to accommodate these changes. In this book, "Sprint" is used in lieu of these other references.

Sprint's early plan was to be the first nation-wide fiber optic cable system operator. The company envisioned a competitive advantage to be the first fiber optic cable operator and gain a competitive advantage in doing so; indeed their initial advertising campaign announced "You can hear a pin drop" over their system. The Union Pacific route, with its merger with the Western Pacific Railroad, well served that plan. In the west, Sprint had a direct route, as well as a willing and accommodating partner, in the Railroad. Their aims required close cooperation; the Union Pacific Railroad provided engineers and supervisors instructed to assist Sprint's desire for speedy construction, and trained their workers for railroad safety.

Sprint achieved its plan to have the first national fiber optic cable service from the East Coast to the West Coast and touted this accomplishment in their "Pin Drop" commercials beginning in 1987. As a result, Union Pacific was also able to expand communications services on one of its own principle routes. This service improvement facilitated dispatcher consolidation at the Harriman Dispatcher Center without the need for leasing similar communications services.

Sprint signed the first Fiber Optic Cable contract with the Union Pacific out of any of the carrier companies and leapt quickly into implementing their construction plan. By August 24, 1984 they had hi-railed St. Louis to Kansas City and were hi-railing Stockton, CA to Winnemucca NV even as they did so, they wanted to get started on lines west of Grand Island, Nebraska.

By September 4, 1984, Sprint identified plans to build fiber optic cables between Dallas and Fort Worth, and shortly afterward (September 16, 1984) extended this request to Sierra Blanca, TX. They then extended the request to construct between Houston-to-Longview, Houston-to-Baton Rouge, and Marshal-to-Dallas, all but Baton Rouge being in Texas.

At the end of August, the announced they would have the entire system (meaning Chicago to California) complete by October 1985.

Some plans submitted by Sprint were merely a right-of-way map with a red line drawn on it. Mr. J. L. Jorgenson questioned the submission, but decided to accept the plan as a survey, though he made clear the Union Pacific would not grant an easement until specific construction plans were submitted.

In mid-November 1984, Sprint discussed many routes, Dallas–Shreveport (hi-rail, canceled); Kansas City–Topeka (red line approved); Omaha–Grand Island, Omaha–Valparaiso; Topeka–Salina-Wichita possible; Daggett-Riverside; Grand Island–Cheyenne; and Denver–Cheyenne. In the following months, construction plans flowed into the Union Pacific Headquarters from the carrier: Kansas City–Topeka November 5, 1984; Dallas–Ft. Worth, January 15, 1985. In May 1985, the Union Pacific Communications engineering advised Sprint of the early Union Pacific DS3 service for 1986, including Omaha-Stockton, Omaha-Salt Lake City, and Stockton-Sacramento.

Sprint's "in service by October 1985" plans were very optimistic, however, lightwave services were in final testing at Omaha, Cheyenne, Salt Lake City, Stockton, and Sacramento during January and March 1987, and in service by the end of March 1987.

Other routes followed shortly: St. Louis, Kansas City, and Ft. Worth, with Kansas City–Omaha in service August 27, 1987.

Corpus Christi, San Antonio, Belt Junction, Amelia, Dallas, Memphis, and Los Angeles, were tested by mid-July 1987.

By the middle of July 1990, Sprint had furnished the following DS3s service to the Union Pacific Railroad, greatly increasing its communications network:

Ft. Worth – Dallas

Kansas City – Ft. Worth

St. Louis – Kansas City #1

St. Louis – Kansas City #2

St. Louis – Omaha 6ea DS-1s via alternate route

Omaha – Cheyenne

Cheyenne – Denver

Cheyenne – Salt Lake City

Salt Lake City – Stockton

Stockton – Sacramento

Houston – Beaumont

Kansas City – Omaha #1

Kansas City – Omaha #2

San Antonio – Corpus Christi

Omaha - Salt Lake City #1

Omaha - Salt Lake City #2

Little Rock – Memphis

Van Buren – Little Rock

Portland – Sacramento Route 6ea DS-1s

Ft. Worth – Stockton 6ea DS1s

Tulsa – Van Buren

To support Sprint's fiber optic cable network, the Union Pacific and Sprint agreed to install their Telephone Maintenance Radio System using Union Pacific Microwave towers and buildings along the microwave routes of Omaha – Salt Lake City and St. Louis – Kansas City with an agreement on April 14, 1988.

By mid July 1990, including all the lightwave systems in service, the Union Pacific had 230,000 DS1 miles.

UNION PACIFIC

Completion of the LDX, MCI and Sprint fiber optic cable routes greatly enhanced the Union Pacific's communications network.

As fiber optic companies presented their construction plans to the Union Pacific, our SAFT group escorted the fiber optic company officials over the route and activated the Union Pacific team. The field inspectors worked to aid in locating the cable on the right-of-way; they knew the cable could not adversely impact the railroad facilities but also realized the benefit of the communication services to the railroad and the nation. As the carrier companies developed and identified their routes, the communications engineers had to quickly review these plans and determine how to integrate and take advantage of these new facilities in the Union Pacific network.

Interface of Fiber Optic Cables and UPRR Communication Services

Critical to activation of these services was the interface between the railroad and fiber optic cable companies was the selection of the cable companies' location of FOP POPs (FOP = Fiber Optic (cable); POP = Point of Presence.) compared to the Union Pacific's local communications office. (The POP was their communications-service interface with local telephone companies). In some locations, the railroad had land ideal for these FOP's, and in other locations, the cable companies purchased land adjacent the right-of-way.

It was important that the UP Communications Department be advised of the location of the FOPs, as construction plans had to be developed quickly to incorporate railroad needs with the cable companies' plans. It was the responsibility of the Railroad to build fiber optic cable from its communications office to the FOP and also to interface Railroad equipment with the cable company's services. In some cases, the Railroad needed a conduit to enter their building. In other cases, the Railroad needed the cable company to include additional fibers in their cable from their lateral off right-of-way or to include a Union Pacific fiber cable in a common trench to where their cable left the right-of-way so that the Railroad services could provide a lateral fiber optic cable to their offices.

An early philosophy in the design of this "Last Mile" interface was established when the UP chose dark fibers between the facilities where possible, in order to maximize the interface with the provider. Using DS3-level interface allowed the communication department maximum freedom to assign and reassign communication services without involving the fiber optic company administratively in the future. Union Pacific had complete flexibility to meet its changing needs within the DS3s provided by allowing for future expansion as needed.

Early coordination was vital to smoothly interface these services. Competition with other telecommunication companies necessitated speed of construction by the builders of these systems. As a result, railroad communication engineers were involved with various cable companies' plans from the start. Once the Fiber Optic Company identified a POP, the UP Communications Engineer needed to quickly develop a plan to use its allocated services and notify the Fiber Optic Company of railroad communications facilities required. For instance, railroad fibers under the Fiber Optic Company's cable; dual placement of Railroad and Cable Company cables in a common trench; splice points; allocation of floor space for Union Pacific equipment relay rack in the Fiber Optic Company equipment building; interface between the cable company-provided DS3 services and the railroad equipment; and power needs associated with railroad-provided equipment.

The Communications Engineer visited many of these sites to develop the details, on the ground, of routing the fiber optic cable between the Fiber Optic Cable Company and the Union Pacific Railroad Communications office. For example, when locating the cable route between the Union Pacific Communications Office in the Kansas City Neff Yard and the Sprint POP, the Communications Engineer walked and drove the route to inspect the potential interface. The route took him past a tent/cardboard homeless shelter hidden in the brush right off of downtown Kansas City, a vision not seen since the depression-era shanty towns.

The location of these POPs was not always in the developed center of the cities and towns, however, and another interface inspection reviewing the proposed Sprint POP in Omaha led the Communications Engineer through high weeds and into a small marijuana plot.

Railroads go through very interesting places sometimes.

During inspection of the potential Houston – New Orleans MCI fiber optic cable route, the Communications Engineer hi-railed over the route to investigate potential radio sites for the drop and insert fiber-optic cable system planned for this route. (This route was along what is known locally as "Alligator Alley.") Most sites were adjacent MCI fiber-optic regenerator sites where dark fibers were extended from the MCI building to the railroad communications building. (This plan was a learning experience for a similar system installed between Longview, TX and Little Rock, AR)

The contracts with the fiber optic companies were very broad, allowing these companies to identify their routes as their plans matured and priorities changed. The Union Pacific developed amical relations with their partners. Our inspectors worked with the cable companies to assist and resolve their needs, as problems, such as physical route location or placement issues, developed in the field. The cable companies modified contracts to meet railroad needs, while our communications engineers identified ways to resolve railroad communications gaps, such as the need identified above with MCI for drop-and-insert capability for local railroad communications service.

The initial focus of the railroad communication engineers was to activate contractually allocated railroad services on each route. As US Sprint placed their Omaha to California fiber optic cable in service, Mr. Steve Bergeron of US Sprint, on August 30, 1989, requested the Union Pacific send a formal letter requesting US Sprint to place the Omaha to Salt Lake City DS3 and the Saint Louis to Kansas City DS3s in service.

Networking of Fiber Optic Cable Services

Initial fiber optic cable company route selection presented point-to-point communications that were limited to the individual end points, creating a potential risk of loss of service should a cable be cut.

As the cable companies expanded their horizons from the initial routes, the UP communications engineers actively worked to merge these fiber optic cable segments into a railroad communication network.

With completion of early fiber optic cables and implementation of Union Pacific communications service into these cables, the fiber optic network allowed relocation of services formerly assigned to the microwave system to be moved to the fiber optic network. These plans permitted rethinking of the design of the railroad microwave system overall.

The UP microwave system, which provided for long distance voice, data, and special railroad-oriented communications services (VHF radio, CTC, Hotbox), was redesigned by moving the long-distance voice and data services to the fiber optic cables. With the elimination of these long-distance services on the microwave, the basic microwave system allowed greater capacity and flexibility for the remaining railroad vital operating services, and new communications services as they developed, such as positive train control (formerly ATCS), multipoint data access radio systems for CTC control, and wireline elimination.

Developing the new communications network required consideration to back up vital services if a fiber optic cable was cut. In later years, the cable companies could reroute some of their services, but in the early days, these reroutes were limited and the railroad had to make its own plans to alternately route these vital services.

An Example of a Major Fiber Optic Cable Fault

A major outage occurred shortly after many of these dispatcher services were first moved to fiber optic cable, prior to the implementation of alternate off right-of-way service. A management decision was made to move forward with using the allocated fiber optic services prior to having the alternate fiber optic routes in service. The decision considered that the CTC services could be placed on dial-up facilities should a failure occur.

A cable cut in western Nebraska, near Potter NE, brought down much of the Harriman Dispatch Center's operations. (The location was identified in email correspondences between Anil Bhalla and Jerry Tichacek two retired communications engineers in personal recollections just prior to publication of this book) This was a major outage affecting train operations, and was quickly observed through alarms, and failure of circuits to perform and usual. Dispatchers normally set track signals many miles in advance of a train movement; however, in a network the size of the Union Pacific, there are always changes to train movements and a continuous need to monitor them. Fortunately, at the time, most of the consolidation only involved the Union Pacific and Western Pacific Railroads, not the Missouri Pacific Railroad whose dispatchers hadn't been consolidated into the Harriman Dispatch Center yet. The Communications Engineer's logbook entry noted the outage occurring on October 13, 1989 about 11:38 AM CDT. The entry noted the CP2000A at the Harriman lost service and transferred to microwave. Services impacted by the outage included Signal Department CTC circuits, Idaho 01 to 10; Oregon 2, 3, 4, 5; Wyoming 5, 6, 7, 8, 9, 11; Utah 04, 05; (The above referenced emails between Tichacek and Bhalla generated a review of the logbook, previously missed, to add specifics to the date, time and impacts).

With the outage, the Signal Department immediately started dialing up CTC services, and the Communication Department started transferring VHF radio and dispatcher voice services back to recently vacated channels on the microwave system.

The initial attempt to dial-up CTC services was successful, but like the Union Pacific, many Sprint customers started using ATT long-distance services. The combined demand on ATT from their normal telephone users and the Sprint telephone customers rerouting their calls overloaded the National long-distance telephone network, causing many customers to run into busy signals. The CTC services, which were to use dial-up back-up, also ran into the busy signals (since dial-up service used phone lines, not fiber optic dedicated "internet" lines).

Meanwhile, the Communication Department moved the CTC services and other dispatcher communications back to the idle microwave channels as quickly as time permitted.

The communication shop immediately shipped lightwave equipment to Ft. Worth TX and Stockton CA by overnight FedEx to provide equipment to alternate-route Sprint communication services originally planned but not activated. Coordination between the UPRR communications engineering and Sprint engineering provided for immediate installation upon receipt of the equipment and activation of these alternate fiber optic service routes. In the meantime, the cable fault in western Nebraska was repaired.

With expansion of the fiber optic cables upon the merged railroads, the Western Pacific Railroad dispatchers were relocated to Omaha, and later the Missouri Pacific Railroad dispatchers as well.

19

Dispatcher Office Consolidations

With the expanded communications services available with the 600-channel microwave across most of the railroad, projects which were once inconceivable were now possible. Thus, management decided to consolidate dispatchers. With the availability of the fiber optic network, a major consolidation of dispatchers is described under the "Harriman Dispatch Center" below. Many dispatcher offices had reduced activity in the evening and at night because of the reduced number of local trains operating at night, so dispatchers' responsibilities could be consolidated by expanding their territories at night. However, balancing the load where there are few or only a single dispatcher console in an office did limit rebalancing the workload during off-hours.

It was decided to move certain dispatcher offices (and consoles) to other locations. One of the first dispatcher's offices to be moved was the move of the Las Vegas dispatcher's office to Salt Lake City in 1967, and the Laramie dispatcher's office to Cheyenne. Many dispatchers' responsibilities were moved from the old location to the new office.

The critical services supporting a dispatcher was the CTC controls and the dispatcher's voice circuit. These are the most important services the dispatcher needs. These services were remoted* to the new locations using the microwave system. Additionally, the dispatcher had a telephone number listed in the old office, and in some cases the chief dispatcher's number was listed. Most times these same single party lines were remoted on the microwave to the new office for ease of communicating with the dispatcher without potential blocking of calls to the dispatcher because of busy tie trunks.

Remoting of a dispatcher to another location meant that all communications and signal services that supported the function were extended by communications services to the new location. Generally new microwave channels had to be provided and telemetry circuits for signal controls and hot box equipment, and voice circuits for dispatcher radio channels voice circuits installed.

Reliable operation of the dispatcher was a must and provisions were provided for protection of this function should the microwave fail. In most dispatch-office moves, a wire-line carrier system provided for alternate protection for dispatcher services. As well, a switch-over system panel was installed at the new and old communications offices in the event that a microwave system outage occurred. In those instances, these panels transferred the CTC code line circuits on **V**oice **F**requency **C**arrier **T**elegraph channels (VFCT) and the dispatcher's voice circuit from the microwave system to the wire-line carrier system automatically. The switchover equipment used a single VFCT carrier on the wire-line carrier-channel to monitor itself to avoid switching into a dead channel. Another VFCT receiver also monitored a channel for a high level of noise, also to avoid switching into a defective channel. As dispatchers' offices were consolidated, this protection pattern was expanded to other locations.

Dispatchers' radios on the mainline microwave system are located at the individual microwave site. The controlling radio voice-channel is inserted directly on the baseband between the microwave site and the dispatcher's associated communications office. With the move of the dispatcher to the new office, many times the base band was continuous between the microwave radio and new office. To move the dispatcher's radio controlling voice-channel, only a new channel module needed to be installed at the new dispatcher's office location to interface with the dispatcher at the new office. Other times, a new channel pairing was needed for the change in channel assignment.

With the early successes, management chose to further consolidate dispatchers. Nampa dispatchers were moved to

Pocatello, Hinkle dispatchers moved to Portland. Later in 1974, the Los Angeles dispatchers were moved to Salt Lake City. Due to the distance and lack of availability of line wire-carrier systems, the move of the Los Angeles office presented some unique solutions. However, the Southern Pacific Railroad had recently completed a microwave system into Ogden, from San Francisco.

The Union Pacific Railroad had an Exchange of Service Agreement (See section on Exchange of Services Agreements (EOS) later in book) with the Southern Pacific; in fact, the Union Pacific had previously furnished channels from Los Angeles to Ogden over its microwave system for the backup of Southern Pacific Railroad CTC service.

With the move of the Los Angeles dispatchers, the Union Pacific routed its dispatcher's backup service via our microwave system to the Southern Pacific's microwave via Holiday Hill (The Southern Pacific Railroad and the Union Pacific Railroad each had microwave buildings at Holiday Hill in close proximity, and a pair of coaxial cables were laid between the two buildings for the exchange of services. Initially, two groups of twelve channels each were installed for the transfer; later additional groups were added). From Holiday Hill, the Southern Pacific routed the backup service from San Francisco to Ogden via Los Angeles onto the Union Pacific microwave system at Salt Lake City. As new communications services were developed, more services were moved with the dispatcher's office, such as the hotbox and other services discussed below.

In December of 1981, the Denver Machine at Cheyenne and the Kansas City Dispatcher were both moved to North Platte.

Installation of Hotbox systems, other trackside services, and additional CTC expansion forced the installation of many "Microwave Legs" between mainline microwave sites and trackside locations. These microwave legs additionally allowed other improved services to depots and maintenance offices.

During the mid-1960s, the railroads, experiencing journal bearing failures which caused many accidents, requested suppliers to develop technology to detect hot bearing before they burned off and caused derailments. Hot box detectors were installed at trackside. Some railroads tied these systems directly to the trackside signals to stop trains for inspection.

The Union Pacific Railroad System, with its extensive communications network, elected to remote these services over wire lines and voice channels to the associated dispatch centers, where the degree of a hot box problem could be evaluated and train crew advised.

Harriman Dispatch Center

During the development of the UPRR fiber optic network time frame, the Union Pacific develop plans to consolidate nine dispatcher offices controlling 21,000 miles of track—including both CTC and dark territory (Track which is operated without a signal system. It normally uses train orders or a timetable to control train movements)—into the Harriman Dispatch Center in Omaha.

Prior to the consolidation of the dispatchers in Omaha, a computerized dispatch center was installed in Portland at the Portland Dispatch Center in 1986. This combined two dispatcher offices controlling a collective 1,500 miles of CTC and 2,000 miles of dark territory. All early dispatcher consoles there were replaced with computer dispatch systems wherein the CTC signal equipment interfaced the WABCO dispatch computer. The dispatchers used CRT terminals and keyboards to monitor and control the train movements with color-coded rear-screen-projection video of trackage, signals, and trains.

The dispatch computers used a program known as computer aided dispatch system (CAD) which not only monitors train movement, but under the input of the dispatcher, sets up a plan of auto routing. It determines train movement, meetings, and schedules under rules established for safe and efficient train control. The CAD system reduces traditional dispatcher workload and assumes many computational, communications, and record-keeping duties. Work requests for track and signal maintenance time is also entered into the system. Dependent upon train movements, track and time permits are issued to the maintenance crews. Hereby, work crews are safely protected against train encroachment, and the trains delays are minimized or avoided through software. Dispatcher territories can be quickly changed through scheduling at a specified time of day, or as problems develop due to changing field conditions under the control of the chief dispatcher.[1]

With the installation the dispatch radio control equipment was updated to solid state equipment manufactured by Avtec. In that system, the dispatcher base station radios are monitored singularly or grouped by the dispatcher, and the assignment of radios controlled can be changed as dispatcher territories change or assigned by the chief dispatcher.

The Portland Dispatch Center proved to be efficient and a plan was set in motion to consolidate all the Union Pacific dispatchers in Omaha. However, this decision presented the Communications Department with some unique problems. The Union Pacific Railroad dispatcher base station radio system was based upon a dedicated voice channel for control of the radio. A locomotive engineer, conductor, or track worker needing to reach the dispatcher pushed a button on his radio, which transmitted a 900 Hz tone.

This tone was detected at the dispatcher center, illuminating a light on the dispatcher console. (In the early days, portable radios had no such button. In the early days the handietalkie user had a 900 HZ tuning fork which he used to signal the dispatcher over the radio, later the 900Hz tone generator was built into the radio). When the dispatcher selected the base station radio, which appeared on his communications console, he was immediately monitoring any transmission occurring in the coverage area of that base station. The dispatcher could wait for the transmission to end or, under push-to-talk control, he could override the conversation if his radio had the strongest signal.

With consolidation of the dispatchers, bringing all of these voice channels under direct control in one place would have required enormous allocation of voice channel capacity. To solve this difficulty, it was decided to terminate the dispatcher radio channels on the nearest PBX, similar to the termination of the mobile telephone radio channels. Thereby, the dispatcher radios were concentrated on the local PBX. The dispatcher radio terminations were unique and required special considerations. The dispatcher radio termination on the PBX used a 900 Hz detector to route the call to a special dispatcher radio trunk appearing on the PBX, and transmitted an identifying code to the dispatcher. The Harriman Dispatch Center used an updated version of the Portland Avtec dispatch radio equipment, which identified an incoming call and routed the call to the appropriate dispatcher. The dispatcher selected the outgoing base station desired and the dial access equipment trunked the call through the appropriate PBX to the selected radio station.

The Harriman Dispatch Center was constructed using an historic freight station. E. H. Harriman and a group of investors purchased the Union Pacific Railroad at a receivership auction on the steps of the UP Freight House on November 1, 1897. The innards of the freight house were gutted and a tornado proof concrete bunker was constructed within the walls of the old freight house. The roof of the concrete bunker initially served for a crew calling center. The initial dispatch area used large TV screens with rear screen projection. With the later Southern Pacific Railroad merger, the rear screen projection TV system was removed to increase the number of dispatchers in the bunker and their consoles. The dispatchers then used console mounted monitors to view train movement.

This consolidation of dispatchers in Omaha created a need for additional long-haul communications across the Union Pacific, and the availability of additional fiber optic cable communication capacity on the railroad was a godsend. It provided service capacity which would have sorely pressed the Communications Department prior to fiber optic cable. Dispatcher VHF radio, dispatcher voice circuits, and Centralized Traffic Control (CTC) services, which control trackside signals, were among the most vital services needed for train operations and the dispatcher consolidation reinforced the need to provide continuity of these services during a cable fault. The dispatcher consolidation preceded the completion of the fiber optic network, but only after many new cable routes were already under planning and construction, including the redundant ones for outage safety.

Dispatcher consolidation, backup routes, and maturing of the communications network created new and expanded opportunities and alternatives to meet these plans. The fiber optic staff (SAFT) negotiated fiber optic telecommunication services off the right-of-way to provide alternate routing should a cable fault occur along railroad-provided routes. In this regard, cooperation between the cable companies and the Union Pacific Railroad worked to the benefit of both companies. Protection of the fiber optic cables along the right-of-way was important to the benefit of the Fiber Optic Companies and the Union Pacific Railroad to maintain its own communications service reliably; the many eyes of Union Pacific trackside workers provided protection of these cables.

Due to the Union Pacific Communication Center at Railroad headquarters in downtown Omaha being separate from the Harriman Dispatcher Center to its south, a fiber optic cable loop was constructed over various routes to protect vital communications services and their interface with the rest of the railroad communications network. The Harriman Dispatcher Center was officially opened on June 1, 1989.

20

Multipoint Distribution Radio System (MDS) and the Elimination of Pole Lines on the Union Pacific

Radio Test leg for CTC

It was discussed in chapter 11, that microwave legs from the main line to adjacent trackside stations were justified because they were needed to extend CTC control to the signal systems in the area. Other trackside services were also included in the trackside microwave legs, such as telemetry for hotbox services, dial telephone services for local track, signal maintenance, and administrative offices.

The original Project Yellow microwave system was located near enough to trackside to provide some other trackside services through short communications cables. As rail traffic service expanded on the North Platte branch, the Communications Department was requested in July 1984 to provide a CTC control circuit to serve a proposed siding at Martin Bay NE. As only CTC service was required, the UPRR communications engineers decided to test the use of a VHF radio leg to this siding for CTC service.

Use of a VHF radio leg eliminated the use of a microwave antenna mounted on an "H" fixture, equipment building with microwave transceiver, multiplex, environmental services (A/C and heat) and a fair size battery backup system—a costly facility to provide for a single telemetry (CTC) service. The VHF radio was housed in a small pole-mounted radio case with signal battery service providing power. The pole served for the VHF radio antenna. (The radio was later relocated to inside the signal CTC building.)

The use of a VHF radio link provided great cost reduction when providing a communications link for trackside CTC control channel service. The VHF radio link service was reliable and successful and proved the way for further use of this technology.

The Martin Bay siding was placed in service in December 1985.

Calnev Pipeline MDS Radio System

Shortly after the successful demonstration of the Martin Bay installation, the managers of Calnev Pipeline, a 270 mile petroleum products pipeline, approach the UPRR communications engineers in December of 1985 for assistance in serving the telemetry (SCADA) of their pipeline system. (Note: The radio equipment used is described as **M**ultipoint **D**istribution **S**ystem—**MDS**. The radio service furnished under the FCC Rules and Regulations is **M**ultiple **A**ccess **S**ystem, **MAS.** The abbreviations used may vary in this book)

CalNev, organizationally, was a subsidiary of Union Pacific Resources Department. UPRD operated the railroad's oil fields, refineries, and other natural resource production on and off the railroad's lands. Traditionally it received communication services as a part of the Railroad.

The Resources Department had offices at the Wilmington oil fields and a refinery on Long Beach CA. Calnev provided petroleum services to Las Vegas from Long Beach. Aviation fuel for Las Vegas McCarren Airfield and Nellis AFB, and other petroleum products, are also transported to the Las Vegas area.

In addition to the pipeline service to Las Vegas, petroleum products were delivered to George AFB and Edwards AFB. Petroleum products including gasoline were delivered to other intermediate fuel depots along the route such as Baker CA, a tourist stop between Las Vegas and Barstow, where seven gasoline filling stations were located serving motorists and tourists. Highways to Death Valley and Mojave National Preserve intersected the main highway (now I-15). In late 1986 and early 1987, microwave legs were constructed by the Communications Department to George AFB, Edwards AFB, and Baker for telemetry readings of product delivery.

Prior to this request, telemetry for the Calnev Pipeline was furnished on leased services provided through six telephone companies. The SCADA system not only provided metering of the flow at various locations along the pipeline, but also control of pipeline pumps en route.

This service, provided via various commercial telephone facilities, included an extensive open-wire pole line, routed through desert California and Nevada, much of it diverted miles from the Calnev pipeline and metering-and-control points. The service was exposed to weather and other service outages and suffered from delayed restoration due to the distances involved.

Since the pipeline was mostly on railroad right-of-way or adjacent to the railroad right-of way ownership, the UP microwave system constructed to serve the railroad was a logical backbone for telemetry to the Calnev pipeline. Most right-of-way companies, including pipeline companies, have FCC radio channels available for multiple access radio services.

The railroad was fortunate in having two engineers with experience in multipoint radio. One a microwave engineer (Dean Gragert) recently hired from a utility company with experience in SCADA multipoint radio systems: the other a highly qualified radio engineer (Mel Bauer) with vast and diversified experience. Mr. Bauer designed the Martinsburg siding CTC radio link.

Multipoint radio equipment designed for this type of service was readily available. UPRR communications engineers selected equipment and designed a system to serve the metering, control points and pump stations along the pipeline. The pipeline metering points were served by a single radio transmitter linked to a transceiver located at a nearby railroad microwave site. Multipoint radio systems operated with a master transmitter at the microwave site and several slave radios at the nearby metering sites. The control point master radios sites had main and standby radios with automatic switchover in case of failure of one radio. A pump station on the pipeline also had a main and standby radio for added protection from failure, due to the critical nature of its function in the system. The backbone of this telemetry system was a channel on the UP microwave system. In March of 1987, the company approved a work order for $350,000 to construct the SCADA system for and funded by CalNev.

In September 1990, the UP Communications Department installed a PBX and microwave leg to the new Calnev office in Colton CA. This was to serve their local telephone switching services and link the office to the Union Pacific Corporation network to the pipeline's SCADA telemetry service central control.

Calnev managers later expressed their pleasure in the reliability the SCADA radio system provided, which their original telephone company leases failed to provide.

Katy Railroad MDS Radio System

Expansion of the railroad to include merger with the Katy Railroad in 1988 provided another challenge to the UPRR communications engineers.

Purchase of the Katy Railroad led for plans to expand rail traffic north of Dennison, Texas. To facilitate the increased traffic, a CTC system would need to be installed to replace a 145-mile Automatic Block System. However, there was no microwave system on this route, and thus limited ability to support a CTC system.

About this same time, Sprint decommissioned a microwave system that paralleled the Katy Railroad between Primrose and El Reno OK. Decommissioning this system meant that the microwave towers would have to be removed and the building leveled unless sold. Removing these facilities would be expensive for Sprint; once it became aware of Sprint's plan to dispose of these facilities, UPRR considered making an offer to acquire them.

Complicating the potential sale of the Sprint towers to the Union Pacific was an offer by the Oklahoma Region for Higher Education (Educational TV) (OETA) to buy the El Reno site. The facilities were more elaborate in the strength of the towers and the building space available than was normally required for a railroad microwave system. The Union Pacific Communications Department looked on these sites as being ideal for a future microwave system that included new voice and MDS radio over a CTC network.

On September 1, 1988, an agreement with Sprint was reached where the Union Pacific offered to buy the nine Sprints sites for $1,000 each (to pay the legal cost of preparing the ownership transfer papers), a significant benefit to the railroad, considering the normal cost to design a new microwave route, acquire property, and build out. The value to Sprint, by sale of the facilities, was saving the cost of facility removal and property disposal. There was a happy ending for the schools as well, however—in October 1988, the Union Pacific agreed to lease tower space to the OETA for their educational TV service.

At that time, funding for a microwave systems was not in the Katy Railroad budget. However, with the successful installation of the Calnev SCADA system telemetry, it was decided to lease Bell Telephone service for the multipoint CTC system and other dispatcher radio systems to the newly acquired Sprint sites. The first installation of multipoint radio system for a railroad was in 1988 at Durant, Oklahoma, using a point-to-point license to serve two remote control points on the same path (because of congestion in the multipoint radio (SCADA) band). The system was later expanded in 1989 and 1990 to Wagoner, Oklahoma, along the Katy Railroad using the multiple access radio band. The system now consists of five master and twenty-six remotes (the master radio equipment is normally located at the nearby microwave site, and the remotes equipment is located at the monitoring location) for a distance of 169 miles to support the CTC system.

To UP knowledge, no other railroad had provided for a multipoint radio system for CTC service. A railroad management decision to proceed with Signal Department approval was made and the installation began on the Katy route. The combination of multipoint radio and the recently developed coded track signal systems eliminated the need for pole lines to support the CTC system. (Coded track systems were in service prior to this system, but usually limited to new CTC areas due to the cost of installation). Multipoint radio and coded track provided many upgraded routes without the need for adjacent pole lines.

Removing Pole Lines

At the Modern Railroads' Special Industry Conference on Communications and Signaling, held at the National Press Club in Washington on January 23, 1991, "Pole Line Elimination" was one hot topic. A recent issue of Modern Railroads quoted the following persons:

Mr. Robert Heggestad VP of Technology for Harmon Industries, "Pole line elimination and the maintenance savings that go with it appears to be one of the more active courses."

Mr. Bill Scheerer of the CSX, "On our railroad, the pole line is probably one of the pieces of plant that is giving us the most problems in terms of reliability and ability to move traffic to meet the needs of our customers."

Mr. Chuck Wheeler of the Sante Fe, "Our big project in the next couple of years will be pole lines. That's the weakest link we have right now in our signal systems. I have to admire anyone who can get rid of their pole lines in the next couple of years, it may be a good start though."

Mr. Herb Rupp of Motorola, "[Motorola] is looking for ATCS for code line replacement."

Mr. James Early of Amtrack, "[The Company] is excited over pole line removal."

At the AAR C&S Section Western Regional Meeting in Omaha, May 8, 1991, Pole Line Elimination was also the main topic. UP Signal Engineer Phil Abary spoke about fifteen minutes on the subject. The Communications Engineer also presented a paper entitled, "Multipoint Radio Utilization of the UPRR," quoting the above industry and railroad officials. Much of the information below was presented at that meeting.[1]

Expansion MDS Radio Systems

The first installation of MDS radios along the main line of the Railroad was an installation of three master stations and fourteen remotes between Gibbon NE and Keith, NE in August of 1990. The masters were located at Brady, Johnson, and Alfalfa Center microwave sites.

By May 1991, the Union Pacific Railroad had installed the following MDS systems

Location(s), Master, Remote (CP), Track Miles

Alexandria, LA, 1, 5, 5

Memphis, TN, 1, 5, 5

North Platte to

Gibbon, NE, 4, 16, 90

North Platte Br.
to S Morrill, NE, 2, 11, 60

Little Rock to
Texarkansas, AK, 7, 41, 143

Kansas City to
Strasburg, MO, 2, 10, 43

For a total of 22 masters, 114 remotes and 515 miles of track.

During the remainder of 1991 the UPRR planned to place in service:

Location(s), Master, Remote (CP), Miles

Longview Sub, TX, 5, 18, 73

Feather River
Canyon, CA, 3, 16, 43

St. Louis to
River Jct, MO, 5, 18, 121

Dallas Sub, TX, 5, 31, 125

Laramie Sub, WY, 3, 12, 33

Coffeyville Sub, KS, 3, 12, 50

Pine Bluffs AR,Sub, 3, 13, 104

Project Yellow, 12, 43, 102

In the railroad industry, many high-density traffic rail lines with CTC, have paralleling microwave systems. These microwave towers thus become logical choices for the CTC/MDS radio systems. By using master and remote radios in a poled fashion, these multipoint data radio systems permit several control points to communicate with a single microwave site, providing an economical alternative to open wire pole lines for CTC code lines. In 1991, the UPRR was replacing 1000 miles of open-wire pole lines with MDS radio and as part of a plan to install 200 control points a year until the 2000 control points are no longer operating on pole lines.

Signal Department Issues with Pole Line Replacement

Pole line replacement requires installation of communications and signal equipment described above in the Multipoint Data Radio Systems section. Signal Department coded track equipment on the track circuit is also required to pass the signal trackside between control points. Without both the MDS Radio and the coded track it would not be possible to replace the pole lines in CTC-controlled territory. In remote areas, it may be necessary to continue using a pole line for transmission of signal power. Solar power can be used to replace the power lines in some locations.

Open Wire Failure Modes

On the Union Pacific Railroad, open-wire pole line CTC failure is probably the greatest source of failure in operation of signal systems. A failure at one location can impact all the control points beyond the fault, and some of the control points near the fault. The faults can be caused by lightning, induction, landslides, floods, wire breaks, right-of-way fires, weeds, and icing. Ice storms have taken down hundreds of miles of pole line in a single storm, causing outages for weeks. In addition, the high price of copper makes open wire attractive to thieves, contributing to outages and replacement costs. (In early times, bison were known to knock the line down from scratching, while native tribespeople knocked or burned them down in protest).

Open Wire Costs

Open-wire maintenance and repair costs are considerable. Poles, wire, and pole line hardware are handled manually with considerable risk of injury to workers both in handling of these materials and repair of the pole lines.

In areas of paralleling power lines, linemen are exposed to the added risk of injury from electrical shock. Thus, it is apparent that open-wire pole line maintenance and repair is costly not only in terms of direct cost, which can be as high as $240 per mile annually, but in the human costs of personal injury as well.

As open wire lines deteriorate, replacement of poles, crossarms, insulators, and wire is necessary for continued reliable operation. Replacement of open wire pole lines is a very expensive process. Dependent upon the pole strengths required and terrain, this cost could be as high as $30,000 per mile in 1991 dollars.

Typical MDS Radio Systems Costs and Configuration

A typical MDS system using microwave towers spaced 30 miles apart along a railroad will operate with an average of five remotes radios at trackside control points for each master radio located at the microwave site. In this configuration, this package would cost about $25,000 total—or less than $900 per mile in 1991 dollars.

MDS Radio has great reliability and great cost savings compared to operating pole line systems, with greater safety to workers. Pole lines are dependent upon facilities exposed to the weather elements, are continuous (where a single break disables the circuit), and many work hazards attendant to pole lines exist (climbing of poles, electrical shock, breakage of poles, tools, and other facilities). Compared to MDS radio equipment installed at discrete locations, antennas on steel towers and in safer environments, pole lines are costly to replace, subject to weather elements, and dangerous to workers.

This is not to say the MDS radio systems don't have risks associated with them. Icing of antennas can reduce radio performance or cause complete outage. Loss of a single trackside control point can cause a slowdown of a train, but dispatchers can give verbal permission to pass a red signal after a stop, proceed at restricted speed to the next signal, or return to normal speed after reaching the next clear signal (Operating Rule 315). Outage of a master site is more serious, but the master site has redundant radio equipment to protect its function; icing of the antenna can also be serious but the antenna has a radome to protect it, and only severe icing can limit its performance.

MCI/UPRR - Fiber Optic Cable Services Interfaced with MDS Radio Service

Opportunity again knocked at the door of the Union Pacific Communications Department when MCI decided to build a fiber optic cable system along the UPRR between Longview, TX and Little Rock AR. This was a Missouri Pacific Railroad route where there was limited communications service, the dispatcher radio services was provided mostly on leased telephone company services at trackside, and leased communications services into North Little Rock yards.

This route had CTC service, but during the rainy season, electrical leakage on the code line wires on the pole line frequently disabled the system until the wires dried out during the daytime.

Negotiations with MCI resulted in MCI provided expanded lightwave repeater buildings with a small room for Union Pacific communications equipment. MCI also provided a single pair of UP dedicated fibers in their fiber optic cable sheath. A radio tower was constructed adjacent the lightwave repeater building for the usual radio communication package; namely, dispatcher radio, mobile telephone radio, maintenance-of-way radio, and the newly designed multipoint access CTC radio. As part of the UP/MCI agreement, MCI was allowed to install their telephone maintenance radio antenna on the adjacent radio tower for radio support of their technicians. UP lightwave drop-and-insert repeaters were installed in the small room to serve the radio equipment. MCI also provided battery power for the UP lightwave equipment and A/C Power for the two-way radio equipment, along with emergency backup power generators.

Immediately upon turn-up service for this multipoint CTC radio service, the nightly CTC failures during the rainy season ended, much to the satisfaction of the Signal Department and railroad operations in general

21

Advanced Technologies ATCS Study

Advanced Train Control System Project (ATCS) was pursued by the railroad industry during the 1980s. In June 1984, the Association of American Railroads joined the Railway Association of Canada in inviting suppliers and consultants to a meeting in Toronto where broad goals of the program were stated. ARINC Research Corporation received a contract to develop the system.[1]

The program envisioned that the system would be capable of performing these main functions:

> *"They will provide the means of detection for the location of the front and rear of a train, its direction, speed of movement, and transmit this information to the control point.*
>
> *"They will provide the capability of conveying all other pertinent information regarding the condition of the railway. This information will include recording electronically those sections of track appropriated by the engineers for maintenance and repair work. The information will also include the position of all switches and reports from all detectors of snow and rockslides, or broken rails.*

> "They will include a "core control" to compute the most favorable sequence of decisions concerning train movement of the next several hours.
>
> "They will specify acceptable kinds of communications of instructions. This will include instruction to the enginemen in the form of an electronic cab display carrying all instructions and other pertinent information.
>
> "And lastly there will be some data link to the railway headquarters to let them know what is going on."[2]

The Union Pacific Railroad participated in the ATCS Program with great enthusiasm and leadership. While improving safety in train operations is a distinct and important benefit, the economic benefits would pay for implementation of the system. The "core control" function of ATCS stipulates calculating the most favorable sequence of decisions concerning train movements of the next several hours. What this means is to operate the meeting trains at their most optimal speed to minimize wait time and maximize fuel savings by avoiding the past tendency to speed to a meet and then wait. Implementation of ATCS system-wide may cost $100 million, but could generate $60 million in annual savings.

This was illustrated in the *Railway Age* feature article from January 1987, page 43. The entire article follows:

ATCS: Will UP be first?

Union Pacific envisions a 60% return on investment from a ground-based system, with in-track transponders and on-board interrogators that could be in place three years from now;

At the end of January, Union Pacific will be winding up a six-month test of an Advanced Train Control System. But months ago, UP began planning for a system-wide application of ATCS which could be completed in about another 36 months, assuming a "Go" decision.

That system-wide application would require a major investment, on the order of $100 million. But UP's system planners are estimating that the annual return on that investment would be about $60 million, perhaps more.

The test that has, been going on since Aug. 1, 1986. is on the North Platte Subdivision, about 200 miles of line from North Platte Yard toward the western coal fields, This is a ground-based system, with in-track transponders and interrogators onboard locomotives. It makes use of available components from such suppliers as Motorola, GRS and Pulse. It involves a basic technology that has been proven in Canada and in Sweden. And it is a natural for tie-in with UP's Transportation Control System (TCS).

The pilot operation. In the test mode, UP has installed 183 transponders, each buried, in the ballast next to a tie. That total includes transponders on many yard tracks along the line because, in the pilot operation, UP wanted to track every movement; in a more realistic application, a transponder would probably be required only at the first switch off the mainline and in the sidings.

UP sees several advantages to such a ground-based system. For one thing, it accuracy needed to determine the precise location of a train. Thus far, satellite positioning systems have come up short in terms of being able to determine which track is occupied where parallel tracks are close to each other. (*This reference to satellite positioning system referred to early Union Pacific tests of train locations by Global Positioning system (GPS) during its infancy and before placement of the full constellation of satellites, and during reduced system accuracy due to military considerations.*)

Then there's the matter of control. And a ground-based, transponder-interrogator system is definitely within the control of its operator, the railroad.

Finally, while the cost of a ground-based system sounds large and is large for a system such as 22,000-mile Union Pacific, it's small-when the annual return on the investment is taken into account.

The usually-stated benefits from ATCS are well-known. Safety will be enhanced. Fuel can be saved because trains can be better paced, Service can be improved because a good ATCS system can handle more trains over a given piece of track, thus making it more feasible to go to a short-fast-frequent operating concept where commercial considerations make that desirable. ATCS can be installed on top of computer assisted dispatch systems, providing trains with more precise instructions as to where to be and when, and what to do to get there. With microprocessors proving that they can function even in a harsh environment onboard locomotives, information needs may be limited only by the imagination of those who make the decisions as to what information is most usable,

For UP, the key is TCS, already in place and working, scheduling work, scheduling car movements,

What remains is to get the data link in place, between trains and a central point.

One system-wide yard office. UP has already moved toward centralizing its billing operations at a single location, St. Louis. With TCS and ATCS, UP planners can see the day when there will be, in effect, a single yard office for the entire system, a central point from which instructions will go to train crews regarding work to be performed. Once the data link is there, with data terminals on locomotives, work orders can be easily transmitted and updated as needed.

Thanks to TCS, the basic information is already available, and what comes next is regarded as "a natural, easy step for UP."

UP officers say that once the data-link is there and the system is in place, the capabilities are such that "we haven't figured out yet what we *can't* do with it."

Even though the ATCS technology UP is using has a track record, the road wanted a hands-on demonstration on a busy territory and under a variety of climate conditions. The North Platte Sub has the traffic and since Aug. 1 it has provided a range of weather-related conditions, even including flooding, 'The system has come through,

In addition, these tests will help UP in determining what type of on-board computer and monitor to install and what functions to include.

It's assumed that the monitor will be able to display data covering such items as train orders, fuel levels, track-segment profiles, locomotive mechanical conditions and emergency instructions. As for the computer, in addition to its function in connection with location-determination, it could also function as a monitor of locomotive and train performance in a number of areas.

In an operational sense, locomotive engineers can operate the power and run the trains as they always have up to the limits of their authority, ATCS also gives some authority to the locomotive itself. If an engineer operates according to the rules and the instructions he's given, he'll never know that the Advanced Train Control System is there-except, perhaps, for the fact that those instructions will be coming to him on a monitor.

Much of what Union Pacific is talking about sounds like 21 Century railroading, and it probably is. Except that in the case of UP and ATCS, "21st Century railroading" maybe here ahead of the 21st Century.[3]

Mr. J. D. Merrick, AVP Communications, reported on the Union Pacific ATCS system at the October 18, 1987 AAR Signals and Communications Meeting "ATCS is going to succeed." Mr. Merrick said "the 1988 ATCS specifications are complete, and by 1989 the Union Pacific will have 3,300 miles in operation. The pilot test has shown an increase of 7.3% improvement in labor productivity."

We anticipate Qualitative Benefits of:

improved quality,

improved capacity (where needed),

improved coordination,

increased safety and

increased information.

We anticipate improved Quantitative Benefits of $50 million annually from:

fuel consumption,

train handling (meets),

reduced accidents and

decreased maintenance costs.

Mr. Jim Strickland AVP Communications CSX Railroad, at the same meeting, said "Communications is the backbone of ATCS."

The ATCS program was the fore-runner of The Positive Train Control (PTC) system required by Congress to be completed by end of 2018. (Under certain conditions extensions may be granted to December 31, 2020 the absolute final statutory deadline). Most of the features ATCS anticipated in achieving in the future have been accomplished. As of May 2018, The Union Pacific Railroad reported that in the first quarter of the year (2018) 176 track segments or 97% of its planned PTC system was complete. Upon completion the Union Pacific's PTC footprint will be the largest of all North American Railroads, encompassing more than 17,000 route-miles.

The scope of the national railroad PTC undertaking is massive and will cost over $15 billion, outfitting 20,000 locomotives, 24,000 wayside locations, involving geospatial mapping of thousands of track-miles with millions of network data points, roughly 2,000 data points per 100 track-miles.[4]

Electronic Research and Development

John L. Jorgenson created an Electronic Research and Development (ER&D) group within the Communications Engineering Department in 1980. One of the first projects assigned to the group was the development of a computer-based hot box detector using a microprocessor. The challenge was great, as not only was the processing of the heat detector element important, the field conditions involved extreme temperature range of from -45° to + 150°.

In order to design equipment to perform reliably in the railroad environment, the ER&D team Mr. Jorgenson hired consisted of a manager named Bruce Burton, an electrical engineer, and other engineers within various disciplines, including electrical, electronic, and mechanical.

The temperature challenge described for the hot box detector required the mechanical engineer to develop an enclosure to limit the ambient field temperature to limits the microprocessor could endure, and operate as designed. While commercial versions of hot box detectors transmitted an analog signal to the dispatcher's office, producing a paper tape of the individual wheel heat signals, the ER&D version transmitted a digital signal. The digital hot box detectors systems were consolidated at the dispatchers' office and alerted the dispatchers when field-reported hot boxes parameters were exceeded, eliminating the need for the dispatchers to monitor each tape individually

The original field test of the hot box equipment was conducted in Wamsutter, WY in January of 1981.

The original hot box detector was replaced with a new version and installed at Harvard NE in July of that same year.

Other equipment designed by the ER&D group included a Fuel Monitoring system to track shipments of Diesel fuel shipped to Union Pacific storage tanks. Tank truck deliveries and fuel drawn from the storage tanks were monitored and a running inventory was maintained on the computer network. Leakage from the tanks was identified due to shortfall in the recorded inventory by occasional physical measurement of remaining volume.

The first Fuel monitoring system was installed in Salt Lake City in March 1981. One of the early benefits of this installation was to discover a leak in one of the Diesel storage tanks.

With the pending introduction of ATCS systems on the Union Pacific Railroad, an onboard computer was needed for locomotives. The ER&D group investigated the need and determined they could design the unit, and produce the quantity needed for the Union Pacific. With early research in need, product, and technology, they could market their unit to the railroad industry.

A decision was made to develop the on-board computer and early development began on the system. These studies lead to the spinoff of the ER&D into as stand-alone company known as AMCI.

During this period, AMCI developed the on-board computer. AMCI also took over responsibility to install most ATCS base station radios.

In June of 2000, AMCI was merged into a new Union Pacific subsidiary called Fenix.

22

Solar Power Systems and Wind Generators

The Union Pacific Railroad operates in areas of the country where commercial power is limited or none existent. To serve railroad operations, the Communications Department's radio and microwave sites, by necessity, are located remotely from the railroad on high ground—in many cases, where power is even more remote.

Because of that, it has been necessary many times for the Communications Department to construct power lines for remote sites. The Mount Emily microwave site in Eastern Oregon above LaGrande is served by a high voltage power cable plowed into the microwave site on the mountain from a commercial power line below. An underground power cable was also installed to serve the Feely, Idaho microwave site.

When feasible, electrical power was constructed to the microwave site from the signal power line below, *e.g.* the Tintic, Utah microwave site. A Communications Department power line was constructed to serve the new Western Pacific microwave site at Floka, Nevada, as well. The Floka power line was constructed from a substation owned by an adjacent gold mine; the power line serving this installation also fed the mine's adjacent site, which previously was powered by solar power.

At a radio site above the Snake River in eastern Washington, a VHF radio repeater was originally served by a wind generator installed in 1969. The unregulated wind generator output boiled the electrolyte out of the battery and damaged the radio.

The Communications Engineer was sent to install an automotive voltage regulator on the automotive-style generator, which was used to supply the 12-volt power for the radio and its battery. Unlike standard automotive generators, the generators field windings were not available for voltage control by the voltage regulator, and the repair wasn't achieved. The solution was to find a different wind generator, or build a power line. In cooperation with the farmer who owned the land where the radio was installed, an REA power line was constructed to serve the railroad's radio, and the farmer's pump for a stock watering tank.

The Communications Department experimented with several other small wind generators at the Omaha communications shop during the late '70s. One was damaged when hail destroyed the blades; the other was destroyed when the wind generator was blown off of the communications shop roof by high winds associated with a nearby tornado.

The use of solar power by the Union Pacific Communications Department was more successful. The first use of solar power was to serve a radio repeater site in 1975 at Woodall Ridge, Idaho. The Union Pacific Railroad operated a mine-haul rail operation on the Conda and Dry Valley branch, serving the Dry Valley mine near Soda Springs, Idaho. A radio survey conducted by the Communications Department consisted of dropping off department supervisors, by helicopter, with portable radios on three potential radio sites, and operating a radio-equipped high-rail automobile 19 miles along the branch from Epco to Dry Valley to determine which potential site best provided the best radio coverage to trackside.

The site selected was the Woodall Ridge site. As there was no commercial power nearby, it was decided to use solar panels for a 12-volt radio power service. As this was the first use of solar power by the department, it served as an opportunity to experiment with many radio configurations to extend the life of solar energy for the radio. As a radio repeater, the site was needed to link to a nearby microwave site. The radio power needed for the VHF control link was minimized by limiting the radio's transmit power to reduce the drain on the batteries. The trackside radio needed the full RF output power of the transmitter to furnish trackside coverage to trains and portable radios. The audio amplifier was disabled and the discriminator output connected directly to the transmitter exciter of the VHF control link radio and vice versa. The original plan for the choice of batteries didn't anticipate these economies, so the net service life of the batteries (considering long winter nights and high snow coverage of the solar panels) was pleasantly extended.

In the Blue Mountains, a UHF radio repeater was located at Meacham, Oregon. The radio repeater served Locotrol train service to provide a radio link between the head locomotive to the remote locomotive near or at the end of the train. Due to the curves and tunnels in the Blue Mountains, direct radio coverage between the head end locomotive and the remote locomotive was not reliable. Locotrol tests results are discussed elsewhere in the book, and is the reason UHF radio service was chosen. Once again, the UHF radio repeater was located at a site to provide solid radio linkage between the two locomotives. However, the site chosen had no nearby electric power service. A solar panel and batteries was the natural solution to power the UHF radio repeater.

After the merger with the Western Pacific Railroad, construction of a microwave system across the Nevada desert became the next installation requiring construction of a solar power installation. A microwave site was chosen on a nearby hill and called South Sandpass (it was near to trackside railroad station Sandpass). Union Pacific microwave sites along mainline rail operations generally use a dual set of microwave radio equipment for main and standby operation to provide reliability of service.

Without commercial power available, solar power was the choice to power the equipment. The trackside signal power line was two miles away, but serving the microwave site from the signal power line, the power load would have caused a voltage drop, making the power line useless.

Additionally, the environmental services of heating and cooling normally provided could not be accommodated with solar energy. Thus, it was decided to bury the equipment room in a concrete vault where the cool earth absorbed the equipment heat in the summer and the buried vault was warmed by the equipment and earth in the winter. A further description of the South Sand Pass microwave installation is described in Chapter 12.

In the end, four solar-power plants provided energy for the microwave site. Two 24-volt solar plants for the main and standby microwave equipment, and two 12-volt solar plants for the radio equipment. The batteries were buried in equipment cabinets adjacent the solar panels, to preserve battery energy capacity during the winter.

In a forest owned by Sierra Pacific International, a lumber company, a site was needed near Kelso, California called Bear Ranch Hill. (During the initial survey, late summer 1991, to select the site, the Communications Department officials did encounter a bear, much to their surprise and the bear's too, which quickly departed). To consider how timber companies operate, the forest was lumbered (it was reported) and replanted near the turn of the century, around the time the Western Pacific was initially constructed; later the forest was harvested again and replanted during World War II in the mid '40s, and now, fifty years later, it was ready to be harvested again. To provide MDS radio service to trackside for a radio link to signal control points, the site was chosen on high ground in the middle of the forest. Again commercial power was not economically available.

The trees at the site were of commercial grade in height and diameter and were being considered by Sierra Pacific to be harvested soon. A lease for the land was negotiated with Sierra Pacific International, the landowner. During the inspection of the site with a Sierra Pacific International forester, Jack Frost said, "He'd get someone to cut the trees." On October 5, 1992, commercial lumberjacks were provided by Sierra Pacific to clear the MDS repeater site and the trees were hauled to the mill. A week later, SPI laid out a new road to the site. Due to the height of the trees adjacent the site, a reasonably large area was cleared south of the facility to allow the low winter sun to illuminate the solar panels. Plans for a helicopter landing pad was considered (similar to Mt. Emily's helicopter pad), but not installed. A 12-volt solar plant was installed to provide power to the radio repeater, with batteries buried in the earth similar to the Sandpass solar plant.

During the installation some problems occurred; for instance, the solar panels were wired incorrectly and the batteries were drained. Communications Supervisor Greg O. Clark visited the site on December 29, 1992, which had two and half feet of snow at the time, to repair the audio. He left, advising everything working and the solar panels putting out 30 amps with no snow on them.

Solar sites are not without problems. The Woodall Ridge solar panel was hit several times by lightning, which destroyed the voltage regulators. Improved grounding was installed to prevent reoccurrence. Heavy snows at Bear Ranch Hill required clearing of the snow and recharging batteries using a portable generator. This was a 16-mile trip by snow cat to reach the site, the reason a helicopter pad was originally planned for the site.

Other failures probably have occurred, but were not fed back to the author.

23

UPRR Subsidiary Communications Expansion

As the Union Pacific expanded, purchased, or acquired subsidiaries, provision of communication services to those subsidiaries became a challenge. At a General Railroad Staff Meeting held in Sun Valley, Idaho in November of 1988, corporate organizations to which the Communications Department provided services listed the following:

Technology

USPCI

UP Resources

Wilmington Refining

CalNev

Champlin Refining Co

UP Realty (UPLAND)

UP Employees Hospital

Overnite Trucking Co.

Outside organizations included:

US Sprint – Telephone Maintenance Radio equipment space, antenna tower support, and radio control channels.

MCI – Antenna tower support.

Traditionally the Union Pacific had a number of departments which operated under the UP corporate umbrella. During the 1988's corporate expansion era of CEO William S. Cook and his replacement Drew Lewis, several departments were created as subsidiary corporations, and integrated with newly acquired businesses. The Communications Department expanded communications services, voice and data to these new and expanded entities, in several cases extending data services to the Union Pacific Railroad computers, as well as integrating their voice network requirements into the railroad voice-based switching network.

Union Pacific Resources (Champlain)

The UP National Resources Department operated the Wilmington CA oilfields, and owned the Calnev pipeline as a part of its system, as described earlier. Communications services between the Union Pacific Communications Office at East Los Angeles and the Wilmington office was served by wire line carrier services from early days.

The UP Natural Resource Department was reorganized as Union Pacific Resources, a subsidiary company. The Union Pacific purchased the Champlin Refinery Company from the Celanese Corporation in 1970 and originally operated as a separate subsidiary. Champlin owned two refineries in Corpus Christi TX and one in Enid OK, and a retail operation. In 1984, they sold the entire retail operation to American Petrofina and closed the Enid refinery. Later, the two Corpus Christi Refineries were sold in 1990 to Petroles de Venezuela S.A. (PDVSA), the Venezuela oil company and merged into Citgo. Subsequently, Champlin was merged with the Union Pacific Resources subsidiary.

With full integration into the Union Pacific corporate structure, two telephone tie trunks were installed between the Long Beach – Wilmington operation and the Denver offices in September 1983. Later, these telephone services were increased by another Long Beach tie trunk, and two tie trunks between Denver and the Rock Springs WY office serving Union Pacific oilfields in Wyoming.

In October 1987, the Communications Department installed a 600-station PBX at the Champlin Long Beach Refinery, to serve the refinery and the nearby Wilmington oil field and related offices.

With the merger with Champlin, Union Pacific Resources established a Houston office in the Allied bank building on the 37th floor. Integrating the Union Pacific Resources office on the Communications network, MCI construction into Houston became an opportunity to extend fiber optic cable into the Allied Bank building. Plans were developed in June of 1987 and MCI requested use of UP Resources conduit in March 1988.

The Corpus Christi refineries were located along the Missouri Pacific right of way. When Sprint elected to construct a fiber optic cable into Corpus Christi, the cable passed the Champlin refineries and the Missouri Pacific Microwave site where the Union Pacific contractual services were terminated. Sprint DS3 service between San Antonio and Corpus Christi was place in service in April 1988. Plans were also developed to extend dark fiber to the refineries for Union Pacific Corporation communications services when the refineries were sold in 1990 to Petroles de Venezuela.[1]

Union Pacific Resources was ultimately separated in September 1996 as an independent corporation by a spin off to the Corporation stockholders.

UP Realty

UP Realty (UPLAND) originally was the Union Pacific real estate department and later incorporated separately. The headquarters was collocated in the Railroad Headquarters building and used dial telephone service of the UPRR network and UPRR computer services. UPLAND later was reorganized and spun off as UR Realty and its headquarters were moved to Dallas TX.

USPCI

USPCI (United States Pollution Control Incorporated) was a hazardous and toxic waste disposal servicing company owned by the Union Pacific Corp between 1988 and 1994. USPCI operated a waste dump at Grassy Mountain UT, about 44 miles East of Wendover. Telephone service to the Grassy Mountain site was served exclusively by leased telephone services. In September of 1988, USPCI obtained a work order of $88,000 to build a 2GHZ microwave link from Barro UT to Grassy Mountain to provide data and PBX telephone service from the UPRR dial telephone network. The microwave link was expedited using spare equipment and was in service by November 1989. The work order included expansion of communications service at USPCI offices in Salt Lake City, Oklahoma City, Kansas City, and Atlanta.

With the installation of an incinerator at Clive UT, USPCI wanted communications service extended there from Grassy Mountain. A 10GHZ microwave link between the two sties was installed in late 1992.

Overnite Trucking Company

During the Union Pacific Corporation diversification period of Chairman William S. Cook in 1986, the Union Pacific purchased the Overnite Trucking Company, which had its headquarters in Richmond, Virginia. Linking this off right-of-way company with the UP communications network presented unique problems.

Initially, an exchange of service agreement (EOS) was reached in January 1990, with the CSX Railroad to grant their communication services to their Union Pacific territory offices, in exchange for using CSX communication facilities to reach the Overnite offices in Richmond. Other exchange of service agreements were similarly reached with the Norfolk and Southern Railroad to reach locations such as Mt. Vernon, Illinois. One channel for Overnite was included in an exchange package of 5 channels, four for the Union Pacific and one for Overnite. Such were the diversified nature of Overnite's operations.

Overnite's communications needs were not easily satisfied with the EOS capabilities with other railroads. Modification of MCI's standard agreement allowed the UPRR to convert excess DS3s into multiple DS1s (T-1), (One DS3 mile equaled to 28 DS1 miles) which permitted the Union Pacific to better serve Overnite's Richmond office in February 1990 and later increase service between Richmond and Atlanta GA in February 1991. It was upgraded again in November 1991 for a second T-1 between St. Louis and Richmond, and between Richmond and Atlanta in November 1991.

Overnite was sold off in August 2005 to UPS.[2]

24

Government Relations

Interface with the Federal Communications Commission

Mr. Hugh Robertson, Director of Communications, a former Union Pacific Communications Engineer promoted to Assistant Superintendent Communications, served as Director of Communications and Signals for the Association of American Railroads (AAR) from 1972 to 1975. The AAR is a lobbying organization representing the Railroad Industry before the Federal Government agencies and Congress. Mr. Robertson was also president of the Land Mobile Communications Council (LMCC) which represented Land Mobile Radio users before the Federal Communications Commission (FCC). The LMCC represented all users of two-way radios service on matters dealing with the FCC, including Police Departments, taxi cabs, utility companies, and local service companies. The LMCC negotiated with the FCC for radio channels, usage issues, and commented on FCC Notice for Proposed Rulemakings, which affected all user's mobile communications.

In this capacity, he represented American Railroads before the FCC (for Communications) and the Federal Railroad Administration (FRA) (for Signals).

Returning to the Union Pacific Railroad, he brought experience and knowledge of procedures used in government rule-making, especially as these procedures pertained to the railroad industry. Mr. Robertson, as Director of Communications, used his expertise to train and educate the UPRR Communications Department engineers on these dealings.

One of the first issues the Communications Department handled after Robertson became Director of Communications for the Union Pacific Railroad Company was a Notice of Proposed Rulemaking (NPR) concerning a Waterways Users Association filing before the FCC.

The Land Mobile Radio channels used by the American Railroads (US and Canadian) occupy a band of radio spectrum in the International Maritime band, allocated by the International Telecommunication Union (ITU), headquartered in Geneva, Switzerland, for world-wide maritime service. The ITU assigns radio spectrum worldwide to coordinate the efficient use of radio and avoid interference between national users of radio channels. In the United States and Canada, this band of radio spectrum channels is assigned world-wide for Maritime Mobile Service. The American Railroads industry, by World Administrative Radio Conference 1959 (WRAC-59) Footnote 287 (Since (WRC-2000, Appendix S18) of the Radio Regulations of the International Communications Union (ITU)), were granted an exception.[1]

Inland Waterways (Maritime Radio)

The Waterways Users Association (WUA) (made up of tugboat and barge operators, many owned by oil companies) wanted to expand their radio communications operations into the maritime band (Footnote 287) along the navigable rivers and inland waterways. (The band occupied in the United States and Canada railroads.) Needless to say, with current congestion in the railroad band, the WUA proposed operation would complicate railroad radio operations.

The WUA Notice of Proposed Rulemaking (NPR) was presented to the AAR by the FCC for comment. Because of his previous position as Director of Communications and Signals at the AAR and familiarity with FCC Rulemaking, the AAR requested the UPRR respond to the NPR. The AAR also recognized that the FCC gave greater weight to responses from users of spectrum than to the lobbying organization representing the industry.

The document submitted by the WUA was almost an inch thick. It contained studies monitoring the railroad usage of radio channels in addition to other documentation. In this manner the WUA attempted to demonstrate the underutilization of these channels by the railroads via periods of silence, thinking the silence could allow sharing of the channel, as is done in other services.

Mr. Robertson turned the NPR over to the Communication Engineer (Who questioned the short time for response) with instruction to submit reply comments and questions to the NPR filing within thirty days. Mr. Robertson said "the FCC feels that the radio spectrum user should be the most knowledgeable about their need and use of these services, and should be able to respond within the 30 day limit." He also advised that "requests for extension weakened the respondent's argument." [The above is paraphrased.]

The Union Pacific Railroad's response was made within the time limit and the Railroad Industry prevailed. Arguments made in the UPRR response to the NPR pointed to the **need for immediate access** to the radio channel for safety (silence did not mean the channel wasn't be used, only that it needed to be available for immediate access when required) and operational purposes. Radio operational rules, in shared services, required users avoid interfering with each other by monitoring the channel before transmitting. The response also attested to the impact on the assets of the railroad involved, including track, engines, and rail car equipment; other railroad facilities; the value of consumer products hauled over rail; and the safety risk to railroad employees and the general public of human life should the railroad industry be required to share the radio channels currently in use. Additionally, the costs to relocate to other radio channels for the industry were identified, both to equipment hardware and training of technicians.

Finding other channels available for such a move was next to impossible as it would be necessary, for technical reasons, to relocate the entire railroad band.

A major issue in defending the railroad argument pointed to the fact that the railroad industry had split radio channels several times from 60 KHZ to 30 KHZ to 15 KHZ to 7.5 KHZ, thereby expanding the number of radio channels available to the industry from within its allocated spectrum and the improved efficiency gained to the railroad industry without expand need for additional spectrum.

At that time, an article in the International Electrical and Electronic Engineers (IEEE) publication "Communications Transactions" was devoted to the Maritime Radio Service in the British Isles. The article highlighted the fact that the Maritime Radio service there had been split, doubling the number of channels available in their coastal waters. (Note exact article could not be found in research for this book, but the issue is verified in IEEE Transactions on Vehicular Technology, Vol.-25, NO. 4 August 1977, "European View of Automated VHF/UHF Radio Systems-Marine Spectrum Usage Alternatives and Trends, author J. D. Parker, Senior Member, IEEE, and may have been the document referenced.)

The number of channels currently available in the United States to the WUA had not been split. The UPRR argument was that, by following the British plan, the WUA could double their channel capacity and negate their need for use or sharing of the railroad channels.

The Union Pacific successfully defended against the Waterway Users Association's NPR request to share usage of the Appendix S18 channels with the railroad industry.

Personal Communications Service (PCS)

Many issues before the FCC involved the reallocation of radio spectrum. Defending the railroad industry spectrum was frequently given to the UPRR by the AAR, likely as the result of Mr. Robertson's previous experience.

Detailed discussion of the loss of the 2 GHZ microwave spectrum to the PCS industry is covered in **Appendix A** because of the complex issues presented. During the early '90s and continuing into 1995, the Personal Communications Services industry initially sought to share the Operational Fixed Microwave Services Band (made up of users including the Railroads, Pipelines, Utilities, Public Safety (Police, Firemen, etc.) and other users).

The original systems, they proposed, used low power spread spectrum portable radios communicating with base stations located on street corners on antenna poles 15 to 30 feet in height. The use planned was for **foot** traffic, since the low power and street corner base stations were not capable of frequent hand-off between radio base stations from vehicular traffic.

Recent interest in 5G cellular networks is focused on using street lamp posts for implementation. As this book is being written, cities are in discussions on how much to charge the cellular companies for rights to use these poles.

Initial interference tests of cellular radio equipment into 2 GHZ microwave were conducted at Orlando, Florida and Houston, Texas in 1991. The tests proved that the portable radios interfered with the 2 GHZ microwave reception.

Subsequently, the PCS industry changed their network design to the current-day PCS radios which included expansion beyond foot traffic into full mobile-radio personal communications.

While the Private Microwave System users continued to recommend other ways for the services to be furnished, the PCS industry remained focused on this specific band.

The Federal Communications Commission sided with the PCS users and determined they should have primary use of the band and delegating the Private Microwave System user to secondary, non-interfering status.

The FCC recommended moving these Operational Fixed Microwave Users to other non-defined bands. However, the PCS users were to pay for the current users' full costs to relocate.

The Union Pacific Railroad received compensation from the PCS industry for loss of many 2 GHZ microwave systems. Use of the 6 GHZ microwave band was used for many rearranged paths. This change of bands required the Union Pacific to construct higher towers for space diversity system to provide the same reliability the 2 GHZ systems inherently provided because of the differences in propagation. These changes occurred after the time period covered by this book.

Microwave Antennas

For reliable 6 GHz microwave design microwave diversity is necessary. Essencially two plans are available. Frequency diversity use by common carriers is not available to the private microwave service. Mr. Jett in his comments identified the limitation the FCC placed on private microwave systems of not allowing more than one 6 GHz on a given path. The alternate design for reliable microwave design is space diversity. Microwave channels tend to fade as proprogation conditions change. These changes vary with frequency; this is why common carriers use frequency diversity for reliable microwave service. Private carriers generally use space diversity on moderate to longer paths. This requires two microwave antennas at each end of the path spaced approximately 30 feet between them. This space varies dependent upon path length and path profile.

Two antennas for a 6GHz microwave path requires a taller tower and associated structural strengthing. Thus there is additional costs for this type of system. Fortunately the 2 GHz microwave path is not as susceptable to as great fading as the 6GHz microwave. A cross-band feed horn was only necessary on one of the two microwave antennas for the 2 GHz underbuild system. This required some costs of the equipment and installation labor, but avoided strengthing the tower.

Interface with Congress (Senate Universal Telephone Bill)

UPRR Communications Engineering was selected to respond for the railroad industry concerning a US Senate Universal Telephone Bill, S1660, 1983.

The Universal Telephone Bill was before the Senate Subcommittee on Communications. The bill, as written, provided an exception for right-of-way companies which had "continuous right-of-way." UPRR Communications Engineering reviewed the wording of the bill. The AAR legal consultants met with the Senate Subcommittee staff. Several iterations of the wording of the bill were reviewed, revised and resubmitted between the senate staff, the AAR legal consultants, and communications engineering.

The issue of "continuous" right-of-way was troubling to the UPRR Communications Engineering staff, there representing the railroad industry. Railroad right-of-way (as opposed to the track) isn't always continuous due to highway easements in place before construction of the railroad, and other real estate instruments which may rule the right-of-way. Also, communications pole lines may deviate from the right-of-way. Microwave systems, by the design, are not on continuous right-of-way, and usually are remote from the track.

Communications Engineering ultimately drafted a letter on September 16, 1983 to Senator Packwood for the AAR to be presented to his staff. In subcommittee discussions, Senator Goldwater wrote, "I didn't like it but didn't show for mark-up."

Besides the Telephone Bill itself, a colloquy prepared to accompany the Bill is a "sense of congress" should a challenge to the Bill be made before the courts. (A colloquy is considered verbal discussions (written down) between senators, which may or may not occur, to understand the issues for developing the resultant bill). The "Bill" and the "Colloquy" developed were perfected to the satisfaction to the Senate staff and Union Pacific Communications Engineering staff.

The ultimate result of this effort was negligible as the Universal Telephone Bill was tabled in the Senate. While the purposed Telephone Bill was tabled, it was important that the Union Pacific Communications Department engineering staff could review the proposal, avoiding the potential production of a Senate Bill which created operational or legal problems for the railroad.

World Administrative Radio Conference (WARC)

While Director of Communications for the Union Pacific, Robertson was the member of the staff serving the US Department of State's participation in the World Administrative Radio Conference. In this capacity, he represented the railroad industry in Geneva, Switzerland before WARC 1979. The International Telecommunications Union regulates the allotment of radio spectrum worldwide. It periodically conducts a conference to consider changes to spectrum allocation.

The railroad band of VHF radio channels occupies a band of spectrum within the international maritime spectrum allocation as described above. Continued allocation of this spectrum is vital to efficient railroad radio operations.

The United States is one nation with one vote in considerations before the Conference, so support by international representatives is required to protect this allocation of spectrum within the international maritime allotment. Lobbying of these international representatives (other nations' representatives) is vital to sustaining this allocation, as the exception only pertains to the US and Canada. Without considerable work and planning, these allocations could be lost to international maritime interests. Footnote 287 of the International Radio Regulations (IRR) is where the exception is noted.[2]

On March 20, 1991 the FCC issued General Docket 89-554 Subject "In the Matter of: An Inquiry Relating to Preparation for the International Telecommunications Union World Administrative Conference Dealing with Frequency Allocations in Certain Parts of the Spectrum." The FCC requested these comments in preparation to the World Administrative Radio Conference scheduled for February 3 to March 5, 1992 (WARC-92) in Spain. Again the Union Pacific Communications Department was selected to give a response in its name for the Association of American Railroads.

The issue concerned reallocation of the 1850-1990 MHZ microwave band to Mobile Satellite Service. The Union Pacific response, in opposition, was similar to the response to the PCS industry taking over the 2 GHZ band. Again it was pointed out the adverse impact on the railroad and the extent services of the railroad provided, and on the microwave services needed for efficient operation of the railroad as was previously given in the NOI 90-314.

The Inquiry was made prior to the final proposed NPR giving the same 2 GHZ microwave band to the PCS services.

The Union Pacific had responded to the Inquiry in April of 1991 defending the railroad's interest in the 1850-1990 MHZ band. However, with the FCC final determination to assign this band to the PCS services, the issue for the railroad became moot.

25

Consulting – Union Pacific Communications

Assisting a Union Pacific Information Technology Team Implement TCS and Yard Inventory Computer Program on Ferrocarilles Nacionales de Mexico

Guerdon Sines, Union Pacific Corporation Vice President of Information Technology, had a close relationship with the Ferrocarilles Nacionales de Mexico (FNM), the Mexican railroad. During his tenure with the Southern Pacific Railroad he served as a consultant to the FNM. In December 1989, FNM interest in the Union Pacific's Transportation Control System (TCS) resulted in the FNM inviting a team of Union Pacific's Information Technology personnel—including computer hardware and software persons, and communication engineers from the Union Pacific—to visit the FNM headquarters in Mexico City.

This initial visit led to discussions on developing a TCS plan for the Mexican railroad. The initial visit also led to further meetings with the FNM Communications Management to discuss communications support for implementation of TCS. An Agreement was signed on July 19, 1991 between the Union Pacific Technologies, the lead UP company, and the FNM to adapt the UP's TCS technology and provide technical support, training implementation, and project management assistance. The project had planned four phases; phase 1 was under development at the time of the signing. The system was renamed SICOTRA (Sistema de Control de Transporte) for implementation on the FNM, replacing the existing SCINCO system, and introducing many other new systems applications to the FNM.

As these discussions progressed, Union Pacific implementation of fiber optic cable installations on its rights-of-way led to revelation that certain US Fiber Optic companies and Telmex (the Mexican Telephone Company) were in discussion with FNM on potential use of FNM right-of-way.

Communications Department Review of FNM Communications Network

The FNM Communications and Signal Department management requested the Union Pacific review the FNM communications network and propose use of their right-of-way for fiber optic cables. An agreement was reached for the Union Pacific communications engineers to study and prepare a report on their communication network and offer advice on ways to improve the network and how the FNM could benefit by allowing the placement of the fiber optic cables on their right-of-way. The Union Pacific Communications group offered ways to proceed strategically with Telmex and the fiber cable companies' negotiations.

The Union Pacific communications study team ultimately issued a 139-page report in English and Spanish with many attachments. This report made detailed recommendations on the microwave system, the existing wireline network, VHF radio service, improvement in the use of the dispatchers radio service, expansion of the data systems, telemetry and control using UHF radio, network management, human resources, satellite services, and a fiber optic strategy to negotiate with fiber optic companies and implementation of fiber optic services[1].

Communications between the Union Pacific and Ferrocarilles Nacional de Mexico Railroads

With an agreement between UP Technologies and the FNM to implement TCS (SICOTRA), it became necessary for Union Pacific Technologies computer technicians to provide technical support to the FNM. To accomplish this support economically, it was decided to link the communications networks between the UPRR and the FNM. A voice and a data link to interface the FNM computer were established via a VSAT Terminal.

Where other communications services were inadequate, the FNM had a Satellite System linking their headquarters with railroad offices throughout Mexico. The FNM's satellite network used the Morelos I satellite for their satellite system. The footprint of the Morelos satellite extended into the southern United States. The availability of the Morelos I satellite footprint at a Union Pacific Communications office in San Antonio presented the Union Pacific with an opportunity to install a VSAT terminal and establish a communication link with the Ferrocarilles Nacional de Mexico Railroad.

The Union Pacific filed for and received an FCC satellite license and permission to establish an international communications link via the VSAT terminal, which the Union Pacific Communications Department installed next to their San Antonio communications office. Here, data and voice circuits were linked between the two facilities and direct voice and data circuits were established between Mexico City and St. Louis headquarters of Union Pacific Technologies. This was the first use of VSAT service on the Union Pacific. On March 19, 1992 VSAT service was established between St. Louis and Mexico City. Data service between the two was transmitted "counter to counter" on April 9, 1992. A Fairchild VSAT terminal was installed for this service.

The use of the VSAT communications aided Union Pacific Technology (UPT) personnel to provide FNM data network support for day to day issues, and data system (SICOTRA) upgrades. The satellite services avoided many trips to Mexico City by UPT support personnel. These services also aided the UP Communications engineers to coordinate many other issues between the two railroads, *i.e.* establishing printer service at Nuevo Laredo for Mexican custom officials to expedite railcar movement across the border.

At the author's retirement, these programs and services were serving the two railroads extremely well. However, Telmex avoided using the FNM rights-of-way at that time. It is believed that some use of railway right-of-way was subsequently used, but has not been verified at the time of publication.

Epilogue

Education of a Communications Engineer

Experience with the Union Pacific Communications Department was a learning opportunity.

Mr. C. Otis Jett, besides being a great engineer, was a brilliant teacher. During a period of expansion of computer services and communications technology to support railroad operations, he greatly expanded the Communications Department's operations and services.

Selling railroad management on funding expansion of communications facilities was not always an easy task. Pole lines and wire were expensive, but they were recognized as a traditional means to support operations.

Enlightened management was not always controlling the budget. E. H. Harriman (early in his career) and William Jeffers (late in his career) were not typical. At times funds were tight and very stingily released. In some years when excess cash remained, it was spent on facilities which the railroad knew would always be needed in the future, such as rail and tie plates.

Mr. Jett was very frugal in his spending for expansion of communications. For important equipment he choose the best; early carrier wire-line equipment was purchased from Western Electric Company, a Bell Telephone Corp. subsidiary. Some had also been purchased before his employment.

With the introduction of microwave, he purchased the best available, like Collins Radio microwave equipment. To economize the cost of constructing the system, he managed to stretch the funds by using truck batteries which were much cheaper than the standard communications stationary batteries. Rectifiers were purchased from scrap yards which were telephone company discards and were reconditioned in the communications shop.

Later, when he wished to expand his Private Branch Exchange network, in many cases replacing leased Bell Telephone Company PBXs, he found discarded telephone switching equipment in scrap yards. Some of the equipment was still in good condition; some of it had to be repaired before use. The equipment repaired by communications department technicians served as on-the-job training. Replacement of leased PBXs with Union Pacific-owned ones saved a considerable expense to the department and required additional technicians, which were then available to expand other services.

As a lawyer, Mr. Jett was aware of the legal rights he had to defend the railroad from encroachment of power lines, which caused harm to the Railroad's wire-line facilities. He got several states to require the power company to provide advance notice of construction plans, giving the railroad an opportunity to object to the construction and to accommodate the railroad interests mutually with the power company's interest. With this understanding, he was able to surrender Union Pacific rights to avoid harm to its communications facilities in exchange for funds used to build alternate communications facilities, many times microwave or radio.

Mr. Jett was a visionary seeing the right-of-way as an asset he could leverage for construction of communications facilities for a commercial communications common carrier venture. Due to circumstances beyond Mr. Jett's control, the project didn't develop; however, it laid the groundwork for future use of the right-of-way for placement of fiber optic cables, which were of great value to the railroad and the Communications Department.

Legally and professionally, Mr. Jett took an aggressive stance in attitude which benefitted the railroad beyond his influence as Superintendent of Communications. Examples include consultation by the Stoddard president on implementation of computer system[1] and other company issues not documented here.

Mr. Hugh M. Robertson provided education of the Communications Engineer in matters dealing with governmental bodies. He had experience as Director, Association of American Railroad's Communications and Signal Section, which represented the railroad industry before the Federal Railroad Administration and the Federal Communications Commission. He also served as President of the Land Mobile Communications Council, an organization of radio users which lobbied the FCC on distribution of radio channels and other radio user interest. Because of his experience at the AAR with government organizations, upon returning to the Union Pacific Railroad Mr. Robertson many times was chosen by the AAR to use his position with the Union Pacific to respond to Notice of Proposed Rulemaking (NPRs), which originated with those agencies.

He delegated this response to the Communications Engineer, with guidance, many times for the company and for the Association of American Railroads. Mr. Robertson taught that in dealing with governmental agencies, the affected user's voice was greater than a lobbying organization.

Mr. John L. Jorgenson, as Director and later Vice President of Management Information Services (MIS), required information, recommendations, or proposals submitted to him to be pointed and brief. He wanted these limited to a single page. On one occasion, the Communications Engineer had to use a sheet of legal paper to meet this requirement.

The Communications Engineer learned from many sources, especially from direct reports, whose needs, insights, and ideas educated him with knowledge he lacked until it being presented.

Throughout the Union Pacific there were individuals whose influence made impressions which further educated the Communications Engineer. The Agricultural Agent, who talked about harvesting tomatoes in the Central Valley of California was one such person. This Agent also aided in acquiring a microwave site in Montana, as the only Union Pacific employee the rancher respected. The Accounting Department Auditor, who counted sheep at Sun Valley Idaho…didn't know the Union Pacific owned sheep.

Appendix A

Move of Operational Fixed Microwave User from the 2GHZ band for Personal Communications Services

A Notice of Inquiry (NOI) which precedes the issuance of a Notice of Proposed Rulemaking (NPR) for reallocation of 2GHZ microwave spectrum to the Personal Communications Service (PCS) was forwarded to the UPRR Communications Engineering for a response. General Docket No. 90-314 was released June 28, 1990. By this NOI, the FCC began an investigation into the concept of using 2GHZ microwave spectrum, allocated to Private Right-of-Way Users, consisting of railroads, pipeline companies, and utility companies, for PCS co-shared usage.

Paragraph 9 of the NOI reads: "PCN America *(a petitioner, PCN America, Inc.)* request that the commission allocate the 1700-2300MHZ band for PCN. Under PCN America's proposal, PCNs would be digital cordless telephone radio networks with extensive service areas built on microcell technology..."

Success with early cell phone services and demand for expansion of these services resulted in a search for new spectrum.

Initially, the PCS users' association planned a micro-cell technology with the use of a low power portable spread spectrum radios and low power radio base stations. Part of the initial plan contemplated PCS radio base stations on Poles fifteen feet to thirty feet in height on each street corner, limited to foot traffic (mobiles in vehicles would move quickly from base to base on street corners). The argument planned on the sharing of this 2GHZ spectrum, with the belief that the PCS service user, with low power portables and base stations, wouldn't interfere with the 2GHZ microwave systems.

Paragraph 9 of the NOI reads: "We (FCC) request information on the technical feasibility of operating PCN-type services in the 1850-1990 MHZ band on a shared basis as proposed by PCN America and the effects such operation would have on existing and future microwave operations in the 1850-1990 MHZ bands...."

Referenced in the NOI, the FCC had previously issued experimental licenses for a series of tests to determine if interference would result. The tests were conducted in Florida (Orlando) and Texas (Dallas) by the United Telecommunications Council (UTC)—an association of utilities and other users of FCC-licensed private microwave impacted by the NOI.

Interested parties were required to furnish comments on or before October 1, 1990.

To address this NOI, the Union Pacific filed a response to the NOI on September 28, 1990, P.R. Docket 90-314. In response to questions raised by the FCC, the Union Pacific responded by describing the type of common carrier railroad service we provided, and the extent of service (23,000 miles of mainline and branch track in nineteen Western, Midwestern, and Southwestern states). We described the usage of Union Pacific microwave services in the 1850-1990 and 2110-2200 MHZ band, the number and length of paths, channels, and services, and undepreciated investment. We also estimated the cost to relocate our microwave service to another band at $130,000,000.

We further responded to "Reply Comments filed by PCN America Inc. to RM 7175 dated January 16, 1990, Pg. 18." The comments were based upon a study by a Dr. Shilling. In his study, Dr. Shilling considered issues with mis-described conditions in microwave systems which did not fully addressed the conditions encountered by the Union Pacific's, especially to average path lengths, propagations variations, number of PCN uses in proximity to our receive antennas, and the further adverse impact.

In seeking comments to the NOI, the FCC raised questions on the potential of the microwave licensees in the above bands to use other transmission media, such as fiber optics or satellite facilities.

The Orlando and Houston tests were conducted as planned. At the Houston test on April 5-10, 1991, Union Pacific representatives were present at portions of the tests in the persons of Larry Sailors and Dean Gragert. Their preliminary report indicted interference was observed by both digital and analog microwave terminals.

Variables in networks, such as number of mobiles in proximity to microwave receivers, was shown to cause interference into the microwave communication spectrum. The tests proved interference was unavoidable and sharing was not practical.

An EN BANC hearing was held in Washington DC on December 5, 1991. A representative of the Union Pacific Communications Department was present and made a number of observations which were submitted to the FCC in January 1992.

Tom Stanley, an FCC staff member, questioned a representative of the users group about the reliability of fiber optics. This was a non-issue as the FO cable design is not efficient for drop-and-insert services, especially where radio towers must also be constructed for radio services. FCC Commissioner Barret raised several important questions about expansion of PCS within their current bands to preserve the 2 GHZ band for existing Public Safety (and Fixed) Users. Mr. Craig O. McCaw replied that "nothing" prevented expansion within the current cellular bands.

Commissioner Duggan, meanwhile, made some very interesting remarks. He claimed: "Until this AM I was lulled in this area" and recommended PCS be used in metropolitan areas and fixed microwave user in rural areas." He went on to feel an obligation to public safety and users who were earlier moved from their 12GHZ bands for DBS (direct broadcast satellite). It was "not our intent" to keep moving fixed users to other bands.

"Mr. Stone of AT&T advised that the Bell Laboratories are experimenting at 6 GHZ. The Bell Laboratories feel that there is a potential advantage to implement PCS in the common carrier 6 GHZ band which is being vacated by common carriers."

Another comment was made that "The commission should give the Congress an opportunity to enact the Dingle bill ("Emerging Telecommunications Technologies Act of 1989" (H.R. 2965)), which should make spectrum available at the 1770-1850 MHZ for PCS services."

Additionally, the microwave system constraints involving moving mobile units to street corner base stations proved to be impracticable.

The NPR 90-314 PCS ruling proposed moving the Private Microwave Service users' bands (such as the 6GHZ) from the 2GHZ band. In the UPRR response to the NPR, Communications Engineering focused on the costs to relocate 2GHZ microwave systems to the 6GHZ band stating that, due to differences in propagation between the frequencies, to achieve the same reliability, microwave repeaters would need to be relocated or altered in place. Microwave towers would need to be replaced and/or strengthened and raised. Space diversity design changes would be needed with additional antennas and transmission lines to achieve the same reliability.

Installation of new 6GHZ microwave equipment would require new 6GHZ microwave test equipment, and training of technicians for the different technology. Needless to say, significant costs were introduced for former users forced to relocate their existing communications services.

The Private Operational Fixed Microwave Service Users were required to relocate to other microwave bands or services as summarized in the following FCC publications:

FCC Docket 95-197 dated April 25, 1996.

> *Relocation Rules Established in Emerging Technologies Docket 92-9 paragraph 3. In the First Report and Order and Third Notice of Proposed Rule Making in ET Docket No. 92-9, we reallocated the 1850-1990, 2110-2150, and 22160-2200 MHZ bands from private and common carrier fixed microwave services to emerging technology services. We also established procedures for 2 GHZ microwave incumbents to be relocated to available frequencies in higher bands or to*

other media, by encouraging incumbents to negotiate voluntary relocation agreements with emerging technology licensees or manufacturers of unlicensed devices when frequencies used by the incumbent are needed to implement the emerging technology. The ET First Report and Order stated that, should negotiations fail, the emerging technology licensee could request involuntary relocation of the incumbent, provided that the emerging technology service provider pays the cost of relocating the incumbent to a comparable facility.

Paragraph 5. Should the parties fail to reach an agreement during the mandatory negotiation period, the emerging technology provider may request involuntary relocation of the existing facility. Involuntary relocation provider requires that the emerging technology provider (1) guarantee payment of all costs of relocating the incumbent to a comparable facility; (2) complete all activities necessary for placing the new facilities into operation including engineering and frequency coordination; and (3) build and test the new microwave (or alternative) system. Once comparable facilities are made available to the incumbent microwave operator, the Commission will amend the 2 GHZ license of the incumbent to secondary status. After relocation, the microwave incumbent is entitled to a one-year trial period to determine whether the facilities are indeed comparable, and if they are not, the emerging technology licensee must remedy the defects or pay to relocate back to its former or equivalent 2GHZ frequency.

Modifications to the rule making continued for several years with minor modifications of the rule which addresses issue of payment by PCS licenses and the allocation of costs as other PCS licenses shared the earlier relocations cost in the future.

Appendix B

Miscellaneous Items in Jett's Five-Year Plan

Pole Line Moves to Joint Signal/ Communications and Retirements

Nebraska Division –

Work Order – Replace signal pole line with joint signal communications pole line Schuyler to Paddock, Nebraska.

Proposed Work – Study the costs of refurbishing wire line North Plate Branch O'Fallons to South Torrington a distance of 200 miles or replace with 2 GHZ microwave. The need for a study was unnecessary with the upgrade of the North Platte Branch with Project Yellow.

Wyoming Division –

Work Order – Replace communications line with joint signal and communications pole line Laramie and Green River in segments MP 566.6 to 571.5 and MP818.75 to MP 818.74. also other locations in WY MP 914 to MP 922, MP 605 to MP 614.

Proposed Work –

Idaho Division

Work Order – (1971) - Retire various communications pole lines between Salt Lake City and Pocatello ID.

Work Order – (1972) – Install conversation and dispatchers' circuits between Twin Falls and Pocatello and retire communications pole line.

Work Order – (1971) – Transfer communications wires and crossarms onto signal pole line and retire communications pole line.

Pocatello – Idaho Falls. All crossarms and open wire, except one pair (for train dispatching service), should be retired and removed from the pole line…by removing all extra wires and crossarms, and supporting one pair of wires on pole brackets this pole line could be retained in service for approximately five years or until decision is reached relative to transferring the remain circuit to the signal pole line.

Idaho Falls – Ashton. A study should be made at an early date to determine if justification exist to rebuild 51 miles of pole line to serve Ashton, Rigby, Rexburg, Sugar City and St. Anthony.

Shoshone – King Hills, ID – A joint communication/signal pole line should be constructed at a very early date. The communication pole line is in a much deteriorated condition, as maintenance has been deferred for years in the belief that the Signal Department would construct a new joint pole line soon and the communication open wires (four) and crossarm would be transferred onto the new pole line, and the communication poles and guys retired. Over 50% of the poles in this line are stubbed and constant fear exists that failure will occur at any time. Present communication pole line should not be repaired or rebuilt as cost would exceed cost of joint pole line.

Ketchum Branch. – The communication pole line on this branch is no longer required, as radio service for section forces is available from the main line radio stations. The lower half of this branch has radio coverage. This pole line should not be retired and removed until determination as made as to where the ID Power Company is constructing their 136Kv line to Ketchum In the event this power line, when constructed, causes interference to the voice communications circuits on this branch pole line, then the ID Power Company has agreed to pay the Railroad $40,000, which payment is made for the purpose of permitting the Railroad to retire pole line and use other means of communications in the event same is required.

Oregon Division

Work Order (1969). Between La Grande and Pendleton, Oregon. Retire communication poles, surplus crossarms and aerial wire from cable pole at La Grande, MP 290.10, to cable pole at Pendleton, MP 215.75. Transfer existing crossarms and aerial wire (two pairs) to signal pole line from HP 215.0 to MP 227.0. Work Order 1971 - La Grande to Lone Tree, OR - ML - Replace present signal pole line (35 poles per mile) with joint signal/communication pole line (40 poles per mile) between MP 289.0 and 296.0, and transfer communication crossarms and wires to pole line; retire existing communication pole line.

Proposed Work –

La Grande – Huntington Oregon. During the last several years between La Grande and Huntington, a joint communication/signal pole line has been constructed in several locations at the expense of the State of Oregon in connection with the construction of interstate highway. In those sections where separate pole lines still exist, both lines are in very deteriorated condition, as neither department has maintained their facilities, as each was planning on a joint pole line at an early date, Today, the construction of a joint communication/signal pole line is most urgent from Lone Pine to Huntington, excluding the sections recently constructed. Under present practice, the Signal Department constructs the new pole line, then the Communications Department transfers their open wire and crossarm onto the new poles and the communication pole line is retired.

Various Locations – The following listed Communications Department pole lines should be rehabilitated at an early date. Maintenance has been deferred due to urgency of other projects.

1. Albina to North Portland Tower.

2. Hinkle to Fish Lake via Ayer and Marengo

3. Joseph Branch (to MP 47.1)

4. Yakima Branch (Wallula to Richland Junction),

5. Tekoa Branch

6. Tucannon Branch.

7. Wallace Branch. It is doubtful if any of these pole lines will be replaced by microwave radio facilities in the foreseeable future. The rehabilitation of these pole lines should consist of: Replacing such poles, crossarms, guys and similar items where necessary; pulling slack and cutting out bad sleeves in the open wire; trimming trees and cutting brush where necessary.

Utah Division

Work Order (1971) Between Dry Lake and Garnet, Nevada — ML — Replace present signal pole line, 35 poles per mile, with a joint signal/ communications pole line between MP 356.0 (Apex) and MP 363.0 and transfer communications crossarms and wires to pole line; retire existing communications poles.

Work Order (1971) Between Salt Lake City, Utah and Pocatello, Idaho — Retire various Communications Department pole lines. Note: This work order authorizes the removal of surplus wires and crossarms on the Communications Department pole lines between Salt Lake City arid Ogden, Utah, also between Ogden and McCammon, Idaho. Further, it provides for rearrangement of communication wires on the joint Communications Department/ Signal Department pole line between McCammon and Pocatello. Work on this project has been deferred, as the Signal Department has requested a delay, as they advise they may wish to use some of the wires that are to be removed for their circuits. Follow up as to the Signal Department's plans should be made in July of 1973 and work progressed accordingly.

Proposed Work –

Las Vegas to Moapa, Nevada

Due to the deteriorated condition of both the Communications and Signal Departments' pole lines between Wann, MP 336.7, and Apex, MP 352.0, a new joint Communications Department Signal Department pole line (40 poles per mile) should be constructed by the Signal Department, The Communications Department can move their crossarm and wires onto this new joint pole line and retire the Communications Department poles and guys.

The Signal Department, between Apex, MP 352.0, and Garnet, MP 356,0, should rehabilitate their pole line to joint Communications/Signal Department standards. The Communication Department to move their crossarm and wires onto the new joint pole line and retire the Communications Department poles and guys.

Note: In connection with items (a) and (b) above, there is a good possibility that the Central Telephone Company (Las Vegas, NV) will desire to purchase the retired Communications Department pole line for $1.00 per pole plus $1.00 per pole per year for an encroachment permit between Wann, MP 337, and Dry Lake, MP 363.0, for their use to furnish their customers telephone service. (c) A new joint Communications/Signal Department pole line should be constructed from Dry Lake, MP 363.0, to Crestline, MP 493.7. A new joint pole line is presently constructed, to permit line changes, between 378.3 and MP 382.3. In this section, neither the Communications Department nor the Signal Department pole lines are in sufficiently good condition to permit consolidation. Both pole lines are presently so located that they are very difficult to maintain, as they are remote from the tracks and are up and down over the mountains. The new joint pole line should be constructed by the Signal Department close to the tracks, avoiding going over the mountains, using whichever side of the tracks that permits the best construction and easiest maintenance.

Salt Lake City – Reference Work Order 22314, paragraph (c) of this section. Plans are presently being formulated to utilize the Communications Department pole line between Salt Lake City and Clearfield, Utah (south end of the CTC pole line of the Signal Department from Ogden, Utah) for a joint Communication/signal pole line. The signal cross- arms and wires are to be transferred onto the communication pole line. Further, the Signal Department will use some of the excess communication crossarms and open wire. The Communications Department is to turn over to the Signal Department this section of pole line for maintenance. The Communications Department's requirements are for one cross—arm and two pairs of wires. The communication pole line is being used as it is in better condition than the signal pole line. Further, the signal pole line is too near to a high voltage power line (steel towers) of the Utah Power Company; therefore, the present location of the signal pole line would not be acceptable for communication facilities, Work Order Authority is being requested to start this work at an early date.

Cedar City Branch and Iron Mountain Branch, Utah, Discussion with the Utah Division Superintendent indicates that one pair of wires (copper) used for telephone service can be removed from Milford to Lund and thence to Cedar City. Further, that the Iron Mountain Branch communication pole line and wires can be retired. Such telephones as are left between Milford and Cedar City can be consolidated onto the one remaining circuit.

California Division

WORK ORDERS

The following listed Work Orders remain to be completed: Work Order (1966) Between Daggett, California and Las Vegas, Nevada. ML Retire communication system poles, anchors and guys, transfer crossarms and wires from communications pole line to signal pole line,

Note: This work is complete from Daggett, MP 158+0 (Santa Fe MP 737+16) to Erie, NV, MP 309+14. Approximately five miles of this work must be redone, as recently five track miles of wire (20 wire miles) in place was stolen by parties unknown. The line from MP 309+16 to MP 334+9, a distance of 25 miles, is yet to be completed. It is estimated that it will require an eight-man line crew about eight weeks to complete. Work should be completed prior to July 1, 1973.

Proposed Work –

The Communications Department outside plant facilities (cable and open-wire pole line) re in excellent condition between East Los Angeles and Riverside. The Communications Department pole line has been "turned over" to the Signal Department for maintenance, as they now have the primary interest and the Communications Department has only one crossarm and several wires on this line. Between Riverside and Daggett, the Communications Department has one pair of wires on the pole line of the AT&SF Railway, and the requirement for additional facilities are not foreseen. On completion of Work Order 40821 the Communications Department facilities will be entirely on the Signal Department pole line from Daggett to the Las Vegas office. The need for additional facilities other than those presently existent cannot be foreseen at this time.

Installation of Carrier Systems

Nebraska Division

Work Order (1972) Various Locations ML Install channel carrier equipment at Omaha, Grand Island and North Platte, NE; Cheyenne, Rawlins and Green River, WY.

Note: The work authorized by this work order is progressing well and is approximately 50% complete to date. Some delay in progressing this project will be experienced in the near future while a determination is made as to how to proceed, dependent on COIN II and the Central Readout of Hot Box Scanner programs. It is estimated that this project should be completed in December 1973. (This work was also authorized under the same work order on the Wyoming and Kansas Divisions with same description)

Work Order (1973) Various Locations — ML Install 45C terminals at Omaha and Columbus, NE, 45C repeater at Fremont, NE and associated equipment at Valley and Schuyler, NE

Idaho Division

Work Order (1972) Install mobile-tel radio stations at Lava Hot Springs, Alexander, Montpelier, Pegram, Idaho; Leefe and Oyster Ridge, Wyoming.

Note: It is anticipated that all radio stations will be in service by April 1, 1973.

Work Order (1972) Various Locations — Install dispatchers' radio at Lava Hot Springs and Pegram, Idaho with related channel equipment at Pocatello and Montpelier, Idaho.

Note: 1t is anticipated that all radio stations will be in service by April 1, 1973.

Work Order (1971) Various Locations - ML - Install channel carrier equipment at Pocatello and Alexander, Idaho and at Leefe, Wyoming; rearrange carrier equipment at Cokeville, Wyoming.

Note: It is anticipated that all radio stations will be in service by April 1, 1973.

Work Order (1972) Various Locations — Install dispatchers' radio at Lava Hot Springs and Pegram, ID with related channel equipment at Pocatello and Montpelier, ID.

Note: 1t is anticipated that all radio stations will be in service by April 1, 1973.

Work Order (1971) Various Locations - ML - Install channel carrier equipment at Pocatello and Alexander, Idaho and at Leefe, Wyoming; rearrange carrier equipment at Cokeville, Wyoming. Note: , It is anticipated that all radio stations will be in service by April 1, 1973.

(The above work orders installed shop prefabricated buildings at trackside radio sites at Lava Hot Springs, Alexander, Montpelier, Pegram ID and Leefe WY. Mobil-tel radios were added to dispatcher radios which were moved from wire-line control to the prefabricated buildings with carrier equipment installed for radio control channels for radio coverage of the Oregon Short Line Railroad Granger to McCammon ID. The radio installed at Oyster Ridge had the control extended from Kemmerer WY carrier equipment on a cable extended from the depot to the radio site.)

Microwave Projects - Divisions

Idaho Division

PROPOSED WORK

Pocatello to Montpelier, Idaho, Install a 2GHz microwave radio system between Montpelier and the Elkhorn microwave radio repeater site (Salt Lake City-Pocatello microwave radio system). Terminals at Montpelier and Elkhorn; repeaters at Georgetown, Soda Springs, Fish Creek and McCammon. Presently, the Communications Department has three physical open-wire circuits in service on which have been superimposed 19 voice telephone carrier channels no voice channels can be added; therefore, expansion of wire line voice communications is not possible, Further, like all open-wire pole lines, this line is subject to failures due to many causes at frequent intervals. Project was submitted for 1973 Budget but was rejected. Analysis of types of communications, dial voice channel, train dispatching voice channels, CTC coding, dispatchers' radio circuit and mobile telephone service indicates that a higher degree of reliability is required than is now provided.

Pocatello, Idaho to Butte, Montana. Install a 2GHz microwave radio system from Menan Butte repeater site to Butte, Montana. At the same time, provide microwave radio legs from main system to Dillon and Lima. When this microwave radio system is completed, train dispatchers' radio circuit and mobile-tel radio service can be provided. Further, if desirable, radio service for Maintenance of Way Department can be made available. The communication pole line should be retired, copper wire salvaged for sale as junk, and good crossarms salvaged for reuse. The poles should be sold to outsiders, or if sale is not possible, cut down the poles and haul off the right of way. The cost of rehabilitating this pole line for 10 or more years of service is not economically justifiable. Cost will be in excess of $1000 per mile.

Nampa to Boise, Id. Install 2 GHz microwave system from Lucky Peak Microwave site to Boise. No additional voice channels can be provided on railroad facilities to Nampa. This project was proposed for the 1973 budget but was rejected. Later as documented in the book this project was installed, however the microwave path was from Squaw Butte to Boise as the original plan was not supportable to the lower "H" fixture adjacent a remolded container, in lieu of the Boise Depot bell tower.

Nampa-Snowbank-Cascade, Idaho. Replace present 960MHz microwave radio equipment with solid-state type. Present equipment is over 10 years old and requires too much maintenance to retain in service at an isolated location such as Snowbank. Furthers present electronic tube-type radio used for train dispatching and mobile-telephone service at Snowbank should also be replaced with solid-state type equipment. Install second-hand 5KW emergency electric generator at Snowbank to protect against electric power failure. Also, operate new solid-state equipment from storage batteries. *(Snowbank, Idaho is a remote mountain-top radio site. It is locate in a building owned by the State of Idaho adjacent a FAA radio site. Winter access is via a road plowed by the FAA because of the need for government technicians to access to their manned radar site. At times access is limited to snowcat operation after frequent snow storms. This project was approved as a work order and installed as recommended in 1973.)*

Oregon Division

Work Order (1971) Various Locations — Bend Branch and Portland, Oregon — ML — Install microwave radio system between Haystack and Bend, Oregon on the Bend Branch and Portland, Oregon Main Line for Bonneville Power Administration,

Note: This project is now under construction, all material is on hand, Estimated in-service date about early May 1973 with closeout in July 1973 accounts. Completion of this project will provide Maupin, Madras, Redmond and the Bend Traffic Office with direct connections to the Albina telephone PBX, also party–line telephone service to the joint stations at Metolius and Bend.

Work Order (1972) Spokane International Railroad Between Black Mountain and Bonners Ferry, Idaho - Install microwave radio system and VHF radio stations at various locations. Retire communication pole line and wire line radio stations.

Note: This project has been completed, except for the installation of the Black Mountain—to-Eastport microwave radio link and the retiring of the pole line. It was necessary to discontinue work on this project due to bad roads and deep snow. On completion of the microwave radio link into Eastport, the pole line can be dismantled and retired. It will be necessary to retain the last three miles of this pole line at Eastport, as a direct microwave radio path cannot be economically established to the Eastport Depot. Therefore, communication circuits (voice and data) from the microwave radio station to the Eastport Depot will be *via* wire line and carrier. Further, the Pacific Gas Transmission Company desires to also use this portion of the pole line for their circuits under a lease arrangement. Estimate completion in early August of 1973.

It is proposed to sell certain portions of this retired pole line to outside companies at $1.00 or more per pole. The buyer will obtain an encroachment permit at $1.00 per pole per year from the Oregon Division. These sales are to be consummated after the copper wire is removed, unless buyer is willing to pay salvage value for copper wire left on pole line. The balance of the pole line will be removed from the railroad right of way. The Railroad has an option to purchase the Black Mountain microwave radio site from the Pacific Gas Transmission Company for $8,000. This option should be exercised at the earliest date possible. The electric power company supplying power to the Black Mountain site is charging an excessive amount for power. Investigation should be made as to how the rate can be lowered. It may be desirable to construct Railroad—owned power line.

Utah Division

PROPOSED WORK

Caliente, Nevada — A low density microwave radio system is desirable into Caliente to provide more reliable communication facilities than are now available--especially with the open—wire pole line needing rehabilitation. This microwave radio leg should extend from either the Enterprise or Morman Mesa repeater stations, Use of microwave radio facilities would permit eliminating one or two pair of wires on the Communications Department pole line between Las Vegas and Milford, together with a 12—channel carrier system between Las Vegas and Caliente. *(A 2GHZ microwave system was constructed into Caliente from Arrow Canyon to a site at Ella Mountain to Caliente via a shop built passive reflector outside of Caliente.)*

California Division

PROPOSED WORK

Los Angeles — The baseband of the Los Angeles—Sierra Peak microwave radio channel is now filled to capacity. It is a "high band," 24-channel assignment. Efforts should be made to obtain, as soon as possible, a "low band," 300-channel assignment so that room for expansion will be available at a future date. This effort should be started at once, as microwave radio channel assignments are becoming more difficult to obtain by the day. *(This upgrade from a "high band" 2GHZ 24 channel microwave to a "low band" 2GHZ 300 channel microwave was accomplished).*

Miscellaneous Communications Work

Oregon Division

Seattle, Washington — Plans are being developed to retire the Seattle Union Station and move all the present occupants to other locations. The Communications Office, together with the unattended telephone PBX, will move to space in the Argo Yard Office, either into existing space or into space in the new addition.

In connection with the move of the present Communications Office, no new or additional facilities will be involved; therefore, all charges should be to Operating Expense (Account 247).

The present unattended telephone PBX is installed in a trailer. On completion of a new telephone PBX in the new Communications Office, this portable telephone PBX should be retired. It was provided under a separate work order as a temporary expediency until a permanent unit could be installed. A work order will be required for the permanently—installed 200—line unattended telephone PBX in the Argo Office.

As a part of the installation of the telephone PBX in the Argo Yard, all leased (from local telephone company) key systems should be replaced by Railroad—owned units. This replacement is economically justifiable, as the sayings by elimination of lease will pay for the facilities in a very short time.

One very serious problem will arise in moving the Communications Office out of the Union Station to the Argo Yard. The problem is, how will interconnect with the Burlington Northern at their King Street Station be achieved? The Union Pacific has an interest or ownership to the extent of 60 voice telephone channels in the microwave radio system of the Burlington Northern between Portland, Oregon and Seattle, Washington. The terminal equipment for this system is located in the King Street Station. Presently, two cables about 2000—feet long connect the Communications Office of the Burlington Northern in the King Street Station to the Union Pacific's Office in the Union Station. By extending these cables to the Argo Communications Office, a distance of about four miles, service could be continued; however, this problem has now become exceedingly complex. Recently, the Burlington Northern announced that they were going to construct a twin tower, 16-story office building near the north end of the Alaskan Way, opposite the park. Informally, advice has been received that on completion of this new office building, the Burlington Northern Communications Office and all the equipment therein will move to the new building. It will be physically impossible *for* the Union Pacific to extend cable facilities to the Burlington Northern's new office building. Even if a route could be established, the cost would be prohibitive; further, the timing of the moves could not be coordinated

There is a solution to this problem that will be little, if any, more expensive than installing cable between the Argo Yard Office location of the Communications Office and the Burlington Northern's office in the King Street Station. Further, the timing of the move will be independent of the Burlington Northern's plans.

1. Construct a 2GHz microwave radio system from the Argo Communications Office to Centralia. This system would involve two repeaters and two terminals. Repeaters would be located at Highland Park (Seattle) and Fife Heights (Tacoma); terminals at Argo and Capitol Peak. An adequate microwave radio link already exists from Capitol Peak to Centralia.
2. Interface the Burlington Northern at Centralia, where facilities are already existent for such connections,
3. In connection with the installation of this microwave radio system, the two VHF base radio stations (dispatcher and mobile—telephone) would be moved from a point near Black River Junction to the new Highland Park location. This will eliminate annual rental for the base stations and provide improved radio coverage of the Seattle area.
4. At Tacoma, the dispatchers' VHF base radio station located at Point Defiance should he moved to the Fife Heights repeater site, which move will eliminate annual rental for the VHF radio station site and rental to the telephone company for a control circuit to this station and, further, provide much better coverage.
5. Installation of this microwave radio system Centralia—Seattle) should be progressed immediately so that it may be placed in service at the time of the move to Argo Yard. Further, when the Union Pacific-owned microwave radio system is placed in service, payments to the Burlington

Northern for use of their facilities can be discontinued. This payment consists of maintenance charges, interest on investments, etc.

6. A second—hand, six—channel microwave radio system should be installed between the Fife Heights repeater site and the Tacoma Freight Depot. This installation will provide improved service to the various offices of the Railroad located in the Tacoma area.

   (i) The addition of a microwave radio repeater at a site above Kelso, Washington on a hill to the east would then permit the Union Pacific to have its own microwave radio system from Seattle to Portland. This would permit complete independence from the Burlington Northern and eliminate any further payments on their microwave system.

If this repeater is provided, a six—channel system should be installed from this repeater (Kelso) to the Railroad's Longview Traffic Office.

Presently, the Burlington Northern could, if they so desired, monitor all conversations to Union Pacific offices in Longview, Centralia, Tacoma and Seattle.

It is definitely recommended that serious consideration be given to the foregoing proposal, as future years' savings will be material and communication facilities between Portland and Seattle can be easily and economically expanded independently of the Burlington Northern.

System

Oregon, Utah, California Divisions

Work Orders (1972) Various Locations Install 10-KW generators, air conditioning and electric heating units at various microwave radio stations. Retire existing 5-KW generators *at miscellaneous locations across the microwave system, propane heaters replaced with combination electric heating and air conditioning system. The increased electric load requires replacement of 5-KW generators with 12 KW generators (in lieu of 10 KW). Eastern District was previously upgraded as above).*

Idaho Division

Work Order (1972) Various Locations - Install air conditioning and electric heating units in microwave radio stations at Magna, Willard and Garland, Utah and air conditioning unit only at Twin Falls, Mountain Home and Menan Butte, Idaho.

Note: This project will be started on the Idaho Division in June of 1973 and should be completed in that month. Waiting on material for Mountain Home site. *(Unlike the above installation of Heating and A/C systems in Oregon, Utah, and California these sites already have 12KW generators.)*

Appendix C

The development of the FCC Railroad Radio Service And Assignment of Frequencies to the Railroad Industry

> "In early 1945 the railroads met with the Federal Communications Commission and requested an allocation of a band of frequencies in the 158-162 megacycle portion of the spectrum. The railroads were assigned 60 channels with 60 kilocycle separation between each channel. In 1949...they reduced the number of channels to 39, however, keeping the same 60 kilocycle spacing between channels. These channels were then allocated to the various railroads throughout the nation on an area basis. The Union Pacific was allocated a number of these channels. On consulting the several leading manufacturers of radio equipment for use in this portion of the radio frequency spectrum, we decided that it would be much to our advantage to arrange to secure our frequencies in the middle of the band, spaced on alternate frequencies or channels."[1]

On January 16, 1945, the Federal Communications issued a report bearing the title "In the Matter of Allocations of Frequencies to the Various Classes of Non-Government Services in the Radio

Spectrum from 10 Kilocycles to 30,000,000 Kilocycles" (Docket No. 6651).

This report lists proposed allocation of radio channels to the railroads.

The report concluded that carrier current radio (Inductive Radio) is not a practical solution for communications needs of the railroad industry.

Railroad Radio Will Contribute to Safety.

The Commission is convinced that a properly engineered railroad radio service will contribute to the safety of life and property both in preventing rail accidents and in reducing the seriousness of injury and damage after accidents by permitting the prompt summoning of aid to the scene of an accident.

Railroad Radio will Benefit Public.

Establishment of the railroad radio service will contribute to the safety and efficiency of these public utilities which play so important role in our national life will result in a direct benefit to the public.

The Railroads Should Make Prompt Use of the Frequencies allocated.

At the time of the hearings in this proceeding, 58 separate class II experimental stations have been authorized for experimentation. **Proposed Allocation.** 100-200 megacycles, 88 channels were requested for railroad use. (The request detailed the specific use of these channels).

Other channels were requested below 3 megacycles and above 1000 megacycles.[2]

On May 17, 1945, the Federal Communications Commission announced its final frequency allocations for non-government radio services in the portion of the spectrum between 25 and 30,000 Megacycle with the exception of the 44 to 108 megacycle region of the spectrum. (The FM Broadcast Band).

The railroad industry was allocated channels in the 25 Mc and 162 Mc band on a Non-Sharing basis. Specifically 152 to 162 Mc. Non-Govt. Fixed and Mobile Note 7 – On the basis of an average channel width of 60 kc. Railroads 60 channels[3].

The Communications Section of the Association of American Railroads issued an explanatory letter to member roads dated June 8, 1945 explaining the FCC's decision concerning the 60 KC channel width. It also explained the uses of End-to-End, Yard and Terminal Communications, and the flexibility in assignment of use. I identified the frequencies by railro9ad extend from 158.4 mc. to 162.0 mc., and frequency No. 1 will be 158.43 Kc. No. 2 will be 158.490 kc. And so on at intervals of 60 kc. Frequency No. 60 being 161.970 kc[4].

In response to a petition filed with the FCC on June 1, 1945, railroad employees will not be required to hold a radio operators license for radio equipment installed by the railroad. This ruling was issued by FCC Order No. 126. Certain provision s were included in the Order requiring the railroad to include an examination given by the railroad to railroad employees on the rules adopted and published "Attached Railroad Radio General and Operating Rules"(by the FCC). The complete rules were included as "**General and Operating Rules**"[5].

On November 15, the FCC announced establishment of the Railroad Radio Service effective December 31, 1945. A hearing on the needs for radio communications on railroads was held by the Commission in September 1944. On the basis of this hearing, the Commission allocated channels for such purpose in it is Frequency Allocation Report of May 25, 1945 (May 17 above). In the ruling the FCC identified the specific 60 frequencies allocated to the railroad industry. They also included specific requirements for eligibility, application procedures, and technical standards including modulation, emission frequency stability and input power. Operating Specifications and Scope of Service, along with records to be kept, tests required, station identification and identification of who may operate the stations. By this ruling the FCC standardized the Railroad Radio Service and its operation[6].

During the years following the establishment of the Railroad Radio Service and the formalizing of frequencies and standards, the railway industry was pressing for the expansion of radio channels beyond the original 80 channels allocated. At a hearing before the FCC in November of 1947 Mr. L. J. Prendergast superintendent of communications for the Baltimore & Ohio Railroad representing the Association of American Railroads said that the 60 frequencies allocated for train communications could constitute only 30 usable channels and will not provide enough frequencies for all railroad yard and terminal services in congested areas such as New York and Chicago. He outlined a need for 34 in these areas within the next three years and 85 channels will be required within 10 years. The FCC itself found that the railroads would ultimately need 53 channels for yard and terminal service. The issue revolved around the potential interference between adjacent channels operated in nearby proximity[7].

However, by July 1948, the FCC was proposing to take away nineteen radio frequencies, leaving the Railroad Radio Service with only forty-one channels to work with. That lead several railroads, the Association of American Railroads, and the American Short Line Railroad Association to file objections[8]. The AAR pointed out that the Railroad Radio Service had only been in existence for two-and-one-half years. It conceded that the railroad installations may not have progressed as rapidly as those in some other radio services. The AAR pointed out a number of factors "which militate strongly against rapid installation of railroad radio communications on a large scale."

"One such factor was listed as the lack of incentive for manufacturers to develop "highly specialized" equipment to meet railroads needs when they could maintain full production of equipment "of less exciting requirements" for other mobile services". Also mentioned was the unfavorable post-war financial situation of the railroads, and the dieselization programs which prompted many roads to delay ordering and installing radio equipment until new diesel-electric locomotives were delivered.

The AAR said there was "every reason to believe" that progress on railroad radio installations "will be much more rapid during the next few years" if carriers "are assured of the availability to them of the necessary frequencies." The AAR indicated that "approximately $15,000,000" will be spent by the railroads of radio equipment during the next three years[9].

The rail industry had strong opposition to the loss of frequencies, which was voiced by many railroads and manufacturers before the FCC in hearings during the weeks of October 3-16, 1948. Many issues and arguments were made in the presentations before the agency, concluding in identifying the expansion in railroad radio authorizations and equipment installations. Among other things, the AAR charged that the development of the use of radio by the railroads was "probably set back" as the result of the "unsympathetic attitude shown by the predecessor of the FCC toward such use. "There is every reason to believe that it will retard still further if this commission goes forward with its present proposal." The AAR counsel to the FCC that the railroads came out of World War II with a large part of their equipment and other facilities "sadly in need" of replacement or rehabilitation at a cost of several billions of dollars over the next few years.

Many other railroads and manufacturers made presentations during the hearing, concluding in Mr. Harry Ockershauser representing the General Railway Signal Company, asserting that the proper equipment has not been developed "to provide operation with 60 kc channel separation. It appears that further development work must be done. It is our opinion that such equipment will not be available for installation for several years[10]."

The reduction in frequencies under the FCC's order went into effect on July 1, 1949. Leading into the implementation of the order, "the Communications Section of the AAR issued a list of the authorizations which the FCC has made to the railroads to use radio. This list includes installations already in service, as reported in our annual statistical issue each January, as well as FCC authorizations for proposed installations, as reported currently each month in our news columns. The Communications Section list includes 73 land stations and 907 mobile units in road train service; 136 fixed stations and 1,324 mobile units in yard and terminal service; and 5 fixed stations and 129 portable units in railroad utility service. The railroads have not been able to carry all these projects to completion promptly because of numerous problems encountered in apply radio communications equipment on locomotives and cabooses[11]."

This development of statistical information became the basis for filing before the FCC to vacate the proposed loss of nineteen frequencies. The filing was submitted on May 26, 1949 and shortly afterward withdrawn. "The withdrawal petition said that the petitioners did not wish to be understood as admitting the adequacies of the frequency allocations to the Railroad Radio Service under the commission's order, or as wavering their rights to seek the allocation of such additional frequencies as their needs may require[12].

The FCC, on June 29, 1949, "dismissed without prejudice" the petition of May 26, 1949 of the railroads and the AAR[13].

Motorola Inc. announced that "technical limitations influencing radio operations in the 25 to 30 and 152 to 162 mc. bands have been overcome in two-way communications equipment the recently perfected." "New equipment designed for these frequencies was recently demonstrated in a special showing for engineers in the communications field at the company's headquarters in Chicago."

"The Chicago demonstrations made by Motorola provided four transmitters working on four adjacent channels. The test stations were operated separately, in pairs, and as three stations in combination, to simulate every possible situation found in practical broadcasting. All transmitters were held within the bandwidth of the assigned frequency by instantaneous deviation control, Motorola development which was designed in accordance with the new FCC rules.

"The receivers operated on four adjacent channels during these tests, and were designed for extreme selectivity, providing complete rejection of unwanted signals. "Intermodulation within the receiver itself has also been overcome[14]." The selectivity achieved in the new receive, used with VHF transmitters specially designed with low spurious emission to keep signals in channel, was shown to make possible clear reception on the four adjacent channels, even in vehicles lined up side by side[15].

"Means of doubling available FM-frequency channels for mobile radio communications, without increasing frequency allocations, were successfully demonstrated in tests conducted in Camden, NJ recently by the Engineering Products Department of the Radio Corporation of America. Observers included engineers of the FCC and the US Army signal Corp. and representatives of public utility transportation industries.

During the past year (1949), improvements in radio technology resulted in the FCC removing radio frequencies. "Under this arrangement the railroads now have for use in the Chicago area 41 frequencies, 49 of which are also available for use in other areas. In addition, during the year several manufacturers announced production of a new line of so called highly-selective mobile radio equipment for adjacent channel operation. With this technical limitation lifted, allocation of frequencies will be more flexible, although probably require some equipment changes[17]." (

During late 1949 and 1950, the railroad industry made moderate installations of yard and road radio systems. In 1949 there were 132 locomotive radios installed, 75 caboose radios, and 81 fixed stations. 1950 saw 205 locomotive radios, 183 caboose radios and 29 fixed stations. The railroad industry limited installations because of the newness of the technology, limitations of the channel spacing, and the anticipated development on the horizon of narrow band radios. Yard radio systems were on a similar increase, 1949 saw 129 locomotive radios and 21 fixed stations; 1950 saw 188 locomotive radios and 54 fixed stations.

1951 saw rapid expansion of railroad road radio systems, with 615 locomotives, and 926 caboose radios installed and 95 fixed stations. Yard radio installations saw some moderate increases also with 253 locomotives, and 50 fixed stations. Expansion of road radio continued increase with over 800 locomotive radios being installed annually through 1958. Caboose radios fluctuated between 400 and 600 being installed annually. Fixed stations also fluctuated between 80 and 175. Yard radio installations stabilized around low to mid 400s locomotives and 100 to 125 fixed stations.

The editor of *Railway Signaling and Communications* questioned, "Will radio become standard equipment on locomotives?" He answered it himself: "Yes! And for the simple reason that for its low proportionate cost (less than one percent of the price of a diesel locomotive unit), radio greatly increases the utilization of a locomotive[18]."

The technology reported on in 1949 resulted in the FCC incorporating it in the FCC Docket No. 11253, the so-called "Split Channel" docket released in the spring of 1956 after several alternative solutions to channel congestion were eliminated. In mid-April, The Office of Defense Mobilization, issued a statement that: "National security, and the needs of air navigation and air communications, precludes the release for non-government use of any of the very high frequencies not utilized by the federal government[19]." (Railway Signaling and Communications, June 1956, Pg. 39).

FCC docket No. 11992 provided for 23 primary frequencies on 60 Kc spacing, and 22 secondary frequencies interleaved at 30 Kc from the primary frequencies along with 46 tertiary frequencies at 15 Kc spacing[20]. The docket was made effective April 1, 1958[21]. The FCC further clarified the split channel issue in Docket No. 12295 with effective date August 1, 1958, which established engineering information needed to support license request for channels and stated that all stations must meet all requirements of narrow band standards stated in Docket No. 11253 by November 1, 1963[22].

Acknowledgments

My son Fred asked if he could write the foreword for this book. I had not considered having a foreword for the book for no particular reason. His offer was quickly accepted. What developed is a personal statement that went well beyond what I expected; it certainly defines me. I appreciate his comments which choke me up. Most importantly, the personal comments about me as a husband and father, demonstrates, I believe, the most important things that defines my life.

A special thanks to these four people and the Communications Department retirees lunch group:

Jack Baird, who added and corrected information on PBX installations, and the Universal Numbering Plan.

Jim Kilby, whom I met at DoSpace (an Omaha organization which assists people in computer technology and education), helped in my quest to convert correspondence files from MS Works to MS Word.

John Larsen, grandson of Director of Communications Bob Brenneman, my boss who, by identifying an article that his grandfather wrote in the *Railway Signaling and Communications Journal*, opened up a whole new world in the history of the subject, which was subsequently researched and incorporated into this book.

Brian Brundige, Director of the Railway Education Bureau in Omaha (a subsidiary of Simmons-Boardman Publishing Company), who made file copies of the parent company's publishing works available for research which had not been digitized.

Several research resources assisted in development of this book.

The Library of Congress, which made available information on old newspapers, and assisted in locating other information included in this book.

The Nebraska Historical Society, especially Andrea Faling, both of which assisted in furnishing information on several leaders of the Union Pacific Telegraph Department and links to their impact on the telephone industry in NE and other western states,.

The Omaha Public Library, which assisted in development of information on Edward Creighton.

The University of Nebraska Library, which furnished information from the Library of Congress on the Union Pacific Railroad and telegraphy.

The Omaha World Herald, for information on the UPRR.

The Babel Haithi Trust Digital Library, for files on the telegraph industry.

Others:

Jeanne Ahern Dempsey, who furnished biographical data on her father, Michael Ahern (a General Director Communications).

Virginia Brenneman, who furnished biographical information on her husband Bob Brenneman and family discussions, which led to her grandson John Larsen furnishing the information described above.

The Union Pacific Museum, which furnished several pictures used in this book.

University of Southern CA, which furnished information located by the Library of Congress.

Simmons-Boardman Publishing Company, for use of information from their publications. Namely, *The Signal Engineer, Railway Signaling, Railway Signaling and Communications, Railway System Controls, Telegraph Age, Telegraph and Telephone Age,* and *Railway Age.*

Metropolitan Community College, which provided courses in "How to Write a Book" by Sandra Wendel. "How to Publish a Book" and "How to Market a Book" by Lisa Pelto.

John W. Barriger III National Railroad Library within the St. Louis Mercantile Library at the University of Missouri – St. Louis for information on Union Pacific's use of teletype equipment.

The Teletype Corporation, for information on the Union Pacific Railroad company.

Ed Kemp, for directing me to report by theAAR before the National Telecommunications Commission on the subject of WRC-2000 footnote S18.

Brad Zielie, for use of pictures he took at Bear Ranch Hill, CA.

And moral support from the Union Pacific Communications Department retirees lunch group, namely: Don Allison, Virginia Brenneman, Bob Hague, Dan Maher, Jim and Barb May, Pete and Nadeen Palmer, Craig Johnson, Gerry Pilakowski, Leo and Jane Rau, Dave "Ozzie" Nelson, Bill Buhrman, Ed Furman, Larry Kopiaz, Scott Kinyon, Steve Jensen, Jerry Tichacek, Paul Blain, Dana Messerschmidt, Rod Bilderback, Dale Dress, Anil Bhalla and my son Steve Kuhn, a retired senior signal manager, whose presence was requested by some of these men who knew him for having worked with him.

This group of former engineers and managers of the Communications Department were very smart and talented group persons I ever worked with. Each of them has had their own experiences about which they can write their own book.

I wish to acknowledge and thank my editor, Thalia Sutton of Des Moines, IA for the review, editorial corrections and valuable suggestions and especially her challenges to improve documentation and expansion of details which improved the quality of the book.

Author Profile

Gene H Kuhn

As stated in the "Preface," I wrote the book to identify the leadership of the Union Pacific Communications Department and preserve the events and issues faced by these leaders. Mr. Jett's General comments at the beginning of his "Five Year Plan" inspired me to research further into the history of the Communications Department. When Mr. Jett interviewed me, for potential hiring we discussed communications technology and his current efforts to enter into commercial communications services with several railroads for a nation-wide communications network based on using high capacity coaxial cables on railroad right-of-way.

At that time I was an Assistant Communication and Signals engineer with the Norfolk and Western Railway. Mr. Jett offered me the lead in building this network on the Union Pacific Railroad if I came to the railroad. While the venture fell through as related in Chapter 16, the introduction to the use of fiber optic cables on railroad-of-way, and implementation of railroad service in these cable was one of my principle assignments in later years, as Director Telecommunications Transmission.

I was born in St. Louis Missouri at the depth of the depression in 1930, which I believed influenced me in the value of a dollar. When of age I joined the Boy Scouts of America and developed enjoyment of camping and fishing. My first paycheck was in the communications industry. At age 14 I delivered telephone books. I received one-half cent for each book delivered, and one and one-half cent for each old book recovered. The mechanical telephone exchanges of that era had a limit of the number of calls which could be handled at one time. Thus it was important to get incorrect telephone numbers out of their books.

I graduated as an Industrial Engineer from St. Louis University. After serving two years with the United States Air Force, I took a job with Southwestern Bell Telephone Company in a training program where I learned all phases of the telephone industry, and worked in several capacities as an outside plant facilities engineer, telephone switching engineer and as a transmission engineer.

I went to work for the Wabash Railroad which later merged with the Norfolk and Western Railroad, in the position described. The railroad had just left the telegraph era and entering the expanded communications era using voice carrier systems and communications systems with greater communications capacity such as microwave. The railroad industry presented many opportunities for introduction of new communication technologies. For example the Wabash Railroad had limited use of two way radios on road locomotives when I started. A couple of yards did have radio equipped locomotives, and associated base station radios.

I was hired as a staff engineer, a term never used before or since until they determine how to use me. Shortly after I was hired, a supervisor at Salt Lake died, and another was promoted from Salt Lake to replace a retiree in the Omaha office. I was asked if I would consider taking a job in the Salt Lake office because of the unanticipated changes.w

After serving in the Salt Lake office with assignments across the railroad, I was moved to Pocatello with principle responsibility for railroad communications throughout the state of Idaho.

With Mr. Jett's retirement and Mr. Brenneman's Promotion to Director, I was promoted to Manager of Communications in Omaha in April 1974.

With reorganization of the Communications Department under Mr. Jorgenson with the Computer Department I was promoted to Asst. Director Communications Engineering and Planning, in

December 1978. Merger the three railroads saw my promotion to Asst. Director Communications, in December 1982 and later to Director Communications Engineering. With introduction of fiber optics, I was appointed Director Telecommunications Transmission February 1984.

I retired in December 31, 1992, in that capacity to live a very fruitful life. I later did some consulting work in communications for the South African Railroads, the Mexican Railroads and a Midwestern Railroad.

Bibliography

Key to Abbreviations

The following abbreviations for cited sources – Principally trade journals - are used through the notes:

OBD, *Omaha Daily Bee or Sunday Bee*

OWH, *Omaha World Herald*

JETT , Jett, C. O., Five Year Plan, Communications Department Union Pacific Railroad, , May, 1973

JT, *Journal of Telegraph*

RA, *Railway Age,* Simmons-Broadman Company

RS, *Railway Signaling and Communications,* Simmons-Broadman Company

RS&C, *Railway Signaling and Communications,* Simmons-Broadman Company

RSC, *Railway Signals Controls,* Simmons-Broadman Company

SE, *Signal Engineer,* Simmons – Broadman Company

TA, *The Telegraph Age,* Simmons-Broadman Company

TG, *The Telegrapher*

TTA, *Telegraph and Telephone Age,* Simmons-Broadman Company

WIKI, *Wikipedia*

WP, *Washington Post*

Footnotes

PREFACE

1 Klein, Maury *Union Pacific - The Birth of a Railroad 1862-1893*, 337-338

CHAPTER 1

Railroad Communications Industry Summary

   4 TG, Jan. 1868, 155.

   5 WIKI,, Russian American Telegraph.

   6 TG, July 2, 1868, 154.

   7 ODB, Feb. 10, 1888, 2.

   8 Klein, Maury, *Union Pacific The Rebirth 1894-1969*, 28

   9 TA, Jan. 1, 1903, 3.

 10 TA, Jan. 1, 1902, 14.

 11 TA, June 1, 1902, 232.

 12 TA, Jan. 1, 1906, 9.

 13 TA, June 16, 1906, 271-272, Aug. 16 1906, 380-381.

 14 Klein, Maury, *Union Pacific the Rebirth 1894-1969*, 64.

 15 TA, July 16, 1902, 289-291.

 16 TA, Mar. 1, 1902, 97

 17 TA, Jan. 1, 1901, 14.

 18 Ibid.

 19 16, TA, Mar. 1, 1902, 97 ,

 20 17, TA, July 16, 1902, 299-300.

 21 18, TA, Jan. 1, 1903, 29.

 22 19, TA, Feb. 16, 1906, 68

 23 20, TA, May 16, 1903, 248

 24 21, TA, May 19, 1906 224.

 25 TA, Sep. 1, 1906, 420.

 26 23, TA, Nov. 1, 1906, 550

 27 TA, Jan. 1, 1909, 57.

 28 Ibid, 58.

29 TA, Apr. 1, 1909, 259-262, Apr 16, 285-288.

30 TTA, Jan. 1, 1910, 57.

31 TTA, July 16, 1911, 504-505.

32 29, TTA, Dec. 1, 1914, 651-652.

33 30, TTA, Jan. 1, 1910, 57.

34 TTA, Feb. 1, 1910, 130.

35 TTA, Mar. 15, 1915 134-136

36 TTA, Aug. 1, 1919, 384.

37 TTA, Jan. 1, 1913, 25.

38 TTA, Dec. 16, 1913, 752.

39 TTA, Mar. 1, 1915, 120

40 TTA, Mar. 1, 1921, 111-112.

41 RS, Jan. 1925, 32.

42 RS, Oct. 1929, 373.

43 RSE, Oct. 1922, 408.

44 RSE, Jan. 1922, 2.

45 RS, Jun. 1925, 237

46 RSE, Dec. 1922, 491-495.

47 RSE, Jan. 1923, 1.

48 RS, Jun. 1925, 237.

49 RS, Sep. 1935, 496.

50 RS, July 1936, 372.

51 RS, Sep. 1936, 494.

52 RS, Sep. 1937, 540.

53 RS, Oct. 1937, 585-588.

54 Ibid, 589-590.

55 RS, Jan. 1944, 26.

56 RS, Jan. 1943, 27.

57 RS, Oct. 1944, 557-558.

58 RS, Nov. 1943, 590.

59 RS, Jan. 1945, 47.

60 RS, Oct. 1944, 561-571.

61 RS, Feb. 1945, 107-110.
62 RS, Jan. 1946, 68
63 RS, Mar. 1946, 220
64 RS, Jan. 1948, 28.
65 Ibid.
66 RS&C, Oct. 1949, 681-683.
67 Ibid, 692.
68 RS&C, Jan. 1949, 58.
69 RS&C, Oct. 1949, 692.
70 RS&C, Jan. 1950, 23.
71 RS&C, Jan. 1951, 30.
72 RS&C, Jan. 1952, 41-43.
73 RS&C, Jan. 1953, 39.
74 RS&C, Jan. 1957, 29.
75 RS&C, Jan. 1958, 22-27, Nov. 1958, 25-29.
76 RS&C, Jan. 1956, 38, 68.
77 RS&C, Oct. 1959, 22-24.
78 RS&C, Jan. 1955, 29.
79 RS&C, Jan. 1962, 16.
80 Ibid, 18.
81 RS&C, Jan. 1961, 18
82 RS&C, Jan. 1963, 19.
83 WP, Dec. 2, 1982.
84 RS&C, Jan 1963, 20
85 RA, Jan. 1985, 31-33.
86 RA, May 1985, 23.

Chapter 2

Telegraph/Communications Department Leaders

87 Burkley, *The Faded Frontier*, 296.,
88 Ibid.
89 Ibid.

90   *Chicago Tribune*, May 11, 1869.

91   Ibid.

92   *Salt Lake Daily Telegraph*, Sep. 7, 1869.

93   Tents of Golden Spike National Historical Society – VI Appendices 158.

94   *Chicago Tribune*, May 11, 1869.

95   He reported as an eyewitness in a *Southern Pacific Bulletin* May 1927.

96   Comments developed from two publications, ""*Driving the Last Spike at Promontory, 1869* by J. N. Bowman from California Historical Society Quarterly, Vol. XXXVI No. 2 June 1957"; "*Tents of golden Spike National Historical Society* – VI Appendices 158-159".

97   JT, VOL.1, Dec. 2, 1867.

98   TT, Sep. 25, 1869, Letter dated Sep. 5, 1869.

99   ODB, Dec, 1885.

100 TA, Jan. 1903, 285.

101 ODB, Sept. 14, 1892, Also Article by Hall 50 Years of Telephone History Quoting Korty, *Telephony* July 31,1926, 16-19, Nebraska Historical Society.

102 TTA, VOL. 39 part 1921 357 re Korty.

103 Ibid

104 ODB Oct. 1911.

105 TA, Aug. 1, 1909, 553-556.

106 TTA, June 16, 1913, 386

107 TTA, Apr. 16, 1910, 285.

108 TTA, July 1911, 465.

109 ODB, Nov. 5, 1911.

110 ODB July 30, 1914.

111 ODB Aug. 13, 1914.

112 Klein, Maury, *Union Pacific the Rebirth* 1894-1969, 504

113 ODB, Nov. 5, 1911.

114 RS&C, Jan. 1921 to Jan1926, Statistics developed from January edition over the period.

115 TTA,Oct. 1919.

116 RS, Sep. 17, 1925 and Oct. 27, 1927.

117 JETT

118 RS, July 1936, 372.

119 Klein, Maury, *Union Pacific the Rebirth* 1894-1969, 504-505.

120 RA, VOL. 110, 548.

121 Klein, Maury, *Union Pacific the Rebirth* 1894-1969, 506

122 OWH, Jan. 1, 1939.

123 Internal UP Correspondence.

124 RS, June 1942, 328.

125 OWH, May 29, 1942.

126 Klein, Maury, *Union Pacific the Rebirth* 1894-1969, 506.

127 Ibid.

128 RS&C, Oct. 1951, 714.

129 RS&C, Mar. 1957, 70.

130 RS&C Jun. 1958, 40.

131 OWH, Jan. 29, 1978.

132 RS, Sept. 1946, 620.

133 Klein, Maury, Union Pacific the Rebirth 1894-1969, 506

134 Ibid.

135 RS&C, Feb. 1961, 34.

136 Klein, Maury, *Union Pacific the Rebirth* 1894-1969, 506

137 Interview with Mrs. Virginia Brenneman, wife.

138 Progressive Railroading, Sept. 1974.

139 RS&C Dec. 1955, 26-27

140 RS&C Feb. 1957, 30, 32, 51

141 RS&C, Various publications over the period.

142 RS&C, Sep. 1973, 33.

143 RS&C, Various publications over the period.

144 Progressive Railroading, May 1979, 31.

145 Ibid.

146 Email from daughter Jeanne Ahern Dempsey, May 1, 2017.

Chapter 3

Constructions Transcontinental Telegraph

1   Western Union History of Pole Lines 1912.

2   First Telegraph Line across the Continent – Charles Brown's 1861 Diary – Edited by Dennis N. Mihelich and James , , , , E. Potter – Lincoln State Historical Society Books – Lincoln page 12.

3   Ibid.

4   Ibid.

Chapter 4

Union Pacific Telegraph and Related Telegraph Companies

1   Wikipedia.

2   Western Union History of Pole Lines 1912.

3   Klein, Maury, The Life and Legend of Jay Gould, Pg 141, and Klein, Maury, The Birth of a Railroad 1862-1893 pgs. 337.

4   Klein, Maury, The Birth of a Railroad 1862-1893 pgs. 337.

5   Ibid.

6   TG, Vol. VIII no. 63, Nov. 2, 1872.

7   Klein, Maury, The Life and Legend of Jay Gould, Pg 141.

8   Klein, Maury, The Birth of a Railroad 1862-1893 pgs. 337

9   Ibid.

Chapter 5

Judicial and Legislative Government Actions

10   *Nebraska Advertiser*, Brownsville Dec. 8, 1870.

11   OBD, Jan. 21, 1873

1   *New York Times*, Apr. 5, 1880.

2   OBD, Mar. 12, 1883.

3   OBD, Dec. 26, 1884.

4   OBD, May 27, 1884.

5   OBD, Mar. 12, 1885.

6   OBD, Jan. 19, 1888.
7   OBD, Jan. 30, 1889.
8   OBD, Nov. 19, 1895.
9   WH, June 27, 1909.
10 Inter office memo UPRR, July 29, 1968.

Chapter 6,
TECHNICAL ISSUES ON OPERATION OF POLE LINES

1   Western Union History of Pole Lines 1912.
2   Klein, Maury, The Birth of a Railroad 1862-1893, p. 221.
3   RS&C, Aug. 1955, p. 40.

Chapter 7
Carrier Telephone and Telegraph

1   Carrier Current Telephony and Telegraphy – E. H. Colpitts and O. B. Blackwell - Presented at the 9th, Midwinter Convention of the American Institute of Electrical Engineer, New York, N. Y., February 17, 1921

Chapter 8
Union Pacific Railroad Officials Involvement in Nebraska Telephone History

1   Hall, Charles E., *Telephony*, Fifty Years of Telephone History, July 31, 1926, p. 18

2   Vanden Berge, Peter Nicholas, The History of the Telephone in Nebraska, 1877-1912, His thesis for the Graduate College of the University of Nebraska, Lincoln, NE. May 27, 1938 pg. 15.

3   ODB, Aug. 4, 1887, p. 2

4   Wikipedia, Elisha Gray and Alexander G. Bell, Telephone Controversy

5   Vanden Berge, Peter Nicholas, The History of the Telephone in Nebraska, 1877-1912 His thesis for the Graduate College of the University of Nebraska, Lincoln, NE. May 27, 1938 pg. 16.

6   Vail, Theo. National Bell Telephone Co. Letter of Apr. 15, 1879 to Louis H. Korty, Collection of Nebraska Historical Society.

7   Paraphrased from Hall, Charles E., *Telephony*, Fifty Years of Telephone History, July 31, 1926, p. 18

8   Vanden Berge, Peter Nicholas, The History of the Telephone in Nebraska, 1877-1912 His thesis for the Graduate College of the University of Nebraska, Lincoln, NE. May 27, 1938 pg. 16.

9   Vail, Theo. National Bell Telephone Co. Letter of Apr. 18, 1879 to Louis H. Korty, Collection of Nebraska Historical Society.

10   OBD, Oct. 3, 1879

11   OWH, June 4, 1933 p. 24

12   Vanden Berge, Peter Nicholas, The History of the Telephone in Nebraska, 1877-1912 His thesis for the Graduate College of the University of Nebraska, Lincoln, NE. May 27, 1938 pg. 17.

13   Ibid. p 20

14   Ibid

15   TTA, Aug. 1, 1910 p. 527.

16   Ibid.

17   TTA, Feb. 16, 1915, p. 90, April 1, 1915, p. 151.

18   Picture of William M. Jeffers, Telegraph Operator Sidney NE age 20 became UP President, Courtesy UP Museum.

19   TTA, Jan. 1, 1911, p. 19.

20   RS, June 1942, p. 328.

Chapter 9

Early UP Telephone Service

1   Kratvile, William, Railroads of Omaha and Council Bluffs, Arcadia Publishing Co. 2001, p. 15.

2   OWH, July, 10, 1904

3   OWH, July 31, 1904

4   TA, Apr 1909, p. 287.

5   TA, VOL. 24, Nov. 1, 1906.

6   TA, Jan. 1, 1909, p. 58.

7   TA, May 1, 1910, p 323.

8   TA, Feb. 16, 1911, p. 171.

9   TA, June 16, 1909, p. 424-425.

10   TA, Jan. 1, 1909, p. 58

11   TTA, For months and years quoted.

12   TTA, Apr. 16, 1910 p. 285,

13   TTA, Apr. 16, 1910 p. 285, May 1, 1910, p. 285-322 with breaks.

14   JETT,

15   RS, Jan. 1924, p. 34-35.

16   Ibid

17   Klein, Maury, The Birth of a Railroad 1862-1893 pgs. 49.

18   Ibid, p. 52.

19   Ibid, p. 53.

20   Ibid, p. 61

21   Ibid, p. 64.

22   Tucker, D. G., Electrical Engineers, Proceedings of the Institution, Volume 121, Issue: 12.

23   OWH, Dec. 24, 1899.

24   Carrier Current Telephony and Telegraphy – E. H. Colpitts and O. B. Blackwell - Presented at the 9th Midwinter Convention of the American Institute of Electrical Engineers, New York, N. Y.; February 17, 1921.

25   JETT.

26   OBD, Nov. 5, 1911.

27   Ibid. Aug. 13, 1914

28   RS&C, VOL. 14, 1921 p. 306.

29   RS, Oct. 1929, p. 373.

30   RSE, Jan. Jan. 1921, p. 28-29.

31   Ibid.

32   RSE, Jan. 1924-1926 Issues.

33   RS, 1926, 1926 p. 290.

34   Klein, Maury, The Birth of a Railroad 1862-1893 p. 505-506.

35   RA, VOL. 110, p. 548.

36   Klein, Maury, The Birth of a Railroad 1862-1893 p. 506.

37   OWH, Jan 1, 1939.

38   RS, Feb. 1939, p. 104.

39   Copy of Memorandum of conference held at Omaha, November 25 and 26, 1941, dated Nov. 26, 1941, in Authors File.

40 RS&C, Aug. 1942.

41 RS&C, Nov. 1945, p. 784.

42 RS&C, Sep. 1950, p. 574.

43 RS&C, Feb. 1961, p. 34.

44 OBD, Nov. 5, 1911.

45 Copy of "Memorandum of conference held at Omaha, November 25 and 26, 1941", dated Nov. 26, 1941, in Authors File.

46 Copy of Telegram addressed to FAC OMA, from GRV. SA, Mar. 3, 1942, in Authors Files.

47 Jett, C. O. AIEE Summer General Meeting, Paper 60-815, Wire Line Carrier Communications on the Union Pacific Railroad", June 19-24, 1960.

48 RS&C, Jan. 1942 – Jan. 1957 issues.

49 RS&C, Jan. 1946-Jan. 1961.

50 OMW, May 29, 1942.

51 RS&C, June, 1956 p. 48.

52 RS&C, July 1956, p. 24-29.

Chapter 10

Early Radio Experiments and Developments

1 TA, Oct. 16, 1909, p 737.

2 TA, May 16, 1910, p. 357

3 T&TA, Jan. 1, 1914, p. 25

4 SE, March 1911, p. 87.

5 Klein, the Rebirth, p. 504

6 Documents in Authors File.

7 Millener, Dr. Frederick H., Paper "RADIO COMMUNICATION WITH MOVING TRAINS, Presented before the Institute of Radio Engineers, New York, December 5, 1917).

8 Klein, the Rebirth, p 504.

Chapter 11,

Jett Era and influence

1   RS&C, Jun. 1959, p. 29-31
2   RS&C, Jan 1949, p. 22
3   RS&C, Mar. 1949, p. 169-177
4   RS&C, Jan. 1949, p. 54
5   RS&C, Jun. 1953, p. 416-419
6   RS&C, Jan. 1954, p. 50
7   RS&C, Mar. 1954, p. 46-50
8   RS&C, Jan. 1955, p. 24-29
9   Ibid.
10 RS&C, Jan. 1956, p. 34-38.
11 Ibid.
12 RS&C, Apr. 1956, p. 34-35.
13 RS&C, Jan. 1951, p. 24-29.
14 Ibid.
15 RS&C, Jan. 1958, p. 35-40
16 Ibid.
17 Ibid.
18 RS&C, Jan.1960, p. 24-28.
19 RS&C, Jun. 1959, p.416-419.
20 RSC, Jun. 1972, p. 7
21 Ibid.
22 Ibid.
23 Author's Files
24 JETT.
25 Ibid.
26 Ibid.
27 TA, VOL. 224 Nov. 1, 1906.

28 American Railway Association, The invention of the Track Circuit, Signals Section, 1922.

29 RS&C, Mar. 1958, p. 67-68.

30 UTAHRAIL.NET, publication – Intermountain Power Project (IPP), Jan 21, 2019.

CHAPTER 12

Private Branch Exchanges PBX and the Jett Era and Influence

1. OWH, July 31, 1904.
2. OBD, Nov, 1911.
3. RS&C, Mar. 1956, p. 27.
4. RS&C, May 1956, p.76.
5. RS&C, Feb. 1960, p. 40.
6. JETT.
7. Baird, J. B. email April 28, 2017.

CHAPTER 13

Radio Systems In The Jett Era And Influence

1. RS, Dec. 1947, p. 796-798, Paraphrased.
2. RS, Mar. 1946, P. 220.
3. RS, Jan. 1947, p 28-29.
4. OWH, Dec. 7, 1947, p. 8.
5. RS, Oct. 1947, p. 626-630.
6. Jett, C. O., paper "FROM PONY EXPRESS TO MILE LONG TRAINS," presented to the Chicago Section of the Institute of Radio Engineers, November 18, 1949.
7. RS, July 1947, p. 431-434.
8. RS, Nov. 1947, p 727.
9. RS&C, Mar. 1949, p. 169-177.
10. RS&C, Aug. 1949 p. 524.
11. RS&C, Dec. 1951, 873-874.
12. RS&C, Jan. 1952, p. 64.
13. RS&C, Sep. 1953, p. 624-626.
14. RS&C, Dec. 1953, p. 894-896.
15. RS&C, Dec. 1955, p.26-27.
16. RS&C, Mar. 1956, p. 60
17. RS&C, January edition of year following installation year listed.

CHAPTER 14

Communications Shop and the
Jett Era and Influence

1   OWH, Nov. 15, 1942.

2   RS&C, Feb. 1957, p. 47

3   RA, Feb. 1985, p. 27-30

4   Ibid.

CHAPTER 15

The Rise of Computers and Real Time
Reporting in the Jett Era and Influence

1   Teletype Corp. paper "Union Pacific Railroad Company recently "streamlined" its coast-to-coast Teletype com communications" 1949, Quoting G. R. Van Eaton.

2   RSE, Jan. 1921, p. 25.,

3   RS&C. VOL. 19, 1926 p. 29.

4   JETT.

5   Teletype Corp. Publications "The Teletype Story", 1957.

6   Ibid.

7   RS&C, Dec. 1950, p. 795-796.

8   Teletype Corp. paper "Union Pacific Railroad Company recently "streamlined" its coast-to-coast Teletype communications" 1949, Quoting G. R. Van Eaton.

9   Klein, the Rebirth, p 507,

10 RS&C, Jan. 1958, p.22-27

11 Ibid.

12 Klein, the Rebirth, p 503-501

13 IBM, J. Develop. VOL. 25 NO, 5 September 1981 "IBM Data Communications: A Quarter Century of Evolution and Progress, Authors David R. Jarema, Edward H. Susenguth, Pg 393.

14 RS, Feb.1974, p15-20

15 JETT

16 Jett, Speech + Paper,

17 RS&C, Jan. 1958, p 22

18   IBM, J. Develop. Vol. 25 NO, 5 September 1981 "IBM Data Communications: A Quarter Century of Evolution and Progress, Authors David R. Jarema, Edward H. Susenguth, Pg 393.

19   RSC, Feb. 1973, p 14.

CHAPTER 16

Expansion of Telecommunications and the Jett Era and Influnece

1 RSC, Dec. 1970, p. 27-28, HVDC comments are paraphrased.

2 RSC, Jun. 1972, p. 7.

3 UTAHRAIL.NET, publication – Intermountain Power Project (IPP), Jan 21, 2019.,

4 Proudfit, G. J., Special Representative (VPO), internal correspondence to Mr. Bailey, December 13, 1968.

Chapter 17

MoPac WP and UPRR Merger

1   Merger Handbook, A Summary of Mergers of Union Pacific, Missouri Pacific, Western Pacific, p. 2-3.

2   RA, Feb. 1986, p. 23.

3   Ibid.

Chapter 18

Fiber Optic Cable and Construction Planning

1   RA, Oct. 1984, p 22

Chapter 19

Dispatcher Office Consolidations

1   RA, March 1988, p. 556-557

Chapter 20

Multipoint Distribution Radio Systems and Elimination of Pole Lines on Union Pacific

1   Authors paper entitled "Multipoint Radio Utilization of the UPRR", Presented at the AAR C&S Section Western Regional Meeting in Omaha, May 8, 1991.

Chapter 21

Advanced Technology

1   RA, June 1984, p. 21.

2   RA, May 1985, p. 23.

3   RA, Jan. 1987, p. 43.

4   RA, May 2018, p. 21

Chapter 22

Solar Power Systems and Wind Generators

Chapter 23

UPRR Subsidiary Communication Expansion

1   Citgo.com website.

2   UPRR.com website.

Chapter 24

Government Relations Interface with FCC and Other Governmental Agencies

1   Filing of the AAR before the United States Department of Commerce, National Telecommunications Administration, June 8, 2001.

2   *Progressive Railroading*, May 1979, p. 32.

Chapter 25

Consulting

1 Ferrocarilles Nacional de Mexico Systems Plan.

Epilogue

1 Klein, Maury, Union Pacific the Rebirth 1894-1969, 503-509

Appendix A

Move of Operational Fixed Microwave Users from 2GHZ Band for Personal , Communication Services PCS Rulings on 2GHZ Microwave Band

Appendix B

Miscellaneous Items in Jett's 5 Year Plan

Appendix C

The Development of the FCC Railroad Radio Service and Assignment of Frequencies to the Railroad Industry

1 Jett, C.O. Paper from Pony Express to Mile Long Trains – Presented to the Chicago Section of the Institute of Radio Engineers, Nov. 18, 1949).

2 RS, Feb. 1945, 107-110

3 RS, June 1945, 384-385.

4 RS July 1945, 481-482.

5 RS Sept. 1945, 593-595.

6 RS Dec. 1945, 849-851.

7 RS Jan. 1948, 27.

8 RS July 1948, 432.

9 RS Aug. 1948, 497.

10 RS Nov. 1948.

11 RS&C June 1949, 385.

12 RS&C July 1949, 441.
13 RS&C Aug. 1949, 522.
14 RS&C July 1949, 462.
15 RS&C July 1949, 464.
16 RS&C July 1949, 462.
17 RS&C July 1950, 23.
18 RS&C July 1955, 26.
19 RS&C June 1956, 39.
20 RS&C June 1957, 46
21 RS&C Mar. 1958, 55.
22 RS&C Sept. 1958, 62.

PHOTO GALLERY

John J. Dickey
Superintendent Telegraph,
Sept. 5, 1869–Aug. 1, 1887.
Photo courtesy Find a Grave

Louis H. Korty
Superintendent Telegraph,
Aug. 1, 1887 – 1908, Photo
courtesy Nebraska History
Museum

Hugh M. Robertson
Director Communications
Jan. 1, 1976–1981
Photo courtesy Progressive
Railroading

C. Otis Jett
Superintendent Communications
1965–June 30, 1973
Photo courtesy Virginia
Brenneman

John B. Sheldon
Superintendent
Oct. 22, 1911–July 29, 1914
Photo courtesy *Daily Bee*

Frank A. Coulter
Superintendent Telegraph
Jan. 1, 1939–May, 29, 1942
Photo courtesy Railway Age

Peter F. Frenzer,
Superintendent Telegraph
Aug. 13, 1914–Dec. 31, 1938.
Source is the Nebraska
Historical Society.

Robert H. Brenneman,
Director Communications
July 1, 1973–Dec. 30, 1975
Photo courtesy Virginia
Brenneman

Glen R. Van Eaton,
Superintendent Telegraph
May 29, 1942–1965 Exact
Date not determined Photo
Courtesy Railway Signaling

Building Telegraph Line Weber Canyon,
Courtesy UP Museum

Esther Rowland, Telegraph Operator, Gibbon NE,
Courtesy UP Museum

William M. Jeffers Telegraph Operator, Sidney NE Age 20 became President UPRR, Courtesy UP Museum

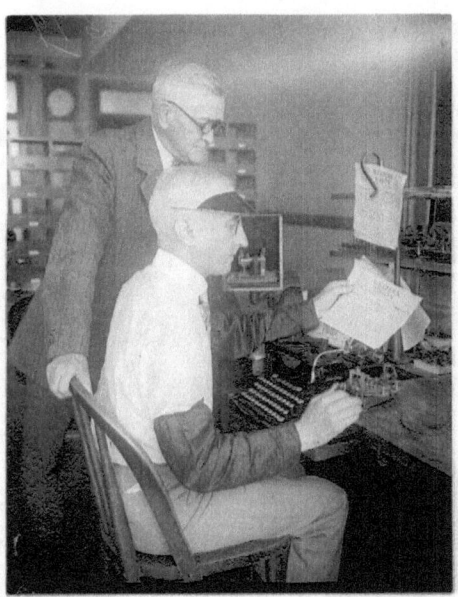

Telegraph Operator with Western Union Telegraph 1929, Courtesy UP Museum

Switchman using Portable Radio (Lunch Box) Armstrong Yard, Kansas City KS, Courtesy UP Museum

Locomotive Engineer using Business Dispatcher Radio, Courtesy UP Museum

> L.H. Korty,
> Omaha.
>
> 18 April 1879
>
> My dear Sir, I will have sent to you as soon as possible a couple full sets of our instruments in order that you may exhibit them, and shew their work. I wrote Mr Dickey to day in regard to the switch board and apparatus to be used in connection with the Exchange. I think it would be well to let our Mr Watson supervise the construction of the apparatus for your central office system, as he can bring to bear upon it an experience of over two years.
>
> Very truly yrs.
> Theo N Vail
> Gn

Vail Letter to Korty, Shipping two telephones and recommending Watson install swbd Apr. 15, 1879, Courtesy Nebraska Historical Society

THE NATIONAL BELL TELEPHONE CO.

Louis M. Korty.
Omaha. Neb.

Boston, 15 April.

My dear Sir,

I enclose your appointment as Agent as made with M Madden. It is affording me more than usual pleasure in doing so, for I had some fears that Omaha would not avail herself of the advantages of our system for some time to come, and, remembering all associations I had more than usual desire to see Omaha for Trusting you will succeed.

I Am. Faithfully,
Theo N Vail

Vail Letter to Korty, Appointing Korty as Bell Agent to install Bell equipment Apr 15, 1879, Courtesy Nebraska Historical Society

Omaha Electric Co.

Boston, May 12th 187_

Dear Sir.

Yours of May 6th rec'd. I am glad to hear that Omaha Electric Company has organ[ized] and I am sure with the list of stock holders that you give opposite will simply be impossible.

Please let us have your probable orders as far in advance as possible, so that we may no[t] delay you, and before orderin[g] your Switch board for the central office I would advise you to co[r]respond with Mr. Watson as we have a very simple pr[i]n[ciple], and o[ne] by which it is possible to run [a] Central office very expeditious[ly] and economically.

Trusting to hear from y[ou] soon,

I am Yours,
Theo. Vail

Mr. L. H. Korty,
Omaha. Neb:

Vail Letter to Korty, Re: Organizing Omaha Electric Co May 12, 1879,
Courtesy Nebraska Historical Society

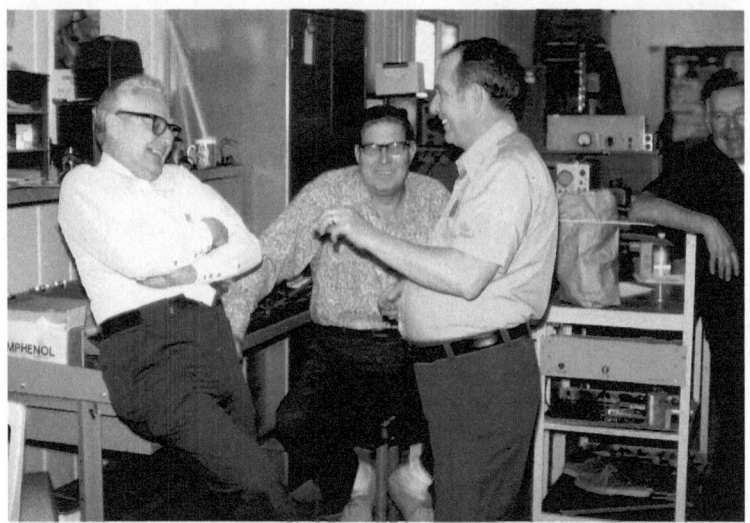

Bob Brenneman's Retirement Party December 15, 1975, Frank Pankiewz, Don Goranson, sequentially Shop Foremen, Jack Freelin, Groundman at Right, Author's Photo

Woodall Ridge, ID, Radio Repeater & Solar Power, First Use of Solar Power by Communications Department, Author's Photo

Sand Pass M/W Site North of Reno NV in Buried Vault, Author's Photo

Bear Mountain MAS Radio Repeater Site near Keddie CA, Photo by Brad Zielie, UP Communications Engineer

Caliente, NV 16'x12'
Passive Reflector
in Assembled in
Communications Shop,
Author's Photo

Oyster Ridge, WY Shop Built
32' x 32' Passive Repeater
Above Kemmerer WY,
Author's Photo

MCI Inspection Special Reno to Denver, July 12-14, 1989, Locomotive View, Author's Photo

MCI Inspection Special Reno to Denver, July 12-14, 1989, Observation Car View, Author's Photo

Western Pacific Wire Line Floating on Barrels Southside of Great Salt Lake UT, Photo by Jerry Chatwin, UP Construction Engineer

Flash II M/W Site Near Barstow CA, Author's Photo

Kelso CA M/W Site, Author's Photo

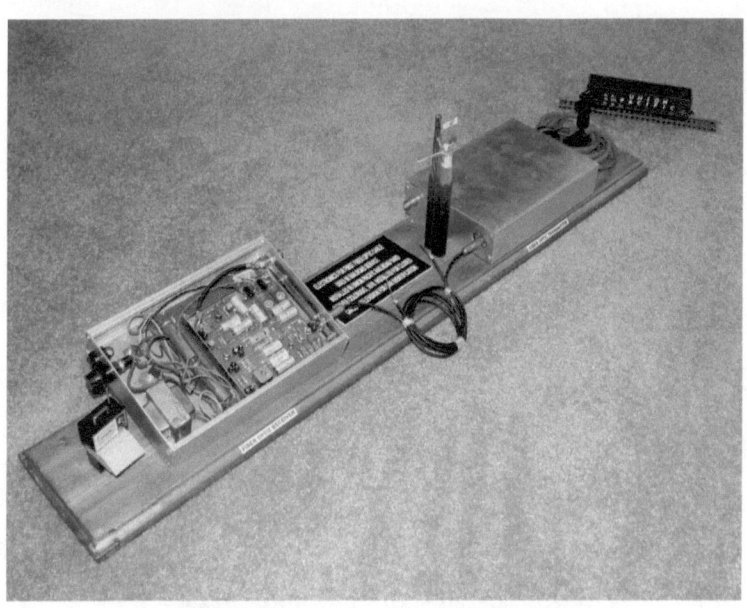

Denver Fiber Optic Cable and Electronics Display Donated to UP Museum Council Bluffs, Author's Photo

Mt. St. Helens in Distant Cloud from Mt Skamania, WA, M/W Site, top of Microwave Building in Lower Left Hand Corner, Author's Photo

Car Identification Camera Site, Denver, CO, Author's Photo

Road to Mt. Skamania, WA, M/W Site, Author's Photo

Car Identification Video Display, Author's Photo

New North Platte Dispatchers' Office with shop built communications consoles. Courtesy Union Pacific History Museum.

North Platte Installation Crew: Front Row Left to Right - Virgil White, Steve Hill, Mike Holland, Bill Stone, Ken Kruger, Wayne Driver. Back Row - Jack Baird, John Hunt, Dennis Schoen, Don Allison, Gary Howard, Ken Moss, Gary Essels, Randy Koch, Don Swedenberg. Photographer Unknown

Mock up of North Platte dispatchers desk with shop built communications console. Courtesy of Union Pacific History Museum.

Evanston, WY Microwave site at sunset. Photo by Author.

Minam, OR UHF-VHF radio repeater. Photo by Author.

Mt. Emily, OR Microwave site with UHF radio antenna. Photo by Author.

Fiber Optic Cable Route on Ead's Bridge across the Mississippi River in St. Louis, Authors Photo

Installation of Fiber Optic Cable in Omaha, Author's Photo

Sunset in Union Pacific Salt Lake City UT Yard. Photo by Author

Index

Alaska, 18
Allison, Don, 178, 329
Anderson, 19
Atlantic Cable, 18
Babel Haithi Digital Library, 328
Baird, Jack, 146, 150, 327
Barriger, John W. III., National Railroad Library, 329
Beach, Joe, 13
Bear Ranch Hill, 274-275, 329
Bhalia, Anil, 241, 329
Bilderback, Rod, 329
Blain, Paul, 94, 329
Brenneman, Robert (Bob), 50-51, 80, 147, 161-163, 167, 327-332, 355, 362
Brenneman, Virginia, 328, 340
British Columbia, 18
Brundige, Brian, 328
Buhrman, Bill, 329
Burlington, 22, 35, 83, 112, 131-132, 156, 196-197, 202, 205, 211, 314-316
California, 18, 56, 67, 200-203, 222, 226, 233-236, 240, 255, 274, 295, 308, 313, 316-317, 339
Chicago, 20-24, 28-29, 34, 38-41, 56-60, 83, 90, 94, 103, 109, 131-133, 137-139, 142, 146, 156, 182, 195-198, 207, 217, 222-223, 236, 322-325, 339, 347, 351
Communications Department, 4-11, 17, 37, 50-54, 80, 116, 120-146, 171-175, 204, 211-213, 220, 226-227, 230-233, 238, 249-250, 253-256, 262, 271-274, 277-278, 282, 287-291, 293-294, 299, 305-310, 313, 327-332, 335, 338, 362

Computer Department, 8, 52, 186, 332
Convention of Railway Telegraph Superintendents, 20
Delaware, Lackawanna, and Western Railroad Company, 22-23
Dempsey, Jean Ahern, 328, 340
Dispatching, 21-25, 31, 35, 43-45, 57, 83-88, 120, 304, 311
DoSpace, 327
Dress, Dale, 329
Erie Railway, 21
Foley, L. B., 22, 25
Furman, Ed, 329
Google, NO ENTRIES
Gould, Jay, 9, 19, 58-61, 341
Hague, Robert, 329
Harriman, E. H., 19-20, 35, 81-82, 87, 105, 153, 235, 241-242, 245, 248-251, 293
Hearst, Rep. William, R., 20
Holiday Hill, 13, 121-122, 152-153, 212, 247
Illinois Central, 21-23, 30, 34-36, 196-198, 217
Jackson, Rep., 19
James, Thomas L. Postmaster General, 20
Jensen, Steve, 329
Jett, C Otis, 7, 10, 49-51, 92-98, 107-117, 123-126, 135-146, 155-168, 171-177, 181-186, 195, 199, 205, 223-224, 286, 293-294, 303, 331-335, 340-354
Johnson, Craig, 329
Journal of Telegraph, The, 18, 37, 40, 335

Kansas, 19, 30, 35, 42, 51, 141, 160, 223, 309
Kemp, Ed, 329
Kilby, Jim, 327
Kinyon, Scott, 329
Kopiaz, Larry, 329
Kuhn, Mary Ann, 3, 13
Larsen, John, 327-328
Library of Congress, 328
Maher, Dan, 329
May, Jim and Barb, 53, 329
Mechanical Department, 8
Messerschmidt, Dana, 329
Metropolitan Community College, 329
Mexico, 18, 54, 230, 289-291, 351
Ahern, Michael, 52-53, 80, 328
MIS, Management Information Service, 8, 52-54, 113, 190, 220, 227, 295
Moscow, Russia, 18
Nate, J. J. , 20-21
Nebraska Historical Society, 328, 339, 342-343, 359-361
Nelson, Dave (Ozzie), 329
New York City, 20
Northern Pacific Railroad, 19-21, 197
Omaha Public Library, 328
Oregon, 18, 92, 182, 200-201, 204, 242, 271-273, 305, 310-317
Pacific Railroad Act,The Pacific Railroad and Telegraph Act of 1862, 62-63
Pacific Railroads, 9, 17-18, 36, 57, 64, 150, 230, 242
Palmer, Pete and Nadeen, 329
Pelto, Lisa, 329
Pilakowski, Gerry, 329
Post Office, 18-20
Postal Telegraph, 63-64
Railway Age, 264, 329, 335
Railway Education Bureau, 328
Railway Signaling and Communications Journal, 31-33, 70, 109-111, 136, 162, 171, 325-329, 335

Railway System Controls, 328
Rau, Leo and Jane, 329
Rayko, Paul Albert, 13
Russian, 18, 336
San Francisco, 18, 48, 56, 60, 86, 93-94, 152-153, 196, 202, 212-213, 247
Secretary of Treasury, 20
Signal Department, 8, 128-130, 196, 215, 234, 242, 257, 260-262, 290, 304-309
Signal Engineer, The, 328, 335
Simmons-Broadman Publishing Company, 335
Smith, Rep. Samuel W., 20
St. Louis Mercantile Library, 329
Telecommunications Department, 9
Telegraph Age, 20, 23, 82-83, 99, 329, 335
Telegraph and Telephone Age, 24, 329, 335
Telegraph Department, 9-11, 40-43, 46-48, 76, 80, 88-90, 328
Telegrapher, The, 18, 37, 40, 335
Teletype Corporation, 329
Tichacek, Jerry, 241-242, 329
Transcontinental Telegraph Construction, 17
U. S. Government, 18
Uncle Sam, 19
Union Pacific Museum, 328
Union Pacific Railway, 64, 75
University of Nebraska Library, 328
University of Southern California, , 328
Washington, 18, 30, 34, 42, 65, 75, 92, 100, 143-144, 182, 197, 200, 203-204, 222, 257, 271, 314-316
Wendel, Sandra, , 329
Western Union Telegraph Company, 38, 41, 48, 55, 60, 76, 81, 94-97, 195
Wikipedia, 335, 341-342
World Herald, 50, 328, 335
Zielie, Brad, 329, 363

www.ingramcontent.com/pod-product-compliance
Lightning Source LLC
Chambersburg PA
CBHW020048170426
43199CB00009B/202